Space and Political Universalism in Early Modern Physics and Philosophy

Edinburgh Studies in Comparative Political Theory and Intellectual History
Series Editor: Vasileios Syros

Edinburgh Studies in Comparative Political Theory and Intellectual History welcomes scholars interested in the comparative study of intellectual history/political ideas in diverse cultural contexts and periods of human history and Comparative Political Theory (CPT).

The series addresses the core concerns of CPT by placing texts from various political, cultural and geographical contexts in conversation. It calls for substantial reflection on the methodological principles of comparative intellectual history in order to rethink of some of the conceptual categories and tools used in the comparative exploration of political ideas. The series seeks original, high-quality monographs and edited volumes that challenge and expand the canon of readings used in teaching intellectual history and CPT in Western universities. It will showcase innovative and interdisciplinary work focusing on the comparative examination of sources, political ideas and concepts from diverse traditions.

Available Titles:
Simon Kennedy, *Reforming the Law of Nature: The Secularisation of Political Thought, 1532–1689*
Lee Ward, *Recovering Classical Liberal Political Economy: Natural Rights and the Harmony of Interests*
Evert van der Zweerde, *Russian Political Philosophy: Anarchy, Authority, Autocracy*
Haig Patapan, *Modern Philosopher Kings: Wisdom and Power in Politics*
Montserrat Herrero, *Theopolitical Figures: Scripture, Prophecy, Oath, Charisma, Hospitality*
Leandro Losada, *Machiavelli in Argentina and Hispanic America, 1880–1940: Liberal and Anti-Liberal Political Thought in Comparative Perspective*
Pablo Bustinduy, *Space and Political Universalism in Early Modern Physics and Philosophy*

Forthcoming:
Filippo Marsili and Eugenio Menegon, *Translation as Practice: Intercultural Encounters between Europe and China and the Creation of Global Modernities*
Miguel Vatter, *Machiavelli and the Religion of the Ancients: Platonism and Radical Republicanism*
Alessandro Mulieri, *Marsilius of Padua and Ibn Rushd: The Political Philosophy of Averroism*
Vassilis Molos, *The Russian Mediterranean: Shaping Sovereignty and Selfhood on the Island of Paros, 1768–1789*

Space and Political Universalism in Early Modern Physics and Philosophy

Pablo Bustinduy

EDINBURGH
University Press

Edinburgh University Press is one of the leading university presses in the UK. We publish academic books and journals in our selected subject areas across the humanities and social sciences, combining cutting-edge scholarship with high editorial and production values to produce academic works of lasting importance. For more information visit our website: edinburghuniversitypress.com

© Pablo Bustinduy, 2024, 2025

Edinburgh University Press Ltd
13 Infirmary Street
Edinburgh EH1 1LT

First published in hardback by Edinburgh University Press 2024

Typeset in 11/13 Adobe Sabon by
IDSUK (DataConnection) Ltd

A CIP record for this book is available from the British Library

ISBN 978 1 3995 2780 4 (hardback)
ISBN 978 1 3995 2781 1 (paperback)
ISBN 978 1 3995 2782 8 (webready PDF)
ISBN 978 1 3995 2783 5 (epub)

Contents

Introduction: Political Cosmologies

The study of natures itself has a history,
and its own nature, if any, must be approached
through the study of that history.[1]

A city "open to all": this is how Pericles describes democratic Athens
in his funeral oration.[2] Under one form or another, the association
with openness, transparency, and accessibility has marked the political philosophy of democracy with a recurrent, intriguing relationship
to space. In their abstraction, for instance, the notions of "public
space" and the "public sphere" have been repeatedly romanticized
as an unobstructed realm of participation, or as Doreen Massey
puts it, as an "emptiness which enables free and equal speech."[3]
The phantom of the *agora* animates our imagination of democracy,
mobilizing the language and the properties of space, loading them
with ethical and political significance, linking together, for instance,
the ideas of an empty sphere, political freedom, and the equality
of rights. But where does such an association come from? What is
its ultimate political and philosophical significance? Is it possible to
think about democracy from the perspective of a philosophical critique of space?

The Return of Space

This kind of association had long been neglected by a critical tradition
which did not deem it worthy of philosophical attention. That tradition has been said to be enveloped in a "temporal master-narrative":
dominated by the thoughts of time, it tended to associate the realm

of the political with the promising indetermination of temporality and the winding movements of history.[4] Space, Foucault affirmed in a famous declaration, "was treated as the dead, the fixed, the undialectical, the immobile"; time, on the contrary, was "richness, fecundity, life, dialectic."[5] By the 1970s, however, this relegation of space came to be increasingly contested. Space became then the object of renewed interest and attention; its political subordination to the temporal appeared as something insufficient, sterile, incapable of capturing the particular essence of the time. The present epoch, Foucault announced then in a premonitory conference, will

> perhaps be above all the epoch of space. We are in the epoch of juxtaposition, the epoch of the near and the far, of the side-by-side, of the dispersed. We are at a moment, I believe, when our experience of the world is less that of a long life developing through time than that of a network that connects points and intersects with its own skein. One could perhaps say that certain ideological conflicts animating present-day polemics oppose the pious descendants of time and the determined inhabitants of space . . . The anxiety of our era has to do fundamentally with space, no doubt a great deal more than with time.[6]

In line with this intuition, a wide and heterogeneous line of enquiry has since then tried to reclaim the centrality of thoughts of space in the constitution of our ethical and political worldviews.[7] Many attempts have been made at investigating the political resonances of spatiality, showing how particular places acquire meanings that are socially bestowed on them, or conversely, how political institutions and processes become embodied in the specific localities of our immediate, everyday experience. The politics of space, and the production of space, time, and space-times as a result of social processes and power relations, have thus been at the center of intense debates reaching across disciplines and schools, often fueled by the ideological warfare concerning the ascent of globalization and its many theoretical discontents.

This rejuvenated consideration of space betrays perhaps a feeling of agitation, a sort of instability within our cultural formations (the "anxiety of our era," as Foucault described it in his premonitory speech). In our metaphysical imaginaries, space had represented indeed the "fixed" and the "immobile": since the publication of Newton's *Mathematical Principles of Natural Philosophy*, and for at least 200 years, the concept of space offered an absolute framework for modern mechanics, but also an ideal of permanence and grounding, of coherence and universality, a source of reliable reference and attachment – in other words, a political foundation. Perhaps this "return of space" expresses the attempt at coming to terms with the crisis of that paradigm, a need to recover some form of shelter and stability, to reawaken a sense of rootedness or meaningful belonging in a world that, after the traumatic experiences of the twentieth century, has become groundless and hostile again. Perhaps the celebrations of the principle of "reunification" at the end of the Cold War, and the many mythologies modeled after the image of a "global space," represent the attempt at easing that acute form of metaphysical anxiety, the nostalgia for a kind of experience that broke down in the world of relativity and the atomic bomb. Space appeared then as a promise of integrity and coherence: after all, it was history, and not space, that was supposed to end with the fall of communism.[8] In the idea of a smooth and unified world-space, even in the virtual space of a digital sublation of reality, perhaps an antidote could be found to that deep form of cultural trouble: a different form of grounding, no matter how superficial; a simulacrum of coherence and stability again.

That such an attempt was fated to fail has only been confirmed by an even deeper form of metaphysical malaise. In the time of the pandemic, the imagination of an open and pacified space was turned into its exact reversal, a nightmarish breakdown of isolation, separateness, and discontinuity, in which the old verses attributed to Petrarch resonated as an eerily contemporary form of pain:

In what annals has it ever been read
that houses were left vacant,
cities deserted, the country neglected,
the fields too small for the dead
and a fearful and universal solitude
over the whole Earth?[9]

Since then, the promise of a stable and pacified Earth appears before us as an idol broken into pieces. What not long ago was presented as a destiny is now besieged by its own fragility, by its own absence of foundation: instead of providing certainty, we fear that space now "hides consequences from us."[10] Nearly all forms of universality – in science, in culture, in politics too, as the insistent narratives on "deglobalization" and the "crisis of democracy" make sufficiently clear – seem ineffective, threatening, or unavailable. Our futures, one would say, have stopped carrying the old promises of progress and abundance, and torment us instead with the imagination of an impending catastrophe. As a result, we feel weak, we feel anxious, and we feel impotent about it.

Among the many reasons for those feelings, perhaps one has to do with a certain form of forgetfulness, with an erasure of the origins of what we now find missing. For we assume that space once offered a secure grounding for the world only by forgetting the kind of shock that was first produced by its assertion, by ignoring that the proclamation of modern space created another form of anxiety, a cultural crisis of proportions that are still today difficult to imagine, and of which the logic of space may still bear the marks. Indeed, the assertion of space as the absolute framework of modern physics – the very basis of what we may call, despite all the ambiguities and contradictions, "modernity" – required the dismantlement of a metaphysical edifice that had tightly ordered the experience of the world for over 2,000 years. Before it could fabricate the notion of universality whose absence we mourn today, modern space had to disorder the world first, producing forms of vulnerability that may perhaps resonate in our contemporary malaise.

To Be in Place

In the classical world, "cosmos" does not only stand for the whole of what exists, but also for one specific aspect of that whole: its "orderliness," the fact that it is arranged in a harmonious manner, that its elements are bound together in a beautiful and congruent proportion.[11] The order of the world is what ultimately guarantees its unity, the fundamental continuity of the natural and the divine, of the life of the gods and the transiency of human forms. In a famous passage of the *Gorgias*, Socrates refers to the opinion of some "wise men" who affirmed that "friendship and community and orderliness (*kosmioles*) and moderation bind together heaven and earth, gods and men, and that this whole is therefore called order (*kosmos*), not disorder (*akosmia*)."[12] This is what men and the gods have in common: the orderliness of being, the living harmony that brings together a multiplicity of elements into a beautiful arrangement and a proper order of relations. For exactly like the soul of the cosmos governs the whole by a virtuous arrangement of its elements, so the human soul must strive for the virtuous arrangement of its own powers.[13] Of course, such powers might pull the soul in different directions, making it prone to excesses, to mistakes, to *akosmia*. But the soul can also find a harmonious balance, the orderly arrangement of those powers, which over-comes the threat of conflict and disorder and brings forth what is good for the whole as well as for each of its parts.

This same principle holds for political existence too.[14] Like souls, cities are also composed of different powers, of different elements and kinds; like souls too, their political arrangement must be made in the image of the world, by imitating the order of the cosmos, even if it is only through a "bastard image" that necessarily distorts its true principle and form.[15] Justice in the city, like virtue in the soul, depends hence on a principle of order: for the whole to be well arranged, each of the elements that compose it must be disposed in the place that is proper and natural to it.

The classical cosmos was organized around a physics of place – it was an utterly solid world where everything was, or at least could be, in its "proper place", where the harmony of the whole, whether that whole be the cosmos, the city or the soul, depends on the good arrangement of its parts, on a balance that can only be reached by disposing each of the elements in its proper and natural position. In the absence of impediments, each thing moves to the place that is natural to it; there, a thing finds countenance and stability, it finds harmony and rest. When things are in their proper places, the ensemble is virtuous and well-attuned; when that order is violated, when elements are kept out of the places where they belong, the result is violence and disorder, a troubled state of affairs that calls for healing and restoration. Classical cosmology thus maps onto a topology of being: from the celestial spheres to the powers of the soul, the world consists in an order of places, a combination of limits, positions and capacities, which determines the purpose and the destiny of all things. Little wonder, then, if the destruction of that order was perceived as a cosmological catastrophe.

Broken Spheres

Modern space broke the vaults of that world and deprived it of its logic of order and relation. The modern universe presents itself as infinite and open; devoid of limits and spheres, of natural hierarchies and ranks; nothing in it seems to be proper anymore. All the places of the world are dissolved into an abstract, indifferent sameness: unsheltered and uncontained, bodies roam through an emptiness that is barren of meaning, of qualities and purposes. Every point in space is now equal to every other; the infinite diversity of nature is flattened into a single plane of value and existence. Unbounded and unchanging, independent of thought or matter, space imposes itself as a mere continuous regularity: space is the universal container of all things, the absolute "in which" of all mechanical processes and motions, the empty background of a world that has lost its references, its center, its essential principles of order.

Inevitably at first, in the modern universe things appear to be tragically out of place. The beautiful wholes of nature are broken into meaningless pieces; the chains of being, subverted and dissolved; the cosmic domes that sheltered the Earth, turned into useless ornaments and ruins. Gone is the harmony of a world anchored and protected, a world that held things fast right where they belonged. Displaced from the center of the scene, the very fact of human existence appears now as a problem: the anxiety of Pascal (what is man in the midst of infinity?) expresses a desperate striving for reference in a universe that no longer seems to have any, where men find themselves unable to tell above and below, the true from the false, the virtuous and the corrupt, where everything seems to be displaced and diminished by the unfathomable vastness of space.[16] As a famous madman would say one day, we tumble in a world that has lost its horizons: we seem to err in an infinite nothingness, not knowing where to go, feeling the cold breath of empty space in our face.[17]

In reconstructing early modern ideas of the universe, we tend to forget the kind of violence and terror that its imagination once imposed, the desperate search for certainty and direction, for new forms of anchoring and foundation, for solid ground upon which to stand. Indeed, it would take an extraordinary philosophical effort to turn that sense of loss and rootlessness into the kind of optimistic frenzy that we easily adjudicate to the early spirit of modernity; to assume that if there is nothing that can protect human life in the universe, if our being has no set horizon and trajectory, no defined nature to grow into, it is precisely because that emptiness is constitutive of what we are as human beings, that our place in the universe is empty too, that God himself, as Pico della Mirandola says in his *Discourse on the Dignity of Man*, has given

> no visage proper to yourself, nor endowment properly your own, in order that *whatever place*, whatever form, whatever gifts you may, with premeditation, select, these same you may have and possess through your own judgement and decision.[18]

This is what follows the realization of the loss of places in the modern universe: the aspiration to shape our own place in the world, and then the world itself in our own image, as if human freedom consisted precisely in experiencing the void that had been forcefully imposed by the cosmological transition. This is perhaps the same spatial faith that, in our contemporary anxiety, we take first as a given, erasing the specific kind of loss out of which it emerged, only to find it empty and shattered, unable to give us strength or relief.

The Logic of Space

We forget the kind of anxiety generated by infinite space because that threat was neutralized by a phenomenally powerful logic. Soon, indeed, science unified the world again – in a manner that seemed, in the eyes of its legislators, even more solid than what had been lost. The empty infinity of the universe was not the chaotic abyss that had been feared. On the contrary, the new science of mechanics could demonstrate that a logical architecture sustains the emptiness of the world: a set of unchanging principles apply universally throughout the endless extension of space, which appears thus as a pure domain of rationality, as the very opposite of chaos.

From the encounter of atoms to the motion of the planets, a new form of mathematical harmony expressed itself in the logic of the universe, holding together what had seemed to be falling apart. Instead of places and regional qualities, the world consisted of quantities of matter in motion; instead of a magnificent scale of forms, the entirety of being was expressed in the language of its universal mechanics. Modern space cleared the soil of nature, it deprived it of order, specificity, and form; but with that same gesture space made what exists unconditionally rational and coherent, it unified a world without exceptions, it made nature infinite and whole again.

The imagination of space, this book will argue, was at once the breaking point of the classical cosmos and the philosophical ground where the effects of that rupture became explicit as problems. Analytically, I believe that those problems can be synthesized in four essential dimensions:

1. space breached the boundaries of the cosmos and imposed instead the presence of an actual *infinity*, defying all principles of restriction and limitation
2. space dissolved the physics of natural places in an indifferent *emptiness*, a pure form of homogeneity deprived of all qualities and differentiations

3. space dismantled the idea of nature as an order of hierarchies, and instead affirmed itself as a universal domain of rational *abstraction*

4. in a universe that seemed to lack all foundations, space was proclaimed as an *absolute* framework, a system of reference that is independent, self-sufficient, and forever equal to itself.

These four essential problems – the infinite, the empty, the abstract, the absolute – converged in the physics and the metaphysics of early modern space; conversely, the imagination of space became the main philosophical setting in which those problems could be expressed, articulated, and resolved as vectors of a universal logic.

Of course, many excellent books have reconstructed the history of the philosophy of space, from the ordering of the world in the *Theogony* of Hesiod, to Newton's strange metaphor of space as the "sensorium of God," and then up to our present day.[19] My goal in this work is not to produce what would necessarily be a lesser version of those efforts, but rather to reconstruct the emergence and development of these four philosophical problems as essential vectors of a universal "logic of space," through which the early modern understanding of the world affirmed itself and ramified into all sorts of theoretical and practical domains. Indeed, this book argues that such logic not only sustained the rising edifice of modern physics, but immediately affirmed itself ethically and politically too.

The Empty Space of Modern Politics

It is remarkable that the metaphysical ascent of modern space coincides with the second great theoretical revolution of the seventeenth century: the formulation of the modern philosophy of the state. Like space in the realm of physics, early modern theories of the state strive to give politics a foundation in a world that no longer seems to have any. Gone are the political emplacements, the natural concord of the parts and the whole, the harmonious arrangement of political elements. In the absence of a natural or theological foundation, the political chains of being are also broken and dismantled. In place of the old transcendent orders, a political emptiness remains, metaphysically groundless, now devoid of purposes and determinations.[20] Again, human beings are forced to find in themselves their own principles of order, to fabricate their own political foundation. Around them, there is nothing but an empty space.

The new foundation of the political appears hence as an entirely rational operation. Like the principles of science, the logical vectors of the state are projected geometrically over an abstract and homogenous surface; the fragmented jurisdictions, the organic hierarchies of medieval powers are dissolved in a single plane of coherence and continuity. Political reason legislates over that space according to apodictic principles; everything particular must now be subsumed under the political figure of the universal. All expressions of power must be unified under a single political form, the *puissance souveraine* of the state, which functions mechanically, in the manner of the world-machine. Like matter in space, political bodies now depend on the relation of forces and masses. Sovereignty itself, the "soul" of the political mechanism, ultimately maps onto a physics of extension, a Cartesian space where the dominion of each state is defined by geometrical lines traced over a smooth surface of projection.[21] Within those lines, the political space is unified under the abstract figure of the state: it is a realm without logical interruptions, a rational and universal space.

In that space, it will soon become impossible to anchor distinctions between individuals. If all can voice an equal claim to all things, like in Hobbes's description of the state of nature; if the reality of violence appears now as an original threat, rather than as a distortion of the natural order of things, it is because like points in infinite space, nothing essential distinguishes their being anymore, because no position can be proper to them. All men (and for a long while yet, only men) share an equal dignity, an equal ontological standing in a political space that has been flattened, emptied of qualities and powers, of meaningful distinctions and inequalities. Every natural hierarchy has lost its ultimate grounding; ranks and scales have been dissolved in an empty political space. This is why the "origin of inequality" must be investigated. The principle of subordination is incompatible with the new metaphysics of space.

This is the democratic promise inscribed in the modern logic of universalism: the idea of a smooth political realm, free from inequality and fragmentation; the conception of an abstract domain of free access and equal participation; the image of an empty political space as a condition for our collective exercises of self-determination. At a time of crisis of that promise, when the political energies that it once mobilized seem exhausted or dissipated, this book aims at investigating its origins, and the philosophical presuppositions under which it emerged. It does so by means of a strong hypothesis, according to which the political logic upon which it relied was predicated on the scientific imagination of the seventeenth century, and more precisely, that it was modeled after the logical attributes asserted and formalized in the early modern metaphysics of infinite space. In the open, empty, abstract, and absolute space of modern physics, so the hypothesis goes, the universalist project of modern politics found its logical model and foundation. There, the anxiety of a dislocated world was overcome, and the ontology of modern physics found a specifically political expression.

Spatial Crisis

Almost from the moment of its formulation, the political program of universalism became the target of fierce political critiques, often inspired by the very same values – freedom, equality, democracy – that such a program was formally supposed to promote. Some of those critiques have to do with a form of incompleteness, as if the modern emancipatory promise – to clear the space of politics, to make it rational, smooth, and available to all – had been only partially achieved, as if it remained unfulfilled and still called on us for its completion. The history of democratic politics is thus presented as a process of approximation to the universalist ideal: through the incorporation of different subjects who had been previously excluded from the condition of citizenship, the boundaries of the *demos* are gradually enlarged, expanding the sphere of democratic politics until it almost coincides with its normative imperative: a truly open universal space where everyone is finally included.[22]

Even in that expansive movement, however, the universalist vocation of modern politics has not ceased to stumble upon its own internal contradictions. In a sense, this is exactly the origin of the Marxist critique of liberalism, credited with proclaiming at once the political emancipation of the citizenry, and the containment of the political within a sphere that leaves the sources of social power essentially unaffected. The emancipated citizens are thus forced to live two lives, one as formal equals in an abstract political space (which Marx, in a curious cosmological metaphor, described as the "sky of the citizen"), another as social beings rooted in relations of inequality and exploitation.[23] That separation, Marx argued, is not simply the mark of an insufficiency or an incompleteness: the distinction between the state and the market, between the spheres of the political and the economic, is an essential premise, almost a transcendental condition for the social reproduction of capital. This is the political contradiction inscribed at the heart of the modern liberal project: the political is at once elevated and separated from social existence; the universal is enclosed within the bounds of a sphere.

The prospect emerged then of a new breach of the spheres: the purpose to bring back together what had been estranged, to end the separation of the political and the economic, of the public and the private, the collective and the individual, and hence to complete the unfinished project of human emancipation. In that pursuit, the horizon of a socialist society was understood as implying the overcoming of bourgeois politics, that is its sublation in a reunified social space of actual freedom and equality; or conversely, as a general politization of social life, transformed even in its smallest expressions into a communal, revolutionary practice. In both cases, the final end was the same. Liberated internally from the social segmentation of being under capitalism, and externally from the antagonistic logic of national statehood, the image of the socialist "world revolution" ultimately coincided with the concrete realization of emancipation in a truly open and universal space.

After the end of the Cold War, such horizon lost the last remnants of its political content, but the universalist ideal on which it was based did not disappear: it was perhaps even reinforced under an inverted form. Of course, the liberal tradition depends on a strict ontology of limits, which are understood as the very condition of possibility of political freedom: the distinct boundaries of the political, the containment and separation of the public sphere from everything that is private, individual or particular, appear here not as a hindrance but, on the contrary, as that which makes possible the universalization of freedom, even as a rational premise of democratic politics. In the logic of neoliberalism, this containment of the political is elevated to the status of a geopolitical principle: it is precisely the subordination of politics which allows for the final unification of the world, for its becoming one not as a federation of free peoples or a cosmopolitan republic, but rather as a world-market, as a single economic space (a tendency, Marx wrote in the *Grundrisse*, that is "given in the concept of capital itself").[24] In the absence of political interferences, the logic of capital can finally produce its own form of spatial integration: the founding myth of globalization corresponds precisely to the image of a unified world space, a single economic sphere that corresponds to the entirety of the capitalist Earth, a universal realm that would be smooth, transparent, and common to all at last – another way, presumably, of making true the political project of modernity.

An irony of the present age, and perhaps an explanation for the precariousness of its politics, is that its hegemonic political narratives still operate under a paradigm that broke down a long time ago. All the logical vectors upon which the modern metaphysics of space were based – the openness, emptiness, abstraction, and absoluteness of space – have long been challenged in the discipline of physics; so is the very idea of universality that they contributed to articulate. Interestingly, the traumatic events of the last century inspired a parallel critique of political universalism, identified with a rationale of political violence and domination (what else, if not the construction of space as a blank surface of projection, could support the colonial domination of the Earth? What other philosophical ground could justify the blind erasure of singularity, if not the imagination of an indifferent political void?). Many attempts have since aimed at detaching democracy from the "perilous metaphysics" of modern space, trying to posit the void not as a rational absolute but as a form of contingency, an emptiness that prevents the closure of the political upon itself. Political universals have been discredited to the point of being almost neutralized; in their stead we have seen a renewed political valorization of particularity, of specificity, of the irreducible character of what is already there.

All these defensive moves, however, have not made our sense of vulnerability less acute. A distinct form of spatial anxiety, perhaps comparable to the one that preceded the advent of the modern age, still haunts our political calculations. Paradoxically, we seem to be trapped between two defective versions of the universal: the broken mythology of the global, which now returns only under catastrophic forms; and the perennial crisis of democratic politics, which deepens our incapacity to articulate credible alternative horizons. It is perhaps the task of any philosophy of democracy today to overcome this impasse of the spatial imagination, and to articulate new forms through which the place of the universal, which once inspired the politics of emancipation, can become productive again.

Notes

1. Robert Brandom, *Articulating Reasons: An Introduction to Inferentialism* (Cambridge, Harvard University Press, 2000), 33.
2. "Our constitution is called a democracy because we govern in the interests of the majority, not just the few. Our laws give equal rights to all ... We are open and free in the conduct of our public affairs.

We maintain an open city, and never expel foreigners or prevent any-one from finding out or observing what they will – we do not hide things when sight of them might benefit an enemy" (Thucydides, *The Peloponnesian War*, ed. P. J. Rhodes, and Martin Hammond [Oxford: Oxford University Press, 2009], 2.37–9, 91–2).

3. Doreen Massey, *For Space* (London, Sage Publications, 2005), 132. See also Hannah Arendt, *The Human Condition* (Chicago, University of Chicago Press, 1958), 198ff.

4. Edward W. Soja, *Postmodern Geographies: The Reassertion of Space in Critical Social Theory* (London, Verso, 1989), 11.

5. Michel Foucault, *Power/Knowledge: Selected Interviews and Other Writings, 1972–1977*, ed. Colin Gordon (Brighton: Harvester Press, 1980), 70.

6. Michel Foucault, "Of Other Spaces," trans. Jay Miskowiec, *Diacritics* 16, no. 1 (1986): 22–7.

7. Critical to that reawakening was the publication in 1974 of Henri Lefebvre's *The Production of Space*, which inaugurated a prolific tra-dition of Marxist geography that has turned space into an essential object of political analysis (for an example of the philosophical sig-nificance of this tradition, see David Harvey, "Space as a Keyword," in *David Harvey: A Reader* (Oxford: Blackwell Publishing, 2006): 70–93). Since then, similar conceptual moves have happened across schools, disciplines, and ideological traditions. The work of Johannes Fabian, as well as the books mentioned above by Soja and Massey, provide clear context and narratives to make sense of that philo-sophical resurgence, which Carlo Galli elegantly synthesizes in the introduction to his influential book *Political Spaces and Global War*: "the thesis developed in these pages is that every political thought and institution hosts a spatial dimension within itself, be it implicit or explicit. Political thoughts and political institutions, I shall argue, come into being as relatively stable and durable (epochal) regulating responses to concrete perceptions of the structures of space and their transformations" (Carlo Galli, *Political Spaces and Global War* [Min-neapolis: University of Minnesota Press, 2010], vii; see also Johannes Fabian's *Time and the Other: How Anthropology Makes Its Object* [New York: Columbia University Press, 1983], from which I take the concept of "political cosmologies," and Stuart Elden's *The Birth of Territory* [Chicago: Chicago University Press, 2013]).

8. Francis Fukuyama, *The End of History and the Last Man* (New York: Free Press, 2006).

9. Jerome Roos, "How Plagues Change the World," *New Statesman*, 13 May 2020. Gianni Avallone quotes an Italian translation in a text called "L'Anno Nuovo del Decamerone": "Come crederanno i posteri che c'è stato un tempo in cui senza i lampi del cielo o i fuochi della terra senza guerre o altri massacri visibili, non questa o quella

parte della terra, ma quasi tutto il globo è rimasto senza abitanti? Quanto mai una cosa del genere è stata udita o vista; in quale annali si è mai letto che le case furono lasciate libere, le città deserte, le campagne trascurate, i campi troppo piccoli per i morti e una solitudine spaventosa e universale su tutta la terra?" I could not locate the original source in Petrarch's *Familiares* and *Seniles*, the collections of private letters where the original Latin verses should be included.

10. John Berger, *The Look of Things: Essays* (New York: Viking Press, 1974), 40.

11. According to Empedocles, in the cosmos "all things grow together as one," being bound by love "in a single orderly arrangement" (DK31B26). See also the reconstruction of the cosmological thought of the Eleatics by Diogenes Laertius, which is particularly interesting for its synthetic value: "The term universe or cosmos is used by them in three senses: (1) of God himself, the individual being whose quality is derived from the whole of substance; he is indestructible and ingenerable, being the artificer of this orderly arrangement, who at stated periods of time absorbs into himself the whole of substance and again creates it from himself. (2) Again, they give the name of cosmos to the orderly arrangement of the heavenly bodies in itself as such; and (3) in the third place to that whole of which these two are parts. Again, the cosmos is defined as the individual being qualifying the whole of substance, or, in the words of Posidonius in his elementary treatise on *Celestial Phenomena*, a system made up of heaven and earth and the natures in them, or, again, as a system constituted by gods and men and all things created for their sake. By heaven is meant the extreme circumference or ring in which the deity has his seat" (*Lives of Eminent Philosophers*, trans. R. D. Hicks [Harvard University Press, 1958], book VII, ch. 1, 137–8). Pindar had already established that gods and men "descend from the same mother" and hence "belong to a single race" (see *Pindar's Nemeans: A Selection*, ed. Benjamin Henry [Munich: K. G. Saur, 2005], 6, 55).

12. *Gorgias*, 507e6–508a8. For an interpretation of the passage see Luc Brisson, "Polis as Kosmos in Plato's Laws," in *Cosmos in the Ancient World*, ed. Phillip Sidney Horky [Cambridge: Cambridge University Press, 2019], 122–41.

13. *Republic*, 441d–442d.

14. The wisdom of the cosmos – as the order and inherent arrangement of things – is bound by an essential relationship to the disposition of cities and human affairs. Inaugurating the long tradition according to which we should live in agreement with the "government of the cosmos," Zeno apparently claimed, in a book that was lost and versed precisely on the ideal political order of the city, that "all individuals within the cosmos are unified under a common law," and that consequently we should all live not under laws distinct from city to city

but rather "observing one manner of living and one kind of order" (Phillip Sidney Horky, *Cosmos in the Ancient World* [Cambridge: Cambridge University Press, 2019], 36); the original source is Plutarch, *On the Fortune of Alexander*, 329A–B). The laws of the city become an expression of the nature of the cosmos precisely through the question of their ordering: this is the profound political meaning of the Stoic conjunction to live "in accordance with nature".

15. *Timaeus*, 52B2.

16. Blaise Pascal, *Pensées*, ed. Louis Lafuma (Paris: Éditions du Seuil, 1962), 199.

17. The famous passage of the death of God in the *Gay Science* has in fact a distinctly cosmological dimension: "Who gave us the sponge to wipe out the whole horizon? What were we doing when we unchained this earth from its sun? Whither is it moving now? Whither are we moving? Away from all suns? Are we not plunging continually? Backward, sideward, forward, in all directions? Is there still any up or down? Are we not straying as through an infinite nothing? Do we not feel the breath of empty space?" (Friedrich Wilhelm Nietzsche, *The Gay Science: With a Prelude in Rhymes and an Appendix of Songs* [New York, Vintage Books, 1974], 125. See also the passionate description of the cultural crisis of modernity, also phrased in spatial terms, from the *Birth of Tragedy:* "In vain we look around for a single root with powerful branches, for a spot of fertile and healthy soil: everywhere we see dust, sand, languishing paralysis", *The Birth of Tragedy* [New York: Oxford University Press, 2000], 110).

18. Giovanni Pico Della Mirandola, *Oration on the Dignity of Man*, trans. A. Robert Gaponigri, (Washington: Regnery Publishing, 1996, my emphasis).

19. To provide an exhaustive list of those essential works in the history of the philosophy of space is indeed a difficult task; in this book, I rely extensively for guidance, interpretation, and commentary on a selection of masterpieces that includes, among others, the following books: Pierre Maurice Marie Duhem, *Le Système du monde: histoire des doctrines cosmologiques de Platon à Copernic* (Paris: A. Hermann, 1913); Edwin A. Burtt, *The Metaphysical Foundations of Modern Physical Science: a Historical and Critical Essay* (New York: Humanities Press, 1932); Erwin Panofsky, *Perspective as Symbolic Form* (New York: Zone Books, 1997); Alexandre Koyré, *From the Closed World to the Infinite Universe* (Baltimore: Johns Hopkins University Press, 1979); Edward Grant, *Much Ado about Nothing: Theories of Space and Vacuum from the Middle Ages to the Scientific Revolution* (Cambridge: Cambridge University Press, 1981); Richard Sorabji, *Matter, Space and Motion: Theories in Antiquity and Their Sequel* (Ithaca: Cornell University Press, 1988); A. O. Lovejoy, *The Great Chain of Being* (Cambridge: Harvard University Press, 1964);

Edward S. Casey, *The Fate of Place: A Philosophical History* (Berkeley: University of California Press, 1998); and Nick Huggett, *Space from Zeno to Einstein. Classic Readings with a Contemporary Commentary* (Cambridge: MIT Press, 1999).

20. See Claude Lefort, *L'Invention démocratique: les limites de la domination totalitaire* (Paris: Fayard, 1994), 172ff.

21. The contradictory character of such limitation – an absolute and universal power contained within physical boundaries – was immediately perceived by the defenders of cosmopolitanism, who understood the direct spatial vocation of political universalism. Pascal had already denounced the political incongruence of a world in which "a meridian decides upon the truth" and the meaning of justice depends on the course of a river: "On la verrait plantée par tous les États du monde et dans tous les temps, au lieu qu'on ne voit rien de juste ou d'injuste qui ne change de qualité en changeant de climat, trois degrés d'élévation du pôle renversent toute la jurisprudence. Un méridien décide de la vérité, en peu d'années de possession les lois fondamentales changent. Le droit a ses époques, l'entrée de Saturne au Lion nous marque l'origine d'un tel crime. Plaisante justice qu'une rivière borne! Vérité au-deçà des Pyrénées, erreur au-delà" (Blaise Pascal, "L'économie du monde," in *Pensées*, 60).

22. See for instance Serge Berstein, *La Démocratie libérale* (Paris: Presses Universitaires de France, 1998).

23. Karl Marx, *On the Jewish Question*, in *Marx: Early Political Writings* (Cambridge: Cambridge University Press, 1994), 36.

24. Karl Marx, *Grundrisse: Foundations of the Critique of Political Economy* (New York: Penguin Books in association with New Left Review, 1993), 408.

PART I

Principles of Space in Classical Physics and Cosmology

It has become a well-established philosophical trope that the advent of infinite space acted as a catalyst for the scientific revolution of the seventeenth century. When approaching relations of this order, however, it is useful to bear in mind that the move which makes the formulation of an idea coincide with the advent of an age has been endlessly repeated, producing for instance the many doubtful dichotomies of which the word "modernity" bears the burden, and the glorification of "destiny ideas" as unifying principles of different cultures and ages.[1]

Still, to acknowledge the revolutionary import of new conceptions of space at the dawn of the seventeenth century has become a widely accepted principle in the study of early modern philosophy and physics. Much responsibility for this narrative lies in Koyré's masterpiece *From the Closed World to the Infinite Universe*, an epoch-making book that portrays the concept of space as an essential factor in the great cosmological transition marking the dawn of the modern age. The philosophy of infinite space is presented as the great facilitator of a historical fracture by which the closed, qualitatively meaningful, teleologically governed cosmos of Aristotelian-Ptolemaic cosmology was to be replaced by the infinite, quantitative, Copernican universe of modern physics. Space acquires here the role of a mediator between cultural formations, enabling a historical transition whose effects would be felt way beyond the scientific fields of astronomy and cosmology.

In the cautious spirit mentioned above, however, several voices have warned against a linear interpretation of Koyré's thesis, arguing that from the very title, his book posits too neat a cut and too short a transition between two worldviews, roughly corresponding to ancient and modern cosmological thinking, that should not be simply counterposed.[2] Indeed, it is a fact that infinite space was not "invented" by the radical creativity of the Renaissance, which Koyré emphasizes so much, but extends its roots way deeper into the philosophical past of the West.[3] Against the simple contraposition of the vaulted cosmos of the ancients and the radical openness of the modern universe, there is a more nuanced story to be told about the long ascent of an idea that generated enormous philosophical – but as we shall see, also political – resistances.

Of course, the image of a cosmological break is more powerful, and possibly more appealing, than a meticulous philosophical genealogy. The loss of man's place in the universe, and the titanic effort to rebuild the world after the radical thought of the endlessness of space, is certainly better suited to sustain an epic narrative about the philosophical origin of modernity.[4] But it could be the case that instead of stressing the revolutionary import of an idea, by positing such a clear break one does in fact diminish it. By failing to notice the slow march of its ascent, in fact, and all the mighty obstacles that needed to be neutralized along the way, one might lose sight of the actual weight that the notion of infinite space bore upon itself.

The modern philosophy of space – a space that is not only infinite, but also empty, abstract and absolute – was not just the expression of a radical cosmological idea. Space expressed an entire form of thought and rational imagination, what we will call in this book a new logic of universality, which would end up sustaining not only the scientific edifice of early modernity, but also its emerging political architecture. This is why it is important to interrogate the conditions under which such logic could emerge, to find a balanced approach to its elements of rupture and continuity, to analyze the main rational vectors that it developed and synthesized. To investigate not simply the origins or roots, but the principles of modern space, corresponds hence to an investigation of the philosophical vectors of the universal logic of modernity – a task that even today resonates with theoretical, practical, and political effects.

With that intention, the first part of this book aims at reconstructing four principles of space in classical physics and cosmology (the unbounded, the void, the incorporeal and the immense), which would play a decisive role in the emergence of the early modern philosophy of science and the radical imaginations of space and the infinite universe. The aim is not to provide an exhaustive reconstruction of ancient conceptions of space – a concept that, as such, had arguably no single correlate in classical physics and cosmology – but only to trace the origins, evolutions, and resistances encountered by each of these principles which would be, centuries later, essential to the crystallization of the modern cosmological worldview. The unbounded, the void, the incorporeal, and the immense will appear hence as four logical and metaphysical conditions of the modern imagination of space and, thereby, of a scientific and political logic of universality that contributed to shape the modern world and our experience of it.

Notes

1. Stephen Kern reconstructs for instance the Spenglerian contrast of an "Euclidean – spatially extended, atemporal" classical world to the "Faustian temporal modernity of restless striving" (Stephen Kern, *The Culture of Time and Space, 1880 – 1918*. Cambridge, Massachusetts: Harvard University Press, 2003, 105). But an excess of generality, as we shall see, does not fail to make an image poor.

2. See for instance Edward S. Casey, who meticulously recovers the philosophical seeds and traces of the idea of infinite space in ancient and classical thought, demonstrating that it was "not an invention of the Renaissance" (*The Fate of Place*, 116); Edward Grant emphasizes the centrality that theological debates played in the elaboration of modern notions of space, crediting the scholastic tradition with devising the concept of a "real, infinite, extracosmic void space that they identified with God's own immensity" (*Much Ado About Nothing*, xi); Dirk. L. Couprie emphasizes the Greek origins of modern cosmology: "The cosmology of the ancient Greeks initiated what we may call the Western world-picture" (*Heaven and Earth in Ancient Greek Cosmology: From Thales to Heraclides Ponticus*, New York, Springer, 2011, xxiii).

3. To be fair, Koyré opens the book precisely by acknowledging that "the conception of the infinity of the universe, like everything else or nearly everything else, originates with the Greeks", and signals that "the speculations of the Greek thinkers about the infinity of space" did play an important part in the story that he is about to begin (*From the Closed World to the Infinite Universe*, 5). And yet, the book certainly deflates the import and the centrality of that influence. Edward Grant wonders repeatedly about the possible reasons of Koyré"s "deliberate and conscious policy", given that he was himself the author of a "momentous study on medieval concepts of void" (see for instance *Much Ado About Nothing*, 374, n. 4).

4. This is Koyré"s poignant description of the cosmological transition: "a fundamental process as the result of which man – as it is some-times said- lost his *place* in the world, or more correctly perhaps, lost the very world in which he was living and about which he was thinking, and had to transform and *replace* not only his fundamental concepts and attributes, but even the very framework of his thought" (*From the Closed World to the Infinite Universe*, 2).

Chapter 1

Unbounded: The Limits of Place

For at least 1,900 years, every attempt at producing a positive image of the unlimited would be destined to incite vivid reactions, if not outright condemnations. *To apeiron*, the cosmic principle attributed to Anaximander, stands for that which knows no limits, which is limitless beyond measure and proportion. As such, the unlimited has no measurable quantity, no qualification or determination. As Anaximander's famous argument goes, the boundless knows no origin, because it is itself the origin.[1]

To present the unlimited as a cosmic principle, somehow identified with the existing physical world, was – and perhaps still is – a radical idea that defied the patient work of philosophers trying to discern order in nature.[2] For if the task of thought is to find harmony and balance in all realms of existence, an unending cosmos is an image of the opposite, because there can be neither proportion nor harmony in what is foreign to any sort of bounds or limits. And yet "all philosophers of repute" who have dealt with the natural world, Aristotle explains in his *Physics*, "have discussed the unlimited and have regarded it as in some sense a principle of actually existing things."[3] The imagination of a world that would have no limits – and even, the identification of the unlimited as such with the principle and origin of that world – has thus been present since the beginning, only to encounter formidable resistances and refutations. Indeed, the very idea of limits, and the belief in the existence of a cosmic order by which a principle of reason and proportion governs our world, was born at the same time as the idea of the unlimited, and quite precisely, as a specific form of its negation.

1.1 The Limitless as Principle

In the *Physics*, Aristotle discusses five different interpretations of the idea of the unbounded. That which knows no limits (πέρας) presents itself under the image of (1) endless time; (2) the infinite divisibility of magnitudes; (3) the unending source of "things which come into being"; (4) a refutation of the existence of absolute limits, and closely related to this; (5) the positing of a "beyond" to every possible limit, in a never ending succession.[4] The two latter images of thought are for Aristotle the "most effective and central" of all. Indeed, in these images the idea of the unlimited connects directly with our cosmological imagination. If we posit that there is no absolute limit, and if we assume for every limit the existence of something that is beyond that limit, then it is easy to imagine that there should be no limit either for that which is "beyond the heavens" (ἔξω τοῦ οὐρανοῦ), and even, that there must be "unlimited worlds." The radical idea of the unbounded as principle is hence crystallized in the image of a limitless world.[5] Aristotle would devote an arduous and systematic effort to dismantle that idea and its effects.

The most basic association that the cosmologists of the boundless make, and the most difficult to understand, regards precisely the connection between the principle of the unlimited and the actual physical world that it allegedly governs and embraces. Looking for the *archai* of the sensible world, what the philosophers had to explain was precisely the relation between the origin and the things that exist; in doing so, most of them conceived only of "material principles" as the cause underlying all things.[6] However, when the principle is the boundless, that which has no limits and determinations, which escapes thought and even our attempts to capture it, the relation with the physical world proves to be particularly difficult to grasp.

Indeed, there seems to be a spatial problem in positing the unbounded as the principle of the physical world. Being un-generated, un-original, un-derived from any other principle, it would seem that we can get a grasp on the unlimited only through what it is not: no bounds, no limits, no beginning or end, no relation to the existence of anything else.[7] But if what defines the principle of things is simply the denial of limitation, then the problem arises of how to make sense of the obviously limited, concrete, and particular existence of beings in our physical word. For how does the unbounded come to be emplaced? How does it find a place in the world, and what relation does it entertain with its manifold components? Where can we look for it, and how can we get access to the unbounded in our life and experiences, in our everyday world?

Most approaches, Aristotle says, make the unbounded a predicate of a different substance, such as the elements of air or water, or even of nature itself; but others hold that the unlimited has a substantive existence of its own.[8] Aristotle finds all sort of difficulties associated to this idea. A presumed infinity of any of the natural elements, for instance, "would mean that the other elements would have perished" because of their conflicting natures, whereas an infinity of all of them, that is a world composed of an infinite number of infinite substances, is in itself unthinkable, since each would require to extend without limit in every direction at one and the same time.[9]

The essential argument against the existence of a sensible unlimited, however, has to do with a deeper reason, one that is related to the spatial nature of our physical world. For Aristotle, anything that exists must be situated somewhere, it must have some "proper site."[10] To be a thing means to be in place; different things occupy different places, and a distinction of places implies necessarily a distinction of things too. If anything unbounded existed, it should be in place itself, it should be located somewhere; but being unbounded, its place should be unbounded too, it should extend in all directions and include all places, "through the infinite region of substance indistinguishable from itself."[11] If an unbounded place existed, hence, there would be no other place in the world outside of itself.

An unbounded place would make all other places, and the distinctions between them, ultimately disappear. The world would be everywhere one and the same, a single place with no markers of locality at all. Without up and down, inner and outer, motion and rest, in such a world everything would be un-placed. But for us, there is a deep correspondence between things and the place in which they are.[12] To be is to be in place; an unlimited world, a world without places, would not be ours at all.

1.2 Place is the First of Things

Place and the boundless appear to be exactly opposite things. Whereas place stands for a principle of limitation, of containment and concrete emplacement, the excessive reality of the unbounded depends precisely on the negation of any limit and concretion. But the two terms also entertain a deeper, unexpected relation. Indeed, the connection between origin and locality, between the unmeasurable principle of things and their concreteness in the sensible world, had resonated in Greek thought since the beginning. Their contrast reminds of the vibrant, disproportionate vitality of the opening scene of the *Theogony*:

> Verily first created of all was Chaos (χάος); thereafter
> Earth broad-bosom'd, unshakable seat of all things for ever.[13]

Chaos, in Hesiod's account, is strangely "mixed with emotion": it implies an image of yawning and gaping, "an idea of terror and fright."[14] But chaos does not stand for the scene of destruction and disorder that one could intuitively associate with it. It is rather the opposite: chaos is the name given to the process out of which everything came into being. One can certainly picture it as a scene of excess, of un-determination, somehow unmanageable by thought and yet absolutely seducing. But chaos proves also to be a productive stage, the condition out of which the material world and sensible things come into being, the process through which they are determined and ordered as what we know them to be. Chaos is, so to speak, the first necessary step, the initial phase of their existence.

That transition towards the ordering of things shows an intimate relation to place. In commenting this very passage from the *Theogony*, Aristotle underlines this relation as expressing a kind of priority in the understanding of the order of things. Hesiod, he says, believed that "before there could be anything else "room" (χώρα) must be provided for it to occupy. For he accepted the general opinion that everything must be somewhere and must have a place."[15] To be something, in Aristotle's account, means to be somewhere, to be in place. To have room "before there could be anything else" means that beings and place are linked by an original relation, that one is somehow unthinkable without the other, that place is something like an original condition that makes sensible things what they are, that makes them possible as things. This is why chaos comes "verily first" in Hesiod's account of the genesis of the world. Chaos is what makes room for the world itself; from chaos, things take place in the world in their manifold vitality.[16]

Commenting on the same passage four centuries later, Sextus Empiricus would give a bold formulation of this principle of the precedence of place. Chaos stands here for "the place which serves to contain all things": a place that is distinct from and prior to earth, and without which none of the other elements could have been stabilized and survived.[17] This is why place comes before, welcoming all things as their abode and their seat, making their existence and their permanence possible. This is also why, Sextus Empiricus says, "in planning the order of the Universe" the ancients "laid down place as the first principle of all things."[18] There has been much speculation on the origin of this radical idea, which turns place itself into the very principle of things in the world. Possibly its paternity, and perhaps its most radical formulation, is owed to Archytas of Tarentum, who composed a treatise on place that was lost together with most of his works.[19] Fortunately enough, some fragments survived through their inclusion in Simplicius's commentary on the Aristotelian categories, including an extraordinary passage that still stands out for its audacity:

> Since everything that is in motion is moved in some place, it is obvious that one has to grant priority to place, in which that which causes motion or is acted upon will be. Perhaps thus it is the first of all things, since all existing things are either in place or not without place.[20]

As the first of all things, place is what existing things have in common. Since things can never be without a place, place seems to be something like their condition, something that is necessary for their existence and is yet distinct and independent of them. But if everything that exists is said to be in place, then we are confronted with a peculiar problem: all things seem to be in place, but place itself seems to be in nothing. As Simplicius puts it in another eloquent passage explaining the thought of Archytas, it seems that

> while other things are in it, place is in nothing. For if it were in some place, this place again will be in another place, and this will go on without end. For this very reason it is necessary for other things to be in place, but for place to be in nothing. And so for the things that exist there always holds the relation of the limits to the things limited, for the place of the whole cosmos is the limit of all existing things.[21]

Place has a mysterious relationship with limits, with the capacity to hold and contain, to define what things are. Beyond place, we are told, there is "nothing": as the limit of every existing thing, as the original limit that makes things be what they are, place finds no other entity that could in turn act as its limit. Place has a constraining power that is itself unconstrained by anything other than itself.

Such is the paradox of place: the only thing that is not bounded is precisely that which bounds everything else.[22]

From here follows a decisive cosmological premise. The "place of the whole cosmos," the place in which all places are, becomes for Archytas the ultimate limit, the container of all things that can itself be contained by nothing.[23] There, place becomes not only the first, but also the last of things. For everything is in the place of the cosmos; but the cosmos itself is in nothing, and as such, it is in need of nothing else.

1.3 Is There Something Beyond the Heavens?

Is there a limit to limits? What is the "place of the whole cosmos," and how are we to conceive of it? Is there truly nothing beyond that ultimate limit? These questions are not innocently raised when dealing with the philosophy of Archytas, who is known for formulating a "wonderful thought experiment" that has to do, precisely, with the boundlessness of space and the infinite regress of limits in their relationship to place.[24] The original text being lost, Archytas's conundrum was reproduced by Eudemus, then by Simplicius in his commentary on Aristotle's *Physics*. In the form under which we have received it, the argument goes as follows:

> If I arrived at the outermost edge of the heaven, could I extend my hand or staff into what is outside or not? It would be paradoxical not to be able to extend it. But if I extend it, what is outside will be either body or place. It doesn't matter which, as we will learn. So then he will always go forward in the same fashion to the limit that is supposed in each case and will ask the same question, and if there will always be something else to which his staff [extends], it is clear that it is also unlimited. And if it is a body, what was proposed has been demonstrated. If it is place, place is that in which body is or could be, but what is potential must be regarded as really existing in the case of eternal things, and thus there would be unlimited body and space.[25]

The place of the whole cosmos, a place that is itself in nothing, and hence has nothing around it, is quite a particular kind of place. For when Archytas arrives at the very edge of the world, at the limit of its place, he decides to extend an arm beyond the limit and finds, over the edge of the world, a place for his arm to be in. But how could that place be there? For we were told that the place of the cosmos was the ultimate limit of things, and hence of the places in which those things exist. What lies beyond the edge of the world is nothing; and yet the arm can transcend it and find a place that is already there. But that place must at the same time be nowhere, for place, as we are told, is itself in nothing.[26]

The paradox is profound in more ways than one. Everything that exists, Archytas had told us, is necessarily in place, it is "either in place or not without a place." For a relation always holds between things and their limits: things are located and contained by limits, and as such they relate to one another within a spatial economy of being that, ultimately, finds in the "place of the whole cosmos" the ultimate, absolute limit, the limit to "all existing things." But since place itself is in nothing – not having any further locality of its own, any other dimension than the relation between limits and the things that are limited by them – we are bound to conclude that such place of places, the place of the whole cosmos, must be itself not limited, that it must be beyond the reach of any limit and actually be different from them. For Archytas, this is the deeper meaning of place being the first of things: the fact that ultimately, that which limits cannot itself be limited at all.[27]

1.4 The Last of the Spheres: Aristotle's Cosmology of Place

Aristotle, who was said to have devoted a three-book study of the philosophy of Archytas, may well have been responding to this puzzle when delineating the essential traits of his cosmology.[28] The Aristotelian cosmos neutralizes the impossibility of setting a fixed, ultimate limit to the world as a place. In fact, that very question, the fascinating thought experiment through which Archytas defies our imagination of the relation between place and body, between the spatiality of the whole and the motion of its parts, becomes meaningless in the world of Aristotle.

To understand why this is so, it is necessary to study the conception of place that Aristotle develops in book IV of the *Physics*. For Aristotle, as for Archytas, to be something means to be somewhere; everything that exists is in place, and places do host and encompass every existing being in the world. But to be in place, in his conception, means above all to be in a certain kind of relation not to the place itself, but rather to another, external body; what place is must be determined by a relation of physical bodies between themselves. As he puts it, "if a body is encompassed by another body, external to it, it is 'in a place.'"[29] To be in place, hence, means to be surrounded by another body, which is at once of the same nature and quite distinct from it. In fact, we are told, a place resembles a vessel, "a 'vessel' being 'a place that can itself be moved about.' And just as the vessel is no part of its content, so the place is no part of that which is in it."[30] A vessel contains something from the outside, but is always quite distinct from that which is contained by it; it is neither the form nor the content of a thing, but rather that which surrounds it and holds it from outside.[31] The interesting thing, however, is that in the physics of Aristotle each vessel must be itself contained by a larger, encompassing body, that body again being contained by another, adjacent one. What we obtain thus is something like a continuous succession of places, with each body being surrounded by another body that contains the former and thus acts as its place.

This is why a place that would be empty of body, or independent of it, does not make a lot of sense. For if emplacement means always (and only) that a body is surrounded by another body, there can be no place prior to the relation between those two bodies, and there can certainly be no place in the absence of either of them. A sort of saturation of bodies and places fills the order of physics. The platial density of the world, the perfect correspondence of things and the places by which those things are contained, depicts a physical order in which no place could be devoid of body and, conversely, no body could be placeless.[32]

The consequences of this change of perspective on the nature of place will be of dramatic importance to Aristotle's cosmology. Indeed, we might ask what happens when, following the logic of the continuous seriality of places, we arrive at the end of the series itself, when we, as Archytas suggests, stand at the edge of the very order of place. Is there a vessel of vessels, a place that contains all places and serves as the "ultimate limit" of all existing things? At this point, Aristotle says quite bluntly that while everything that exists has a place in the cosmos, the cosmos itself has no place at all:

> Heaven therefore "rotates" but the universe has not a "where", for to have a "where" a thing must not only exist itself but must be embraced by something other than itself; and there is nothing other than the universe-and-the-sum-of-things, outside that sum, and therefore nothing to embrace it.[33]

The world, Aristotle says, has not a *where*. For the world to be located, it is not enough that it exists and acts as a container for all the things that are in it. It is also required, according to his own definition of place, that another thing exists outside of it, something larger than the world itself, which could encompass it and hold it together as places do with their things. But such a thing, according to Aristotle, does not and cannot exist; there is nothing else besides the whole, besides this world that is "one, solitary and complete."[34] Outside the cosmos there is nothing to be found. And since there is no body outside the heavens, nothing that could surround the cosmos from the outside, it does not make sense to speak of a place for the cosmos as such either. If the cosmos is the place of all things, for all its parts and constituents have places within its encompassing whole, the cosmos as such, we must conclude, is placeless.[35] The world is in no "where" and in no "thing," which is quite different from saying that it is "nowhere" and "in nothing."

From this it follows that Archytas's conundrum makes no sense in its formulation.[36] At the limit of the cosmos there is simply nowhere else to go. Beyond the last vessel, beyond the last limit there is absolutely nothing, no body, no place, no void either. Nothing could reside on the other side of that limit and nothing could come to be there, either naturally or by an act of violence.[37] The cosmos is finite, and closed by an impenetrable boundary that cannot be transcended.

From the center of the universe to the last boundary of the heavens, hence, extends the stable edifice of Aristotle's cosmology.[38] Between those two absolute limits, the world consists of a succession of concentric, contiguous transparent spheres, which revolve carrying the celestial bodies that they contain in a continuous, circular motion, each one in contact with the next, without producing, however, any sort of friction of resistance between them.[39] Hence the last of those spheres, the sphere of the stars that we can properly identify with the "supreme above" of the heavens, acts truly as the last vessel, the last surface containing the entirety of the world. Beyond it, there is nothing to be found or to be thought of. Within it, everything finds its place in a finite, fully saturated plenum. The world is thus perfectly ordered, balanced and contained. The vault of the heavens closes the cosmos upon itself.

The excessive thought of the boundless is thus conjured within a platial cosmology of limits.[40] And yet, from the very moment of its formulation and for the next millenary at least, philosophers, astronomists, cosmologists, and theologians would ceaselessly work to break through the boundaries of that world, searching for a beyond that would not so easily accept its limitation. In that quest, all of them had to confront another unsettling, dangerous idea, that seemed to be somehow associated to the first: the idea of nothingness as a constitutive principle of the world.

Notes

1. *To have no origin* is precisely one of the traits associated with the divinity and the source of motion and becoming. See for instance the formula that Diogenes Laertius attributes to Thales: "What is the divine? That which has no origin and no end" (DK 11A1). In the *Phaedrus*, Plato uses a version of that same argument to prove that the beginning "cannot be destroyed nor generated" (Plato, *Euthyphro. Apology. Crito. Phaedo. Phaedrus*, trans. Harold North Fowler [Cambridge: Harvard University Press, 1914], 245d1-6). This is the same argument that Aristotle uses in explaining that, being a principle, the boundless "can have no beginning or end of existence" (*Physics*, 203b6-10). See Couprie, *Heaven and Earth*, 91.

2. In the *Metaphysics*, Aristotle lists apeiron as a negative term along others such as darkness or evil (see *Metaphysics, Books I-IX*, trans. Hugh Tredennick [Cambridge: Harvard University Press, 1933], 986A22-27; and Radim Kočandrle and Dirk L. Couprie, *Apeiron: Anaximander on Generation and Destruction* [Dordrecht: Springer International Publishing, 2017], 11, note 5). Elsewhere, Couprie notes the deep association between perfection and limit in Aristotle's metaphysics (see *Heaven and Earth*, 9).

3. Aristotle, *Physics*, trans. P. H. Wicksteed, F. M. Cornford (Cambridge: Harvard University Press, 1957), 203a1-4.

4. Aristotle, *Physics*, 203b17-27. In *Physics* 204a14 Aristotle describes the *apeiron* as "that which it is not possible to get through the end of". For an interpretation of this passage, see Kočandrle and Couprie, *Apeiron*, 6. Both in the *Physics* and in the *Metaphysics* (1066a35 and ff), Aristotle's conclusion is clear: there can be no actually existing infinity, no *energiai apeiron*. As Erwin Panofsky puts it, for Aristotle "in modern terms, even the sphere of fixed stars would be an "individual object" (*Perspective as Symbolic Form* [New York: Zone Books, 1997], 44).

5. Whether the *apeiron* of Anaximander is to be conceived as an independent, spatially extended entity, as an attribute of nature, or merely as the generative principle of all things that exist is in itself a matter of discussion. Simplicius describes it as a first principle that "is neither water nor any other of the so-called elements but some other boundless nature" (*Commentary on Aristotle's Physics*, 24, 13, in L. Sweeney, *Infinity in the Presocratics: A Bibliographical and Philosophical Study* [Springer, 2012], 2). Drawing from the same source in Theophrastus, Hippolytus says that for Anaximander "all the heavens and

the worlds within them" have sprung from "some boundless nature" (*Refutatio*, I.6,1, DK 12A11, ibid., 3). For a reconstruction of the fragments and an overview of the different interpretations see for instance Daniel W. Graham, *Explaining the Cosmos: The Ionian Tradition of Scientific Philosophy* (Princeton University Press, 2009), 31, and Couprie, *Heaven and Earth*, 93–5, 120. Couprie, who mentions the stories according to which Anaximander, was the first person to ever draw a map of the earth, characteristically calls Anaximander "the founding father of cosmology" (*Heaven and Earth*, 79, 163).

6. Aristotle, *Metaphysics*, 983b7-13, 987a4-5.

7. "Being a principle, it can have no beginning or end of existence; for whatever comes into being must come to an end, and there must be a term to any process of perishing. So the 'unlimited' cannot be derived from any other principle, but is itself regarded as the principle of the other things, embracing and governing all, as it is said to do by such as accept it" (Aristotle, *Physics*, 203b6-13).

8. The physicists "all make some other nature – one of their so-called elements, water or air or the intermediate between these – a subject of which 'unlimited' is predicate; and only those of them, such as Anaxagoras and Democritus, who hold the elements themselves to be unlimited, admit the principle of the unlimited at all" (*Physics*, 203a17-19). For the Pythagoreans, the unlimited is a separate entity, the essence out of which things are predicated (see *Metaphysics*, 987a14-20).

9. The reason for this is that the elements are opposite to one another. "If any of them should be apeiron, it would long since have destroyed the others" (*Physics*, 204b25-27). Nor could every element severally be unlimited (as for instance defended Anaxagoras of Clazomenae, for whom the "first principles are infinite in number," see *Metaphysics*, 984a12-14). For then we would have an unlimited number of unlimited bodies extending all at the same time and without limit in every possible direction (*Physics*, 204b20-24).

10. "A sensible body or substance must be situated somewhere, and any given body has some proper site, which is the same for the part as for the whole; for instance, for earth as a whole and for a single clod of earth, or for fire as a whole and for a single spark" (*Physics*, 205a10-12).

11. Aristotle, *Physics*, introduction to book 4, p. 239.

12. Being for Aristotle has to do with place, and our world is marked by a deep correspondence between things and their places. Indeed, "we cannot suppose that 'locality' in general and 'body' in general do not fit; since neither can the totality of 'place' have a greater magnitude than the totality of 'body' can have at the same time – and besides, if this were so, body would not be infinite – nor can 'body' be in excess of 'place'; otherwise, in the one case there would be vacant place, and in the other body of such a nature as to have no

locality" (*Physics*, 205A33-36). Ultimately, Aristotle aims at proving that an unbounded place, exactly like an unbounded body, is utterly impossible, either conceptually or sensibly (see *Physics*, 204B5-7 and 205B31-32; *On the Heavens*, trans. W. K. C. Guthrie [Cambridge: Harvard University Press, 1939], 274b33-275b11).

13. I am following the classical translation by R. G. Bury as it appears in Sextus Empiricus, *Against Physicists. Against Ethicists* (Cambridge: Harvard University Press, 1936), II, 1, 11.

14. Max Jammer, *Concepts of Space: The History of Theories of Space in Physics* (New York, Dover, 1993), 19.

15. Aristotle, *Physics* 208b33-35. χώρα is alternatively translated as "space" (see for instance *Complete Works of Aristotle, Volume 1: The Revised Oxford Translation* [Princeton, Princeton University Press, 2014], 355). The difficulties associated with the term will be dealt with in the third chapter. For an authoritative presentation of the problem see John Sallis, *Chorology: On Beginning in Plato's Timaeus* (Bloomington: Indiana University Press, 1999).

16. For Edward Casey, whose interpretation I am following here, in the *Theogony* chaos indicates an action, and not a state. As such, chaos is not "the eternal precondition of a differentiated world" but the process of differentiation through which things come to be. The setting of the *Theogony* thus becomes a "scene of spacing," the scene of an action that creates "a place for the things to be," a process of differentiation by which each thing finds its proper, befitting place (see *The Fate of Place: A Philosophical History*, 9, 370). The order of places appears as a correlation to the order of being; things come to be through the emergence of place. Chaos is the name of that transition to being, to being in place, which brings together the origin and concreteness of our sensible world.

17. Sextus Empiricus, *Against Physicists*, II.1.11-12. Sextus says the following about the importance of chaos as a spatial original condition: "for if this had not subsisted neither earth nor water nor the rest of the elements, nor the Universe as a whole, could have been constructed" (ibid.).

18. Ibid.

19. Monte Ransome Johnson, "Sources for the Philosophy of Archytas," *Ancient Philosophy* 28, no. 1 (2008): 173–99.

20. Simplicius, *in Aristotelis Categorias Commentarium*, as translated in Samuel Sambursky, *The Concept of Place in Late Neoplatonism* (Jerusalem: Israel Academy of Sciences and Humanities, 1982), 37; cited in Thomas Brockelman, "Lost in Place? On the Virtues and Vices of Edward Casey's Anti-Modernism," *Humanitas* 16 (2003): 20).

21. Edward S. Casey, *Getting Back Into Place: Toward a Renewed Understanding of the Place-World* (Indiana University Press, 1993), 15.

22. Place has "the property of setting frontiers or limits to bodies in it and of preventing these bodies from becoming indefinitely large or small. It is also owing to this constraining power of space that the universe as a whole occupies a finite space. For Archytas, space is therefore not some pure extension, lacking all qualities and force, but is rather a kind of primordial atmosphere, endowed with pressure and tension and bounded by the infinite void" (Max Jammer, *Concepts of Space*, 10).

23. Duhem synthesizes in a beautiful passage how the logic of place structures through its tension the very order of the universe: "on peut dire de l'univers, de l'ensemble des choses autres que le lieu, qu'elles ont un lieu; ce lieu, c'est la frontiere meme qui borne l'univers; c'est, en effet, par la puissance du lieu que cet univers est contraint d'occuper telle etendue limitée, de même que chaque corps est reduit a telle dimension par la pression ou la tension que le lieu exerce sur lui" (*Le Système du monde*, 44).

24. Johnson, "Sources for the Philosophy of Archytas," 14.

25. Eudemus, Fr. 65 Wehrli, Simplicius, *Aristotelis Categorias Commentarium*, Iii 4; 541, as translated in Johnson, 14–15. Grant reproduces Cornford's translation of the passage from Simplicius: "If I am at the extremity of the heaven of the fixed stars, can I stretch outwards my hand or staff? It is absurd to suppose that I could not; and if I can, what is outside must be either body or space. We may then in the same way get to the outside of that again, and so on; and if there is always a new place to which the staff may be held out, this clearly involves extension without limit" (Grant, *Much Ado About Nothing*, 105). Archytas's conundrum knew a glorious fate in posterior developments of the philosophy of space. The experiment was famously reproduced by Lucretius, who substituted a spear for the hand, and later by the Stoics, several scholastic philosophers, and even John Locke (Lucretius, *De Rerum Natura*, 1, 968–83; John Locke *Essay*, ii, 13, 21; on the history of the conundrum, see F. M. Cornford, *The Invention of Space*, in *The Concepts of Space and Time* [Dordrecht: Springer Netherlands, 1976], 3–16, quoted by Grant, *Much Ado About Nothing*, 105). The experiment has been termed "the most compelling ever produced for the infinity of space" (Richard Sorabji, *Matter, Space and Motion: Theories in Antiquity and Their Sequel* (Ithaca: Cornell University Press, 1988), 125).

26. I argue that the question here is more ontological than physical or cosmological. In attacking Zeno's paradox ("For if everything that exists is somewhere, he used to say, and place too is something, then place too will be somewhere. Hence place will be in a place; and so ad infinitum," in Jonathan Barnes, *The Presocratic Philosophers* [London: Routledge, 1982], 202). Aristotle explains that places can be said to be somewhere in the same manner that limits are in what

is limited by them (*Physics*, 210b22-30). Archytas's logic is in this respect Aristotelian, except that he draws a radically opposite conclusion: that which limits must be unlimited too.

27. Duhem compares this idea of an "absolute place" to χώρα, and describes it as "[un] lieu dont l'existence ne fut pas subordonnée a celle des corps . . . capable d'agir sur les corps logés en lui" (*Le Système du monde*, 45). For a different interpretation of Archytas as a Pythagorian who believes that the cosmos itself is limited, but surrounded by infinite empty space, see Couprie (*Heaven and Earth*, 225). Casey has a more nuanced interpretation, according to which the cosmic place is limited, but only by itself: "In other words, there can be no other nonplacial entity, medium, or container (not even an infinite and vacuous one) into which place, whether the tiniest locale or the cosmos at large, could be deposited. Instead there is simply the boundary of the physical universe, its own limit. The limit of place is thus the limit of every actual occasion as well as the limit of the universe that contains all actual occasions. Place provides the absolute edge of everything, including itself" (Casey, *Getting Back Into Place*, 15).

28. According to Carl Huffman, "it is probably to Archytas that Aristotle is referring when he describes the fifth and 'most important' reason that people believe in the existence of the unlimited" ("Archytas," *The Stanford Encyclopedia of Philosophy*, ed. Edward N. Zalta (Metaphysics Research Lab, Stanford University, 2018). Indeed, many conceptual moves in the *Physics* and *On The Heavens* seem aimed precisely at dismantling the Archytian problem.

29. *Physics*, 212a32-33.

30. *Physics*, 209b30-32.

31. See *Physics*, 209b32-34: "A place, then, is neither the form of its 'content' (inasmuch as it is not integral to it) nor its matter (inasmuch as it is not the 'content' but the 'continent')." It appears, then, that whatever is "somewhere" is itself a definite "something" and also has a definite "something else" outside it.

32. The saturation of places somehow restricts the capacity that Archytas had put on limits as a foundational aspect of place. Indeed, in the *Physics* "spatial modes are restricted to differentiations of a plenum filled everywhere with extended material bodies" (Grant, *Much Ado about Nothing*, 4).

33. Aristotle, *Physics*, 212b15-18. On the use of the words "cosmos" and "world", and Aristotle's preference for the terms *to ouranos* (the heaven), *to holon* (the whole), and *to pan* (the totality), see Monte Johnson, "Aristotle on Kosmos and Kosmoi," in Phillip Sidney Horky (ed.), *Cosmos in the Ancient World* (Cambridge: Cambridge University Press, 2019), 74–107. As Aristotle himself explains in *On the Heavens*, οὐρανός refers to three possible meanings: "(i) the sphere which bounds the whole Universe, and contains the fixed stars,

(ii) the region between this outermost sphere and the moon, where are the spheres carrying the planets, (iii) the Universe as a whole, i.e. everything enclosed by the outermost sphere, including the earth" (278b11).

34. *On the Heavens*, trans. W. K. C. Guthrie, Loeb Classical Library (Cambridge: Harvard University Press, 1939), 279a7-19. Here, Aristotle explains through a series of arguments and demonstrations on the possibility of simple, composite, and infinite bodies and their motions existing outside the heavens and concludes that since there can be no bodies there, there can be no place, or void, or time either. For alternative demonstrations of the same point see *On the Heavens*, 275b5-12 and 278b22-25.

35. The *koinos topos* that is the world, the ensemble of all places that exist, has no *topos idios*, no proper place of its own (*Physics*, 209a31-b4). For a discussion of the distinction between *koinos topos* and *topos idios* see Graziano Ranocchia, Christoph Helmig, and Christoph Horn, *Space in Hellenistic Philosophy: Critical Studies in Ancient Physics* (Berlin: Walter de Gruyter, 2014), 21. In his seminal study on the history of perspective, Panofsky gives a very useful distinction between the *koinos topos* as "general space," determined by "the furthest frontier of an absolutely large body, namely the outermost celestial sphere," and the *topos idios* as the specific location of individual things, which is for him "the frontier where the One meets the Other" (*Perspective as Symbolic Form*, 43).

36. While dealing with the very question of the place of the cosmos and the alleged infinity of the world, Aristotle says that thanks to his notion of place we are "not compelled," quite literally, "to think of 'place' growing, on its own account, to accompany a growing body" *Physics*, 212b24-5.

37. That is, a body cannot find its natural place outside the cosmos. This is the sense of Aristotle's comment about the possibility of a body existing outside the last sphere, when he says that it makes "no difference whether we ask, 'Is it there?' or 'Can it come to be there?'" (see entire passage, *On the Heavens*, 279a7-19).

38. As we learn, the cosmos does not only come to be limited in its outer edge. The center of the Earth, which in fact is the center of the whole cosmos, also acts as the immobile downward limit for the whole of the cosmos, that in this way comes to be contained by two definite limits equally impossible to transcend: "So the center of the universe and the inner surface of the revolving heavens constitute the supreme 'below' and the supreme 'above'; the former being absolutely stable, and the latter constant in its position as a whole" (*Physics*, 212a21-25). On the motion of the "supreme above" see note 42. On Aristotle's general cosmological structure see, among others, *On the Heavens*, 276a16-18 and *Metaphysics*, 1073b-1074a.

39. Since motion implies a change of place, the placelessness of the outer sphere of the universe must imply, in the strict logic of Aristotelian physics, the impossibility of its motion. To reconcile the rotation of the stars with the Aristotelian theory of place and the finiteness of the cosmos would hence become a difficult problem to solve for cosmologists and philosophers alike. The Aristotelian solution, codified in Simplicius's commentary of the *Physics*, consisted in forcing a risky conceptual move according to which "a rotation does not involve motion out of place so . . . the inner surface of the heavens counts as a motionless place (Nick Huggett, *Space from Zeno to Einstein*, 85). The outer shell of the fixed stars is considered immobile as a whole but composed of parts that do move, and the last sphere becomes *a sort of place*, a place by accident. The solution, however, was far from being satisfactory, and generated vivid reactions from Peripatetic cosmologists and Christian theologians alike. For a reconstruction of the problem see Duhem, *Le Système du monde*, 203, 299–301.

40. As Couprie puts it, "the introduction of a spherical cosmos with the outermost sphere of the stars meant (. . .) the end of the notion of infinity that was at least implicitly present in Anaximander's conception of the universe" (*Heaven and Earth in Ancient Greek Cosmology*, 221).

Chapter 2

Void: Nothingness as a Cosmological Principle

The limitless and the void seem to be bound by a sort of negative relation. Aristotle had made such connection explicit by demonstrating that nothing, not even an "unoccupied place" that would be somehow deprived of body, could exist beyond the ultimate limit of the world.[1] Indeed, his finite cosmology not only deems impossible the existence of void or empty places beyond the outer shell of the heavens, but also within our physical world, which is to be considered full and saturated up to its very limit.[2] At stake in this argumentation, however, was much more than the confrontation of different cosmological images and hypotheses on the composition of bodies and matter in the world.

Before and after Aristotle, radical cosmologists would associate the notion of the void with the idea of an infinite extension lying beyond the boundaries of the natural world. This unsettling relation, according to which what is infinite might be nothingness itself, represented a phenomenal challenge to the cosmic coherence and the ontological stability of the world. At stake in the quarrels on the void was nothing less than the stipulation of the cosmic status of nothingness, and the presence of non-being in the order of reality. The outcome of this confrontation, however, was for a long time all but unquestionable: the denial of the existence of the void crystallized into a major principle of classical and medieval physics, which even the scientific revolutions of modernity would struggle to challenge and refute.

2.1 Against the Void: Infinity and Limitation

The problem of not-being implied from the beginning a problematic cosmological dimension. Perhaps one of the earliest expressions of that problem comes from a famous passage of the Parmenidean poem, which has not ceased to generate bewilderment among its readers and interpreters. In the passage, the goddess likens being to a "well-rounded sphere" that is everywhere identical to itself, and even speaks of a "furthest" or "ultimate" limit in relation to the selfsame reality of being.[3]

Endowing the "sphere" of being with physical extension implies several difficulties and problems. For as soon as a material shape or limit would be ascribed to being, the question could be raised before the goddess: what is to be found then beyond that limit? To answer that there is nothing would imply the Archytian conclusion that being is in nothing, or even more radically, that nothingness begins precisely where being ends, at the "furthest" limit of being, at the exact point where being encounters limitation.

For Parmenides, this must have been an outrageous proposition. In the poem, being saturates the totality of existence, leaving no place for not-being to interrupt its continuity. The density of being must fill up the physical entirety of the cosmos. Nothingness, it follows, cannot assume any form of positive existence; it can have no place, no presence in the order of reality.[4] Of course, one could find an immediate way out of the problem by arguing that the "sphere of being" is not to be understood in literal terms, but simply as a metaphor, a suggestive image of the perfection of being that the human mind can picture, but which implies no cosmological associations.[5] Nonetheless, it is telling enough that at least one disciple of Parmenides did take this problem quite literally, even if that meant earning the philosophical scorn of his peers.[6]

Melissus of Samo, in fact, seems to affirm that the order of being, otherwise endowed with the Parmenidean attributes of unity, identity, continuity, and eternity, is in addition spatially extended, and moreover infinitely so.[7] Being must be without end or limit in the strictest sense of the terms. For if being was to be limited, beyond its limits there could only be something different from it, that is, not-being. But not-being is nothing, and what is nothing by definition cannot exist. For a similar reason, being is also said to be still, because the motion of being would require somewhere to move into, somewhere where being would not be already present, that is, a place empty of being, devoid of being, a void. But such void would once again be not-being, which as such cannot exist.[8]

This is the striking corollary that Melissus derives from the boundlessness of being: that being cannot be "in any way empty"; that "what is contains no void," and that the very idea of an empty place must be ontologically impossible. By extending being in every possible direction, without any kind of imaginable limits, this argument was, however, destined to destroy its own premises. Indeed, the idea of an infinite spatial extension was soon to espouse the very notion of nothingness that Melissus had sought to dispel.

2.2 Thing is No More than Nothing: The Early Atomists

There was another solution to the problem raised by the ontology of the Eleatics, albeit a quite radical one: to embrace the existence of nothingness as a positive element of reality. This is exactly what the early atomists did in the fifth century BC. Instead of demonstrating the impossibility of the void, either through the continuous infinity of a spatially extended being (as did Melissus), or through the saturation of the physical world in a perfect continuity of full places (as in Aristotle), the atomists upheld the actual, positive reality of a form of nothingness that was finally considered as ontologically existent. The void becomes then the "face" of not-being itself, its actual expression, its concretion in the order of reality.[9] Thus Plutarch famously reconstructs the thought of Democritus, according to whom "thing is no more than nothing, calling 'thing' body and 'nothing' the void, since that too has a nature and substance of its own."[10] The consequences of this move are quite drastic on the ontological level. If what-is exists no more than what-is-not, then one is forced to recognize the existence of nothingness as real. As such, nothingness becomes a constitutive element of existence, equaled on the ontological plane with the absolute reality of being. That which is, says Democritus again, this time in the words of Simplicius, "exists no more than that which is not, and both are alike causes of the things that come to be."[11]

The cosmos of the atomists is a material expression of this great equalization of being and nothingness. The countless atoms that compose our physical universe are only one of the constitutive elements of reality. The other, equally fundamental element is the void itself, which spaces a myriad of atoms that clash and collide between themselves, enters into compounds with them, and even moves together with the bodies that exist besides it. Complementary to matter, bounded and interrupted by it, the void is nonetheless its equal: in the world around us, bodies are no more real than the emptiness that exists around and within them.[12] Indeed, our reality would not exist without their combination, without the intertwinement of being and nothingness in the atomic structure of the cosmos, of which they are the two constituent, basic elements. The punctuation of being by nothingness, that is the "differentiation" of being by the negative presence of the void, is a necessary condition and the material cause of everything there is.[13]

Here we seem to reach the extreme opposite of the Aristotelian conception of the cosmos. Far from the picture of a bounded, self-contained plenum where everything finds its proper place, the atomistic universe is marked by the pervasive presence of emptiness. Against the image of the harmonious continuity and naturality of emplacements, the world of the atomists has no pre-established order, no other logos or direction than the endless forming and reforming of matter through the random motion of atoms across the infinite vastness of empty space.[14] Indeed, the universe of the atomists not only welcomes nothingness as one of its constitutive elements; it also embraces infinity – an infinity of atoms, of space, and even of the possible worlds – as an essential cosmological principle.[15] In the vision of Leucippus and Democritus, the primeval conception of the unbounded becomes explicitly cosmological, it espouses without reservations the physical world. The junction of these two radical ideas, the positivity of nothingness and the infinity of the cosmos, would result in a world-picture that was destined to haunt the cosmological imagination for centuries to come.

2.3 Void and Infinite: Empty Space in Epicurus and Lucretius

The early atomists were not alone in their imagination of an infinite cosmos marked by the presence of emptiness. Pythagorean philosophers had already conceived of a "limitless breath" that separated the heavenly bodies and made them distinct from one another.[16] Since Anaximenes at least, the idea of the *pneuma apeiron*, an infinite cosmic air that fills the universe, animating it and ensuring its togetherness, had been likewise associated with the imagination of the principle of the boundless. Unlike the void of the atomists, however, *pneuma* was endowed with a specific form of materiality, identified with a form of thin air (as a matter of fact, Anaxagoras is known to have denied the existence of the void precisely by positing the corporeality of air, an argument that Aristotle repeats in book IV of the *Physics*).[17]

Similar conceptual moves would mark the imaginations of space for centuries to come. The concept of the infinite mobilized the idea of nothingness; it made the existence of non-being felt in a manner that had something threatening or unacceptable about it. Once and again, the void would hence be disguised as ether, as light, as cosmic air, as if it needed to be somehow covered or dissimulated. Consider the case of Heraclides Ponticus, who famously broke into pieces the picture of the closed, stable cosmos contained by the vault of the celestial stars. Heraclides' universe is infinite, populated by an infinite number of worlds, and yet there is no room on it for the void, not even for the idea of emptiness: the entire heavens are suspended in an infinite corporeal ether.[18] Only in the physics of the atomists those two principles – the existence of the void as a purely non-corporeal element, and the boundless infinity of the world – were associated in a single image of thought.

With Epicurus, that image would achieve its full development and refinement. Sextus Empiricus reports that, according to him,

> of "intangible substance" (*anaphès phusis*) . . . one kind is named "void" (*kenon*), another "place" (*topos*) and another "room" (*chora*), the names varying according to the different ways of looking at it, since the same substance (*phusis*) when empty of all body is called "void", when occupied by a body is named "place" and when bodies roam through it becomes "room". But generically it is called "intangible substance" in Epicurus' school, since it lacks resistant touch.[19]

Referred to by the different names of void, place, and room, *anaphès phusis* is an infinite substance: it extends boundlessly, without any pre-established order or direction. As such, the intangible substance is also "complete"; independent of the bodies that are in it and move through it, it is not the quality or the accident of anything else.[20] And yet, the substance remains "intangible": it lacks any positive qualities or proper determinations. Infinite and noncorporeal, boundless and negative, *anaphès phusis* provides the medium for atoms to encounter and clash. Without it, Epicurus says, bodies would not have anywhere to go and anywhere to be. *Anaphès phusis* is the "in which" of the world as such.

Here, the void is no longer conceived of as a circumstantial emptiness, the discrete presence of nothingness in the reality of being, but rather as a stable, unaltered reality that remains forever equal to itself. The intangible substance is not in need or lack of anything; it persists and remains in itself, even in the absence of anything to occupy it at all. Identified with empty space, nothingness is not just an element of reality, but the very scene in which the physical world finds its place.[21] As Lucretius, the great disciple of Epicurus, would put it in a famous passage whose rediscovery would shake decisively the early modern imagination,

> All nature, then, as self-sustained, consists
> Of twain of things: of bodies and of void (*corpora sunt et inane*)
> In which they are set, and where they are moved around.[22]

The only independent, constitutive elements of the real are bodies and void, with the added particularity that bodies are placed in the void and move through it, so that empty space "exists even where body does not."[23] *Qua* extension, the void hosts and exhausts all the possibilities of the real, to the point that, according to Lucretius, it is not possible to imagine any other, "third substance" that would mediate or separate the two, or that would be needed in order to explain the physical structure of the universe.[24] Nothing else needs to be imagined in order to understand the world around us; nothing else could exist independently of atomic bodies and the infinite void in which they are and move through.

Indeed, such void must know no limits at all. For what would happen if someone, Lucretius asks in a familiar argumentation, placed himself at the very boundary of the world and threw an object beyond its limit?[25] Where would the object land? Is there a "where" to be imagined outside of what is, a "nowhere"? The notion of the all excludes the existence of anything beyond it. Empty space (and matter too) must hence be infinite. Except that now, in the rational cosmology of Lucretian atomism, that space is identified with the idea of an infinite void: a form of nothingness which, strictly speaking, coincides with the vastness of the universe itself.

2.4 A Sphere Surrounded by Nothing: Stoic Cosmologies

From different sources we know that Stoic philosophers also incorporated the idea of an infinite void.[26] They did so, however, in a drastically different manner than the atomists. The Stoics coincide with Aristotle in asserting that, within our world, the existence of an actual void is impossible. Similarly, they also conceive of the cosmos as a bounded, finite sphere, with the Earth at its center and the entire system of the heavens, containing all the planets and stars, concentrically surrounding it. Such cosmos, moreover, is said to contain within its bounds everything there is, all existing matter and reality; like in Aristotle, again, beyond the last boundary of the fixed stars there cannot exist any material or spiritual thing of any kind whatsoever. But unlike Aristotle, the Stoics posit that beyond the boundaries of that closed, self-sustained cosmos, there is indeed an infinite, void extension, without any sort of limits or determinations.[27]

Thus, in a passage from his polemic book against the Stoics, Plutarch attributes to Chryssipus the conception of an "infinite void" surrounding the whole of the cosmos.[28] From the *Eclogae* of Joannes Stobaeus we also know that, according to those who followed the teachings of Zeno, in our world the existence of the void must be deemed impossible, since places are always occupied by corporeal bodies that are contiguous to one another; outside the cosmos, however, there is no such thing as matter or bodies, and we can only find an "infinite void."[29] The Stoic philosopher Cleomedes, asserts this in the clearest possible terms:

> [That a void outside the cosmos] extends from all sides to infinity is of the utmost necessity, as can be seen from that which follows. Everything finite is bordered by something of a different kind (. . .) It would, therefore, be necessary, if the void surrounding the cosmos were finite, for it to terminate into something of a different kind. But there does not exist anything differing in kind from the void into which it terminates and therefore it is infinite.[30]

But how, given the cosmological premise of a bounded cosmos in which the void is impossible, can we make sense of the existence of such endless, infinite void surrounding it? Confronted precisely with the difficulties involved in Stoic physics, Galen of Pergamon had observed that, since things cannot contain themselves, a distinction must be established between that which contains and what is thereby contained.[31] The cosmos knows no lack and no emptiness; it comprises all the substance that exists and includes within itself "everything that it needs."[32] But again, this complete and perfect cosmos must itself be contained by something else. And that something can be nothing else than an empty, infinite void of extension, which surrounds its boundaries and hosts the entirety of what exists as its receptacle.

For the Stoics, the nature of this surrounding void must be understood as radically different from the matter of the world; indeed, it belongs to a "very different order of being."[33] The Stoic cosmos is a cohesive, continuous whole, whose entire material substance is pervaded by a spiritual breath that animates it and holds it together, ensuring the sympathy of its elements. That is why no void can exist within the cosmos, for it would interrupt the coherence of its parts. Conversely, no matter or spirit exists in the void, which is limitlessly empty and totally devoid of bodies and life. Any interaction between those two orders would be indeed difficult to imagine. The void cannot affect the cosmos in any way; it neither acts upon the cosmos nor suffers from its action.[34] Beyond the last boundary of the cosmos, it would seem, begins an inane form of emptiness, a nothing where the very idea of nothingness is neutralized.

The most salient feature of Stoic physics may consist precisely in the retracing of that very boundary, the celestial vault that shelters the physical world and guarantees its cohesion. By re-establishing the frontier between the cosmic order and a surrounding void that is separated from it, the Stoics confined nothingness outside the realm of the world. Thus, they disjoined the equivalence of being and nothingness on the same plane of existence, and re-accommodated the idea of empty space where its nuisance was least felt. Perhaps that explains the better fortune of its reception.

Notes

1. Aristotle, *Physics*, 213a15-19 and 213b31.
2. In book 4 of the *Physics*, Aristotle methodically rejects the existence of the void as an extended entity, as an atomic necessity, and as an extracosmic reality. For a reconstruction of the arguments see for example Grant, *Much Ado About Nothing*, ch. x, and note 1, p. 321. Duhem has a particularly illustrative account of the refutation of the atomist's claim according to which the void is what makes movement possible (*Le Système du monde*, 170, 197).
3. The divergences in the translation of DK 28B44-49 reflect the ontological and cosmological implications of the passage. This is the translation given by Gallop (my emphasis): "Since, then, *there is a furthest limit*, [it] is completed, *From every direction like the bulk of a well-rounded sphere*, Everywhere from the center equally matched; for [it] must not be any larger Or any smaller here or there; For neither is there what-is-not, which could stop it from reaching [Its] like; nor is there a way in which what-is could be More here and less there, since [it] all inviolably is; For equal to itself from every direction, [it] *lies uniformly within limits*" (Gallop, *Parmenides of Elea. Fragments: a Text and Translation with an Introduction*, 73). Compare it with Coxon's translation, where the geometrical comparison and every reference to limits are diffused (my emphasis again): "Since now *its limit is ultimate*, Being is in a state of perfection from every viewpoint, *like the volume of a spherical ball*, and

equally poised in every direction from its centre. For it must not be (45) either at all greater or at all smaller in one regard than in another. For neither has Not-being any being which could halt the coming together of Being, nor is Being capable of being more than Being in one regard and less in another, since it is all inviolate. For it is equal with itself from every view and *encounters determination all alike*" (A. H. Coxon, *The Fragments of Parmenides: A Critical Text With Introduction and Translation, the Ancient Testimonia and a Commentary* [Las Vegas: Parmenides Publishing, 2009], 8).

4. In the *Metaphysics*, Aristotle sums up in this way the absolute ontology of Eleatic philosophy: "For holding as he does that Not-being, as contrasted with Being, is nothing, he necessarily supposes that Being is one and that there is nothing else" (Aristotle, *Metaphysics*, 986b27-30). In the *Theaetetus*, Socrates similarly observes that the Eleatics "maintain that everything is one and is stationary within itself, having no place in which to move" (Plato, *Theaetetus. Sophist* [Cambridge: Harvard University Press, 1921], 180E).

5. In his commentary on the image of the sphere, Gallop argues that to preserve the coherence of the Parmenidean logos, it should be taken as an assertion of completeness and perfection, and not as a literal description (Gallop, *Parmenides*, 61). Benjamin Harriman, on the other hand, affirms that the "metaphorical" reading of the passage is "charitable," that there is "no hint in ancient sources that Parmenides was taken to have metaphorical limits in mind," and mentions abundant evidence, among others from Plato's *Sophist*, suggesting that ancient readers of Parmenides "universally understood [him] to have held that Being is spherical" (*Melissus and Eleatic Monism* [Cambridge: Cambridge University Press, 2018], 76). In a similar vein, Enrico Volpe seems to suggest an explanation of the atomists' critique of Eleatic ontology precisely along the lines of a literal reading of the image of the sphere as an actual delimitation or a determination of being: "la natura dell'essere si deduce attraverso una serie di attributi costitutivi tra cui la metafora della sua forma sferica. La relativa critica degli atomisti si focalizza su questa immagine dell'ἐόν come determinato entro i limiti, ovvero inteso letteralmente come sfera; ciò presta il fianco all'obiezione secondo la quale se l'essere fosse effettivamente determinato e delimitato, allora dovrebbe esserci qualcosa che renda possibile questa sua qualità e ciò non può che essere il vuoto, cioè il non-essere" (Volpe, "Melisso e il problema del vuoto: apologia e/o fraintendimento del monismo parmenideo?," *Peitho. Examina Antiqua* 1, no. 8 (2017): 102).

6. In the *Metaphysics*, Aristotle tells us that "It appears that Parmenides conceived of the Unity as one in definition, but Melissus as materially one. Hence the former says that it is finite, and the latter that it is infinite" (*Metaphysics*, 986b20-22). Aristotle also refers to Melissus's notion of the infinite in *Physics*, 185a32 and 207a15-31, where he

attacks precisely the notion that the "indefinite" could surround what is definite: "So one must judge Parmenides to have spoken better than Melissus: the latter says that the infinite is whole, the former that the whole is finite, 'evenly balanced from the middle.' For the infinite is a different kettle of fish from the universe or whole – yet it is from this that people derive the dignity attributed to the infinite, that it surrounds everything and contains everything in itself, because it has some similarity to the whole" (translation by E. Hussey, reproduced in Harriman, *Melissus and Eleatic Monism*, 92; for the reconstruction of Aristotle's scorn of Melissus as a philosopher, see 66ff).

7. See for example DK30B2, where Melissus affirms that being is infinite since it has no beginning and no end, and no limits that could contain its perfection: "Therefore, since it did not come to be, it both is and always was and always will be. And it has no beginning or end, but is infinite. For if it had come to be it would have a beginning (for it would have begun coming-to-be at some time) and end (for it would have ended coming-to-be at some time). But since it neither began nor ended, and it always was and always will be, it has no beginning or end. For whatever is not entire cannot be always" (as translated in Harriman, *Melissus and Eleatic Monism*, 71. For Harriman, "there is every reason to think that Melissus understood Parmenides' point spatially", 76).

8. This is the famous passage in fragment 7 in which Melissus refutes the existence of the void (τὸ κενεόν): "Nor is there any void. For the void is nothing and what is nothing could not be. Nor is there any motion: for it is unable to move aside at any point, but, rather, it is full. If there were void, then it could move aside into de void. But, as there is no void, then there is nowhere for it to move aside into" (DK 30 B7.7, as translated in James Warren, *Presocratics* [London: Routledge, 2014], 156). The void is here explicitly conceived as non-being: "In questo passo vi è la negazione esplicita del vuoto concepito come non-essere: non esiste il vuoto poiché esso sarebbe non-essere, e il non-essere non è, da ciò l'ἐόν risulta essere immobile e pieno" (Volpe, "Melisso e il problema del vuoto," 98). Volpe quotes a passage from Raven Kirk explicitly associating the problem of the limitation of being and the existence of the void: "Melissus in fact is countering the possible objection to the sphere of Parmenides that, if it is indeed 'limited on every side,' then something must surely lie outside its limits, and that something can only be void" (ibid., 99).

9. I borrow the expression from Volpe: "è a mio avviso evidente che l'introduzione del non-essere sotto l'aspetto del vacuum sia un tenta- tivo neanche troppo velato di 'dare un volto' al non-essere" ("Melisso e il problema del vuoto: apologia e/o fraintendimento del monismo parmenideo?," 96). M. Andolfo gives an interpretation contrary to this view, affirming that the void has no real existence of its own

apart from an essentially privative character: il vuoto è definito [dagli Atomisti] come privazione e precisamente come totale privazione di pienezza, ossia di Essere" (M. Andolfo, *Testimonianze e Frammenti Degli Atomisti Antichi* [Milan: Bompiani, 2001], 20). Volpe also alludes to the historiographical problem concerning the temporality of a possible dialogue between Melissus and the early atomists (see Giovanni Reale, *Melisso Testimonianze e Frammenti* [Florence: La Nuova Italia, 1970], 15).

10. Plutarch, *Against Colotes* 4,1108f (I follow the translation in C. C. W. Taylor, *The Atomists, Leucippus and Democritus. Fragments: A Text and Translation with a Commentary* [Toronto: University of Toronto Press, 1999], 142. Numeration of the fragments correspond here to the work by Taylor. For a concordance to DK and Luria see page 265). In *Metaphysics*, 985b5-11, Aristotle employs similar categories in his famous characterization of atomism: "Leucippus, however, and his disciple Democritus hold that the elements are the Full and the Void – calling the one 'what is' and the other 'what is not.' Of these they identify the full or solid with 'what is,' and the void or rare with 'what is not' (hence they hold that what is not is no less real than what is, because Void is as real as Body); and they say that these are the material causes of things."

11. Simplicius, *Commentary on Physics*, 28.4-27, as translated in Taylor, *The Atomists*, 71–2. In the passage, Simplicius remarks how Democritus and Leucippus distinguish themselves from the Eleatics by positing the "infinite principles" of what-is and what-is-not as the equal causes of everything that exists.

12. There are different interpretations of the relation between void and space in the early atomists: the void can be identified with *empty space*, or else posited as a different entity, a form of non-being that is distinct from it and said to occupy space *exactly* as the atoms of matter do. Jammer clearly follows the former interpretation; for him "the void or the empty means clearly unoccupied space . . . space in this sense is complementary to matter and is bounded by matter; matter and space are mutually exclusive" (Jammer, *Concepts of Space*, 11). Grant also makes a similar association, speaking of the "nothingness of space conceived of ontologically as a something, however minimal" (*Much Ado about Nothing*, 3). Casey distinguishes in this respect the notions of "void" and "vacuum," namely the "empty part" of a compound entity constructed of atoms, "a nothing that exists within the compound which in turn exists within the void proper." Vacuum thus has "a place in which to exist – a place provided by the void" (Casey, *The Fate of Place*, 82). In what follows, I adopt David Sedley's reading from this seminal article on the notion of the void ("Two Conceptions of Vacuum," *Phronesis* 27 (1982): 177). According to Sedley, Epicurus refines the notion of the

void inherited from the early atomists, namely a form of not-being which is, however, a component element of reality, capable of occupying space and hence ontologically distinct from it, and develops a conception of the void as purely empty space, wholly independent of bodies and matter. Benjamin Harriman synthesizes the thrust of the argument in the following way: "David Sedley has made that the conceptual difficulties of grasping the notion of the void were worked out over a period of time. As such, he maintains that there is evidence for an early understanding of the void as something like a space/place occupier and a later, more developed view where void is viewed purely *as* 'empty space' and not as emptiness in a space or a place" (*Melissus and Eleatic Monism*, 185).

13. Aristotle says that the atomistic universe "is not continuous", but rather "differentiated by the void": "If the universe is not continuous, but, as Leucippus and Democritus say, differentiated by the void, it is necessary that everything should have a single motion. For they are differentiated by their shapes, but they say that they have a single nature, as if each one were a separate piece of gold" (*On the Heavens*, 275b29-276a1).

14. The processes of cosmogenesis and the explanation of planetary motions posed deep problems for early atomistic cosmology. Couprie provides a nice synthesis of the role that "cosmic whirls" and "vortexes" play in the accounts of the aggregated cosmic motions of atoms (see Couprie, *Heaven and Earth*, 224). As he notes, many of the atomists' problems derive from the curious fact according to which unlike Aristotle, who believed the world was finite in space but infinite in time, they held the universe to be infinite in space but finite in time, that is having beginnings and ends.

15. According to Democritus, the atoms are "small substances infinite in number" that exist in space (see Simplicius, *Commentary on De Caelo*, 294.33-295.36, as translated in Taylor, *The Atomists*, 70-1). That said space, consequently, "must be boundless too: the infinity of space may be deduced from the infinite number of atoms in existence, since these, although indivisible, have a certain magnitude and extension, even if they are not perceptible to our senses" (Max Jammer, *Concepts of Space*, 10). Finally, the infinite atoms in infinite space must give birth according to the atomists to *apeiroi kosmoi*, an infinite number of worlds, constantly being formed and destroyed in a random, never-ending dynamics of cosmic life devoid of any purpose or orientation (a "world" in this context stands for "a "cosmos," consisting of a central body, such as the Earth, together with other celestial bodies orbiting around it. Our familiar cosmos of Earth, moon, sun, planets, and stars is such a world, of which there are, according to the atomists, "infinitely more" [Couprie, *Heaven and Earth*, 222]).

16. See Aristotle, *Physics* 213b22-27: "The Pythagoreans too asserted the existence of the void and declared that it enters into the heavens out of the limitless breath – regarding the heavens as breathing the very vacancy – which vacancy "distinguishes" natural objects, as constituting a kind of separation and division between things next to each other, its prime seat being in numbers, since it is this void that delimits their nature." Max Jammer explains though that for the Pythagoreans, such a notion of emptiness acts only as a "limiting agent between different bodies," that is, the discrete individual numbers that serve as principles of physical reality, as a sort of "spatial vacancy" between them (Jammer, *Concepts of Space: The History of Theories of Space in Physics*, 9).

17. See *Physics*, 208bff. On the Aristotelian elaboration of the notion of ether and its conceptual origins and evolutions, see Konstantinos Kalachanis, Efstratios Theodosiou, and Milan Dimitrijevic, "Aristotelian Aether and Void in the Universe," *Journal of Classical Studies Matica Srpska* 18 (January 1, 2016): 135–50.

18. One of the first thinkers to defend the rotation of the Earth, which earned him the explicit recognition of Copernicus, Heraclides claimed that each of the stars in the infinite heaven is to be conceived of as a world, comprising an earth surrounded by air and suspended in the infinite ether. These infinite worlds are not enclosed by homocentric spheres; the stars do not move, their positions are fixed and located, so to speak, behind one another. Couprie explains how this conception is in many respects more radical than the atomists' vision of the infinity of worlds, for Heraclides makes the infinite begin within our sight: "This conception is to be definitely distinguished from the atomists' infinite worlds beyond our horizon of experience, which means beyond the stars that together make up the spherical boundary of our world. Heraclides' worlds also extend into infinity, but they are a continuation of the worlds we can see as the stars. Otherwise stated: for the atomists, the stars we see are all at the same distance from us, just as they are for Aristotle, but for Heraclides Ponticus they are at different distances from us, continuing infinitely" (Couprie, *Heaven and Earth*, 226).

19. Sextus Empiricus, *Against the Professors*, 10, 2, in A. A. Long and D. N. Sedley, *The Hellenistic Philosophers: Volume 1, Translations of the Principal Sources with Philosophical Commentary* (Cambridge: Cambridge University Press, 1987), 28. In the interpretation of Casey, these are understood as three "roles or functions of generic space in different circumstances" (*The Fate of Place*, 372).

20. In the *Letter to Herodotus*, Epicurus speaks of "bodies and void" as the two only "things grasped in terms of complete substances and not as what we call accidents or properties of these", which together form "the totality of things" (*Letter to Herodotus*, 39–40, as translated in

Sedley, "Two Conceptions of Vacuum," 183). Later in the same text Epicurus will assert the infinity of both space and body, since all that exists "is bounded in no direction" (ibid., 41–2).

21. For Sedley, the opposites that for Democritus were the basic elements of all things, the full and the empty, the thing and the nothing, the existent and the non-existent, were still "names for occupants of space, not for space itself." Epicurus was the first to provide a clear recognition of geometrical space as a three-dimensional extension which persists whether or not it is occupied by body (Sedley, "Two Conceptions of Vacuum," 188–9).

22. Lucretius, *De Rerum Natura*, trans. William Ellery Leonard, The Internet Classics Archive, book I, 420.

23. Sedley, "Two Conceptions of Vacuum," 191. Empty space has become the medium of all atomic existence and motion, it is, as Jammer puts it, "an infinite receptacle for bodies" (Jammer, *Concepts of Space*, 12).

24. "Beyond these there is nothing which you can call distinct from all body and separate from void, to play the role of a third discovered substance. For whatever will exist will have to be in itself something with extension *(augmine)*, whether large or small, so long as it exists. If it has tangibility, however light and faint, it will extend the measure of a body and be added to its sum. Whereas if it is intangible, and unable to prevent anything from moving through it at any point, it will undoubtedly be the emptiness which we call void" (*De Rerum Natura*, I.430-439, as translated in Sedley, "Two Conceptions of Vacuum," 189–90). Casey develops a suggestive analysis of the spatialization of being that is implied by *augmine*: to be is to be in space, to stand through it (see *The Fate of Place*, 79–85).

25. In Lucretius's version, the Archytian thought experiment keeps the same logical structure: "now since we must admit that there is nothing outside the sum, it has no outside, and therefore is without end and limit. And it matters not in which of its regions you take your stand; so invariably, whatever position any one has taken up, he leaves the universe just as infinite as before in all directions. Again if for the moment all existing space be held to be bounded, supposing a man runs forward to its outside borders and stands on the utmost verge and then throws a winged javelin, do you choose that when hurled with vigorous force I shall advance to the point to which it has been sent and fly to a distance, or do you decide that something can get in its way and stop it? For you must admit and adopt one of the two suppositions; either of which shuts you out from all escape and compels you to grant that the universe stretches without end" (as translated in Jammer, *Concepts of Space*, 12). While Epicurus did not use *strictu sensu* the same image of thought, in the *Letter to Herodotus* he had affirmed the boundlessness of the existing universe through a similar logical figure: "The universe is boundless.

For that which is bounded has an extreme point: and the extreme point is seen against something else. So that as it has no extreme point, it has no limit; and as it has no limit it must be boundless and not bounded" (J. E. McGuire, *Tradition and Innovation: Newton's Metaphysics of Nature* [Dordrecht: Springer Netherlands, 1995], 155. McGuire is quoting the letter from its rendition in book X of Diogenes Laertius's *Lives of Eminent Philosophers*, of which he claims that Newton actually owned an edition).

26. Some of those sources include Simplicius's commentaries on Aristotle's *Physics* and *On the Heavens*, Plutarch's *De Stoicorum repugnantis*, the *Eclogae* of Joannes Stobaeus and the *Outlines of Pyrrhonism* by Sextus Empiricus. In what follows I rely mostly on translations and commentary from Pierre Duhem, *Le Système du monde*, and Samuel Sambursky, *Physics of the Stoics* (Princeton: Princeton University Press, 2014).

27. See Sambursky, *Physics of the Stoics*, 108: "The main feature which the Stoic cosmos has in common with that of Aristotle is the geocentric order – the earth in the centre of a finite cosmos and the heavens with moon, sun, the planets and the fixed stars surrounding it." In its turn, that finite cosmos was surrounded by an "infinite, three-dimensional, extracosmic void space was assumed to be totally devoid of body and spirit" (Grant, *Much Ado About Nothing*, 112). In the *Lives of Eminent Philosophers*, Diogenes Laertius identifies three senses in which the Stoics speak of the *cosmos*: "The term universe or cosmos is used by them in three senses : (1) of God himself, the individual being whose quality is derived from the whole of substance; he is indestructible and ingenerable, being the artificer of this orderly arrangement, who at stated periods of time absorbs into himself the whole of substance and again creates it from himself. (2) Again, they give the name of cosmos to the orderly arrangement of the heavenly bodies in itself as such; and (3) in the third place to that whole of which these two are parts. Again, the cosmos is defined as the individual being qualifying the whole of substance, or, in the words of Posidonius in his elementary treatise on *Celestial Phenomena*, a system made up of heaven and earth and the natures in them, or, again, as a system constituted by gods and men and all things created for their sake. By heaven is meant the extreme circumference or ring in which the deity has his seat" (Diogenes Laertius, *Lives of Eminent Philosophers*, VII, 1).

28. Plutarch, *De Stoicorum*, 1053e-1054b, as translated in Sambursky, *Physics of the Stoics*, 111.

29. "Zénon et ceux qui procèdent de lui affirment qu'à l'intérieur du Monde, il n'y a aucun vide, mais qu'à l'extérieur, il y a un vide infini. Ils distinguent entre le vide, le lieu et l'étendue. Ils disent que le vide, c'est l'absence de corps; que le lieu, c'est ce qui se trouve occupé

par un corps; enfin que l'étendue, c'est ce qui est occupé en partie" (Joannis Stobaei, *Eclogarum*, I, XVIII, as translated in Duhem, *Le Système du monde*, 309–10). Duhem explains right before that the void, however, can never become actual within the bounds of the world, because places are always already occupied by bodies of different sorts (ibid., 308). It is only beyond the limits of the world, consequently, that there can be an infinite void.

30. Cleomedes, *De motu circulari corporum caelestium*, I, 1, as translated in Sambursky, *Physics of the Stoics*, 143–4. Duhem quotes another passage from Cleomedes, which he interprets as referring to the thought of Posidonius: "le monde n'est pas infini; il est limité . . . Mais hors du Monde, il y a le vide qui s'étend à l'infini en tout sens. De ce vide (*kenon*) illimité, ce qui est occupé par un corps se nomme lieu (*topos*), tandis que ce qui n'est pas occupé par un corps est appelé vide (*kenon*)" (*Le Système du monde*, 311).

31. Duhem relates this distinction to the physics of Cleomedes: "tout corps doit nécessairement être en quelque chose. La chose en laquelle il est doit différer de ce qui l'occupe et la remplit; cette chose doit être incorporelle et comme impalpable. Cette substance qui est ainsi constituée qu'elle puisse recevoir un corps en elle-même et être occupe par lui, nous disons qu'elle est vide" (*Le Système du monde*, 311–12).

32. Chrysippus borrowed the idea of the cosmos as a self-sustained animal that feeds and grows out of itself from the *Timaeus* and the Neoplatonic tradition (Plutarch, *De Stoicorum*, 1052d; Emile Bréhier, *Chrysippe* [Paris: Félix Alcan, Editeur, 1910], 149–50; mentioned in Duhem, 310–11).

33. David Sedley, "Two Conceptions of Vacuum," 190.

34. In his commentary on the *Physics*, Simplicius defines the infinite void of the Stoics as "indistinguishable and equally yielding everywhere" (*On Aristotle's Physics*, 671, 4, as translated in Sambursky, *Physics of the Stoics*, 144–5). In the void there are no directions, no qualities or determinations; it has no form or shape. Its only apparent relation to the cosmos is marked by the fact that it allows it to *move*, since the whole cosmic sphere oscillates, expands and contracts through an organic rhythm that cyclically renews it to life. "This nothing," wrote Emile Brehier, "is made to give to the world . . . the freedom to move" (*Chrysippe*, 151). Casey calls this void a *négatité* ("not a nothing, but neither a thing nor a place"), and sees in the Stoics the beginnings of "negative cosmology" (*The Fate of Place*, 85). Couprie suggests, however, a possible essential function of the void (or better, of the radical separation between the cosmos and the void): to prevent the dispersion of matter through an infinitely extended space, to dissipate the "fear of falling" that every imagination of an infinite empty space entailed (*Heaven and Earth*, 22, 228).

Chapter 3

Incorporeality: Dimension Distinct from Body

With the Stoic retracing of the cosmic boundary, the quarrels over the infinity of the world lost part of their centrality in the cosmological debate. In Stoic physics, the endlessness of the universe becomes somewhat accessory, in the sense that it is non-fundamental to the physical structure of the cosmos: whatever lies on the other side of the cosmic border, be it finite or infinite, be it empty or full, cannot affect the actuality of nature and our physical reality. Instead, the philosophical investigations on space would center on that intra-cosmic reality itself: for instance, on the relation between space and matter; on the essence of extension; or on the categorial logic that associated the substance and the spatial attributes of bodies.

Paradoxically, this re-centering of cosmological reflections (together with the insistent denials of the existence of the void in the natural world) would prove crucial for the refinement of the general concept of space. In the Aristotelian tradition, place is always intimately connected with body; there is no such thing as a notion of space which could be considered in abstraction of the manifold things that exist in it. The idea of space as an immaterial reality, a kind of physicality that is nonetheless separate and distinct from the corporeality of matter, would move decisively beyond the limits of such tradition. The abstraction of space paved the way for its later assertion as an independent reality and a form of dimensionality that is distinct from, and prior to, the bodies that occupy it and move through it.

3.1 The Cosmological Origin of Incorporeal Space: John Philoponus

In that process, a salient role is reserved for the work of John Philoponus, also known as John the Grammarian, who was responsible for a decisive contribution to the idea of *spatiality* as such. It is interesting to note that Philoponus accepts as a premise the Aristotelian injunction on the finitude of the world; precisely in the name of that injunction; however, he ends up rejecting the notion of place that sustains the whole edifice of the *Physics*.[1] The logic of Aristotelian cosmology, otherwise put, forces him to abandon his physics.

The problem, once again, has to do with the old paradox regarding the place of the cosmos, which could be synthesized in the following form: if everything that exists is somewhere, and if the cosmos exists, then what is the place of the cosmos as such?[2] As Philoponus reminds us, Aristotle had solved the problem through his conception of place as "the limit of what is limited." From that perspective, of course, the heavens as a whole cannot be strictly in a place, for there is no extra-cosmic body that would be capable of surrounding and encompassing the all. But when considered "in respect of all of its parts," Aristotle says, the cosmos is effectively emplaced, for each one of the celestial spheres, being contiguous to one another, acts successively as the place of the sphere that it encloses, so that the concave surface of the first celestial sphere acts as a place for our sublunar world, and the last of the spheres, that of the fixed stars, for the cosmos as a whole – except for the strange fact that such sphere must be considered to include itself, that is, to act somehow as its own place.[3] The cosmos, therefore, can only be said to be in place as "by analogy."

Commentators of the cosmology of Aristotle had struggled for centuries with this solution. For all its merits, this reasoning presented a major problem: places, for Aristotle, are by definition immobile, and all of the celestial spheres move. How are we to imagine that a rotating sphere could play the role of an immobile place? How to assume that the stability and peace of our sublunar world, and even of the cosmos as a whole, must come from an ethereal continuous movement, instead of the embracing solidity of an immobile place?

Philoponus frontally rejects the "orthodox" solution to this problem, according to which the rotatory movement of the spheres is not equivalent to local motion because, considered as a whole, a rotating sphere always remains in the same place. For it is obvious that, even if the sphere as a whole does not change its place, each of its parts does move locally, occupying different portions of space and moving from one place to another as the sphere as a whole rotates. At this point, Philoponus only has three options available to resolve the problem of the placelessness of the world. The first would be to abandon the belief in the finitude of the cosmos. The second, to renounce the principle of the rotation of the heavens. Philoponus rejects these solutions and embraces the third, concluding that Aristotle's notion of place is deficient, and that a completely different understanding of the locality of being is needed if we are to make sense of the world.

This cosmological investigation led Philoponus to develop an astoundingly original conception of space (*diastema*), which departed decisively from the conception of place in Aristotelian physics. Place, Philoponus says, is not the limiting surface of the surrounding body. Rather, in the "Corollary on Place" that he adds to his *Commentary of the Physics*, he says that place should be conceived of as

> a certain interval, measurable in three dimensions, incorporeal in its very nature and different from the body contained in it; it is pure dimensionality void of all corporeality; indeed, as far as matter is concerned, space and the void are identical.[4]

As pure dimensionality, space must be understood in complete independence of the bodies that come to occupy it. Space is not a substance: it has no corporeality and is absolutely different from any form of body-ness or materiality. Space is to be understood simply as the opening of length, width, and height that allows for the corporeal things of the world to take place in it. Independently of which body occupies a particular region of space at any given moment, space will remain always the same, it will not move or change in any way whatsoever. Simply put, space belongs to an entirely different plane of existence.

3.2 The Problem of Motion in Immaterial Space

The physics of Philoponus would find, however, a subsequent problem. As a result of his voiding of spatiality, in fact, Philoponus is forced to reject altogether the intrinsic capacities that had been formerly attributed to the notion of place. The consideration of space as "pure dimensionality," everywhere equal to itself and entirely distinct from bodies and matter, proves to be incompatible with the idea that places can in any way act on matter or direct its motion. It is ridiculous, Philoponus says in a passage from his commentary on the *Physics*, "to pretend that space, as such, possesses an inherent power."[5]

How can we explain then the motion of bodies in the great, empty interval of space? In Aristotle, the dynamics of bodies and matter are explained in close relation to a natural topology of the physical world. Movements, Aristotle says, are either natural or unnatural, "and these terms are defined in relation to places, i.e. the one which is proper and the one which is alien to the body."[6] To each element corresponds a proper place in the world, to which that element is drawn by a sort of intrinsic pull. By their heaviness or lightness, for instance, bodies are directed downwards or upwards, towards the center of the Earth or the lunar orbs, each depending on its nature. When bodies reach the places that are natural to them, they can put an end to their motion and be finally at rest.

Having voided place of its inherent powers, Philoponus finds himself in the difficulty of explaining the natural movement of bodies. For in a general space that is devoid of qualities and determinations, a space that is effectively reduced to pure dimensionality, how could those motions be explained?[7] Why would bodies move in one direction rather than another? Would we even be able to discriminate those directions? Would there still be an "upwards" and a "downwards," a "front" and a "back," a "left" and a right"?[8] The problem of movement reflects a much deeper tension that becomes manifest in the innovative physics of Philoponus: the tension between an incorporeal, undifferentiated space that is everywhere empty and equal to itself, and the order and reference of things in the existing material world.

In a surprising move, Philoponus's solution to this problem consists in introducing a complex, apparently obscure relation between the purely abstract nature of space and a theological theory of physical emplacement. If each body tends to its natural place, he explains, "it is not because it seeks to reach a certain surface; the reason is rather that it tends to the place which was assigned to it by the demiurge."[9] Bodies do not tend towards physical places because those places are natural to them, but rather because they have been ascribed to them by the divine creator of nature. With this move, Philoponus tries to maintain his denial that places can have any sort of power or inherent capacity of their own, while holding to the logic of hierarchy and position that structures and orders the world as it is. His solution, however, makes only more manifest a form of metaphysical tension between the incorporeal and the corporeal, abstraction and emplacement, space and matter, theology and physics, which would keep haunting the philosophy of space for many centuries to come. In that respect, it is not a coincidence that Philoponus's solution echoes the mysterious, alternative grand theory of space inherited from Greek philosophy: the thought of *chora* (χώρα), exposed in Plato's *Timaeus* precisely as an articulation of that very same tension.

3.3 Being, Space, and the Materiality of Things: The Legacy of Plato's Timaeus

In the *Timaeus*, *chora* entertains a difficult relation with the idea of space. Only through a "bastard reasoning," Timaeus of Locri says in his presentation of it, we affirm that everything that is must be in some region (τόπῳ) and occupy some *chora*, the "seat" or "abode" for all things that are generated.[10] But *chora* does not equal locality. *Chora* is somehow prior to place: it is what makes room for things to exist, as the receptacle or the opening in which the physical world can take place. *Chora* is the answer to the paradox raised by Zeno: it is the "where" of places and of the things that come to be in them. That is why Timaeus says that only by approximation can we count it "as a place."

Entertaining Socrates with a grand speech about the origin of the cosmos, Timaeus affirms that between the realms of being and becoming there must be a mediating third kind, the realm of *chora*, which is essential to understand the nature of the world. On one side there is being, the unbegotten and unperishable realm of forms that are always selfsame and equal to themselves. On the other side, the fleeting materiality of becoming, always tied to the concreteness of places and the succession of time. Between the two, stretched by the original tension of being and materiality, *chora* appears as the complex, mysterious opening that makes room for things in the world to take place.

Like the distance that separates two terms while bringing them together, *chora* conditions and limits at once the movement between the anywhere of εἶδε and the concreteness of every possible *there*. *Chora* welcomes and receives the forms in becoming, but its reception indicates a distortion as well, a margin of inadequacy and even perhaps of resistance, a dislocation that obscures the thought of a peaceful equation, of the flat and limpid translation of what is placeless into the commensurable concreteness of our nature and our world. *Chora* at once "enables and limits" the sensible images of the intelligible, dispelling every illusion of a straightforward trajectory between the nowhereness of truth and the thereness and givenness of physics.[11]

To amend such distortion, or to reduce it completely, would become a philosophical obsession for the followers of Plato. The physics of Aristotle reduced *chora* to the corporeality of *topos*, collapsing space and matter on a single plane and thus eliminating the metaphysical source of their tension.[12] To the Stoic, Neoplatonic and Christian traditions, which shared and prolonged the logic of a dual metaphysics of nature, the incorporeal logic of *chora* would offer, however, an invaluable philosophical tool. *Chora* grants an intelligible seat for the actual physicality of bodies. It gives noetic room for the physical world to take place, and offers thereby a spatial solution to the metaphysical scission of being and becoming.[13]

The subtlety and duplicity of *chora* gives then way to different forms of spatial equivalence between matter and mind, body and God, the corporeal and the incorporeal. For the Stoics, "spiritual bodies" contain and give cohesion to the passive substance of matter, with which they coincide. The air-like element of *pneuma* permeates the world and holds it together, guaranteeing its continuity and the spatial coincidence of spirit and matter. Substituting the cosmic breath by light, which Plotinus had already identified as the purest and most perfect element of all, Proclus would conceive of an immaterial body of light in which the physical world takes place. Echoing another image from the *Timaeus*, according to which the demiurge gave to the body of the cosmos the "most perfect and uniform" shape, Proclus pictures hence the existence of two spheres,

> one made of a single light, the other of many bodies, the two equal to each other in volume. But seat one concentrically with the other, and on implanting the other in it, you will see the whole cosmos residing in its place, moving in the immobile light.[14]

Two concentric and coextensive spheres, one of which contains the entire materiality of physics, the other of a purely intelligible nature, with the cosmos rotating in immobile light. With this image, Proclus not only solves the Aristotelian problem of the motion of the outer sphere, granting a stable shell to the cosmos, which finally finds in light its immaterial place. Space also provides a solution for the metaphysical scission that had threatened the very consistency of physics. Identified with nothing more than a "finest light," the incorporeal substance of space now sustains both the soul and the body of the world; space nurtures them and holds them together at last.[15]

3.4 Order and Dimension: The Determination of Space in Neoplatonism

This form of metaphysical mediation between the orders of the corporeal and the incorporeal is not the only legacy of the *Timaeus* to the Neoplatonic philosophy of space. There is a second, decisive contribution which has to do with the concern for the arrangement of matter in space, or otherwise put, with the order and hierarchy of bodies as they exist in the cosmos. This was precisely the problem that Philoponus had encountered when dealing with the explanation of natural motions. If we assume that space is distinct from the things that are in it, how can we explain that things occupy some regions of that space instead of others? Why do things move towards certain places, and when they reach them, remain there? And more generally, how can things be determined and differentiated in a space that is incorporeal and immaterial?

Dealing precisely with the problems of generation and determination of matter, Timaeus makes yet another mysterious statement: *chora* is not merely a passive recipient, like a blank surface upon which the physical copies of being would be simply imprinted. On the contrary, we are told that *chora* moves, that it acts and puts pressure of matter.[16] In the manner of a sieve, we are told, *chora* discriminates the elements, guides them to their proper places, and hence contributes to order the world. Such order, consequently, is not the exclusive result of the action of the demiurge; *chora* participates in the ordering as well. Quite remarkably, this will be the logic followed by Syrianus to explain the process of differentiation in the natural world: both the demiurge and the soul of the cosmos give form and sensible determinations to an otherwise undifferentiated and incorporeal extension.[17] Each part receives from both a purpose and a position that is proper to it within the common receptacle that welcomes them all. Thus things are determined and emplaced in the most fitting possible order, right where they belong, and nowhere else.

Building on his powerful image of the two spheres, the disciples of Proclus would further refine this logic of correspondence and hierarchization of the physical world. The first sphere contains this time the entire material realm of bodies and their movements; the second sphere, of a purely ideal nature, imprints upon the first the arrangement of their proper and essential positions.[18] The elements and motions of the world are hence determined by a cosmic natural hierarchy. The noetic function of space guarantees not only the empathy and continuity of the physical and the ideal, but also the order and position of everything that exists in the world.

Philoponus's answer to the problem of natural motion ("a body tends to the place which was assigned to it by the demiurge") does not differ substantively from this established logic of the ideal determination of matter. With him, however, an underlying paradox becomes perhaps more apparent. There is a tension between the affirmation of space as an independent dimension and the concern for the disposition and order of things in the world, as if the "voiding" of space, a space emptied of qualitative powers and differentiations, required to be "filled back" again to account for the inner workings of bodies and their motions. In Philoponus, that tension could not be resolved without surrendering incorporeal space to determinations of an explicitly theological nature – a logic that Christian thinkers would meticulously refine over the next millenary or so. To achieve its full independence, it was not enough for space to distinguish itself from matter. It needed to be divinized too.

Notes

1. See for instance the description by Jammer: "Philoponus accepts the fundamental tenet of the finiteness of the universe. Since matter is finite, its correlate, space, which is indissolubly connected with it, must be finite as well. Thus the universe possesses a final boundary, a last sphere, which determines its 'upper' regions" (*Concepts of Space: The History of Theories of Space in Physics*, 67).
2. Philoponus also deals with a second related problem, already formulated by Zeno and dealt with by Archytas, which has to do with the infinite regress related to *locality of place* itself: if everything that exists is somewhere, and if place exists what is the place of place? See John Philoponus, *On Aristotle Physics 4.1-5*, trans. Algra Keimpe and J. M. van Ophuijsen (London: Bristol Classical Press, 2012), 599–1, 84.
3. Ibid. 596–7, 82: "So the heavens as a whole, he says, are in a place in respect of all their parts (for each of the parts is contained by the parts surrounding it, and the parts are like a lace for each other);

yet the universe is not in a place. For if it were in a place, it would have what contains it from outside (. . .) all things are in the heavens, because the heavens are the universe: for they contain everything from outside, and have included it within themselves (. . .) According to his exegetes, however, the place of the sphere of the fixed stars in respect of its parts would be the convex surface of the sphere inside it, and different parts of the one sphere are in contact with different parts of the other sphere at different times (. . .) in this respect, then, the convex surface of the inner sphere may by analogy be the place of the sphere of the fixed stars, and the place of the whole of that sphere in respect to its part."

4. *Ioannis Philoponi in Aristotelis physiscorum libros quinque posteriores commentaria*, edited by H. Vitelli (Berlin: 1888), 567, as translated in Jammer, *Concepts of Space*, 56; also cited in Duhem, *Le Système du monde*, 317–8. Philoponus's identification of space with the void, however, is profoundly paradoxical. In fact, the emptiness of space is never realized in the world: space is always and everywhere filled by bodies, to the point that there can never exist a place devoid of the body, nor a body deprived of the space that allows it to extend volumetrically. Jammer calls that void a "logical necessity." Similarly, Grant describes this "vacuum" as a "continuous three-dimensional physical quantity in which the magnitude of bodies is received" (Grant, *Much Ado About Nothing*, 186). Perhaps this identification could be understood as being of a purely metaphysical nature, a signal of the tension introduced by the abstraction of space and its consequent separation from matter. Panofsky could be referring to this tension when he speaks of the "inability of antique thought to bring the concrete empirical "attributes" of space, and in particular the distinction between 'body' and 'nonbody', to a common denominator of a *substance étendue*: bodies are not absorbed into a homogeneous and infinite system of dimensional relationships, but rather are the juxtaposed contents of a finite vessel" (*Perspective as Symbolic Form*, 44). Somehow, the separation of the incorporeal from the materiality of being cannot be fully achieved, and leaves hence a mark of incompleteness.

5. *Ioannis Philoponi in Aristotelis physiscorum*, 581, as translated in Jammer, *Concepts of Space*, 57.

6. Aristotle, On the Heavens, 276a 10–16: "And if this is lacking, there cannot be movement; for movement must be either natural or unnatural, and these terms are defined in relation to places, i.e. the one which is proper and the one which is alien to the body. Again, if when a body rests or moves contrary to its nature, the place of the action must be proper to some other body (a fact which experience leads us to believe), then it is impossible for everything to have weight or everything lightness; some will have one and some the other".

7. Aristotle had explicitly expressed this problem when arguing the impossibility of movement in a void. In the absence of local determinations, he argues, "no one could say why a thing once set in motion should stop anywhere; for why should it stop *here* rather than *here*?" (*Physics*, 215a 19–20). These are precisely the arguments that Hasdai Crescas refutes in his *Or Adonai*, already in 1400. Considered as the great continuator of the theory of Philoponus, Crescas considered space – perhaps for the first time – as a single, infinite, and homogenous empty extension distinct from matter and from the bodies that occupy it. Crescas would anticipate modern dynamics by making the void not an obstacle, but precisely the condition for the possibility of movement (see Harry Austryn Wolfson, *Crescas' Critique of Aristotle*, Problems of Aristotle's Physics in Jewish and Arabic Philosophy (Cambridge: Harvard University Press, 1971).

8. These are the six dimensions that Aristotle attributes in the *Physics* to *topos koinos*, the general place of the world (see Panofsky, *Perspective as Symbolic Form*, 43). In a language evocative of Nietzsche, Duhem sums up the problem of orientation generated by Philoponus's abstraction of space: "Mais comment, dans cet espace doué seulement de trois dimensions, pourra-t-on déterminer, distinguer et placer le haut et le bas? Où placera-t-on le lieu suprême? Jusqu'où l'étendra-t-on? Où mettra-t-on le lieu le plus bas? En outre, le lieu doit être doué d'une certaine puissance naturelle, car les corps graves et les corps légers désirent leurs lieux propres, chacun d'eux se porte vers le lieu qui lui est particulier par une inclination et par un élan naturels; or, cet espace, qui est vide par lui-même, en peut avoir aucune puissance; pour quelle raison certain corps porteraient-ils vers une certaine région de ce vide et certains autres corps vers une autre région?" (*Le Système du monde*, 319).

9. Philoponus, *Corollaries*, 44, as translated in Jammer, *Concepts of Space*, 57. Casey provides an alternative translation of the passage, with even deeper religious undertones: "Things move to their proper place through desire for that station in the order which they have been given by their Creator" (*The Fate of Place*, 96).

10. *Plato's Timaeus: Translation, Glossary, Appendices and Introductory Essay*, trans. Peter Kalkavage (Focus, 2001), 52a). The entire passage reads as follows: "one kind is the form, which is in a self-same condition – unbegotten and imperishable, neither receiving into itself anything else from anywhere else nor itself going anywhere into anything else, invisible and in all other ways unsensed . . . and there is a second kind, which has the same name as the form and is similar to it – sensed, begotten, always swept along, coming to be in some region (τόπῳ) and again perishing from there . . . and moreover, a third kind – that of χώρα- which always is, admitting not of destruction and providing a seat for all that has birth, itself grasped by some

bastard reasoning with the aid of insensibility, hardly to be trusted, the very thing we look to when we dream and affirm that it's necessary somehow (που) for everything that is to be in some region (τόπῳ) and occupy some χώρα, and that what is neither on earth nor somewhere (που) in heaven is nothing."

11. Sallis, *Chorology*, 45. Sallis emphasizes how "in the transition from intelligible to visible something like place [comes] into play, letting things be set apart as they are gathered into the comprehensive visible cosmos. As the chora, which seems like place, will prove always to have come into play in the very opening of difference" (ibid., 60). Indeed, *chora* always has to do with "phantoms that come and go"; it never acts as a mere mirror "in which perpetual being would be reflected and the cosmos thus fabricated" (122).

12. This is what Sallis describes as the Aristotelian "conflation of Platonic chora with matter (. . .) and space" (*Chorology*, 154). Paradoxically, that movement would not be entirely foreign to Philoponus, who in addition to (and distinct from) incorporeal space conceived of a *three-dimensional* "corporeal extension" (*sômatikón diastema*), *an undetermined substance that is "constitutive of body as such"* (Christian Wildberg, "John Philoponus," in *The Stanford Encyclopedia of Philosophy*, ed. Edward N. Zalta [Metaphysics Research Lab, Stanford University, 2018]). For Sallis, such movement would be a paradigmatic example of the reduction of *Chora* to matter. Tracing the instances of such reduction, Sallis reserves a special place to Plotinus's powerful – and paradoxical – descriptions of matter as *incorporeal*: "Matter, then, is incorporeal . . . It is a ghostly image of bulk . . .; it is invisible in itself and escapes any attempt to see it and occurs when one is not looking, but even if you look closely you cannot see it . . . Whatever announcement it makes, therefore, is a lie . . . its apparent being is not being, but a sort of fleeting frivolity; hence the things that seem to come to be in it are frivolities, nothing but phantoms (*eidola*) in a phantom, like something in a mirror which really exists in one place but is reflected in another; it seems to be filled, and holds nothing; it is all seeming" (*Treatise on Matter*, III.6.7, as translated in Sallis, *Chorology*, 151).

13. See Casey, *The Fate of Place*, 90ff.

14. Plato, *Timaeus*, 33b; Simplicius, *In Aristotelis physicorum libros quattuor*, as translated by Sorabji, *Matter, Space and Motion*, 115. Casey sees in Proclus's identification of space with light the "anticipation of Modern ideas of an all-encompassing ether" (*The Fate of Place*, 377).

15. Proclus, *Elements of Physics*, 142a. On the spatial function of mediation between the corporeal and incorporeal orders of existence, see Lucas Siorvanes: "Proclus' Space is an intermediary between the World Soul and Body, i.e. between the immaterial and incorporeal state of existence, on the one side, and the material and corporeal, on

the other, hence the "immaterial body" ("Proclus on the Elements and the Celestial Bodies. Physical Thought in Late Neoplatonism," PhD diss., Department of History and Philosophy of Science, University College London, 1986, 113).

16. Plato, *Timaeus*, 52d.

17. I am following Duhem's rendition of Syrianus's account of the rational determination of extension, as reconstructed in Simplicius's "Corollary on place" (J. O. Urmson, *Simplicius: Corollaries on Place and Time* [London: Bloomsbury, 2014]). This is Duhem's illustrative commentary of that process: "Une étendue (*diastema*) qui, par elle-même, serait homogène et indifférenciée; du Demiurge et de l'Âme du Monde cette étendue va recevoir l'hétérogénéité et la différentiation. Le Demiurge, en effet, contient en lui-même une multitude de formes (*eide*); l'Âme renferme une foule de raisons (*logoi*); en illuminant l'étendue, le Demiurge et l'Âme y engendrent une multiplicité semblable à celle qui réside en eux-mêmes, ils la divisent en parties et, à ces diverses parties, ils confèrent des propriétés distinctes; chacune de ces parties devient, par la, le domaine propre de tel corps . . . l'étendue (*diastema*) compénètre le Monde entier, elle admet, en elle-même, la nature corporelle tout entière . . . fixe, rigide, immobile, exempte de tout changement, elle est établie dans le monde des apparences, elle confère un domaine (*chora*), un réceptacle, une borne, un contour" (*Le Système du monde*, 334–7). On Syrianus's reading of the *Timaeus*, and specifically on the intricacies of his conception of the relations between the demiurge and the paradigm and his influence on Proclus, see Sarah Klitenic Wear, *The Teachings of Syrianus on Plato's Timaeus and Parmenides* (Leiden: Brill, 2011), 11–3, and her translation of fragments 6, 7 and 24 especially.

18. See Duhem: "Selon Damascius et Simplicius, la même surface sphérique délimite encore deux sphères exactement superposées l'une à l'autre. Une de ces deux sphères est corporelle et matérielle; elle est formée de tous les corps, constamment mobiles, que contient l'Univers. L'autre est purement idéale ; elle est formée par l'ensemble des positions propres et essentielles de ces mêmes corps" (*Le Système du monde*, 347–8).

Chapter 4

Immensity: Space as a Theological Problem

The affirmation of space as an incorporeal dimension would prove to be at least as decisive as the assertion of the infinity and emptiness of space for the early modern scientific imagination. To be sure, the connections between those three ideas were at the time far from being developed. Like most Neoplatonic philosophers (and the scholastics who recovered the works of Aristotle), Philoponus clearly rejected, for instance, the infinity of the universe, and only accepted the idea of emptiness as a theoretical entity – which means that according to him, the void could never become actual in the physical world. There is no doubt that the "emancipation of space" is here far from being realized; as we have seen, the very notion of the incorporeality of space is still trapped in deep metaphysical tensions and contradictions.

Nevertheless, the idea of an immaterial, three-dimensional space that is distinct from, and independent of, the bodies that exist in it, was destined to complete its process of abstraction, and to do so precisely by espousing those two other notions, the infinity and emptiness of space, in one and the same concept. That espousal would not happen, however, without the concourse of a very different philosophical power: the corpus of Christian theology, in which space would become an attribute of the divinity itself, or most simply put, the very immensity of God.

4.1 The Spatial Paradox of Ubiquity

The theoretical problem of space runs deep in the Judeo-Christian tradition.[1] In the first verses of the Book of Genesis, God is said to create "the heavens and the Earth" and only then to separate them spatially, motivating a complex interrogation on the spatial presuppositions of creation and on the broader ontology of the relation between God and physical space. The mystery of creation implies spatiality in a deep manner, and conversely, space seems to be a privileged way of accessing the mystery of God's power and his relation and effects on the physical world.

Any approximation to that relation, however, could not fail to trigger serious concerns and theoretical problems. Not only there are obvious questions about the spatial presuppositions of creation and the forms of presence of the divinity (where was God before the creation of the world? Where is he now in relation to it? How to understand the relation to the world of an ever-present, non-extended being? Where is heaven in relation to our spatial existence on Earth?).[2] There is also the added problem that space as such appears as the image and expression of physicality, of our mortal and earthly existence, and hence unworthy of the absolute power and greatness of God.

The relation between God and space acquired, hence, a profoundly paradoxical form. Paul had said "in Him we live, we move and we are": God opens and sustains the space in which all things are, to the point that an early Christian, Arnobius of Sicca, identified the divinity with "the place and space of things created."[3] But while all things are in God, and God himself is said to be present in all things, God cannot be in any kind of space.[4] His ubiquity, essential to the form of divine presence, cannot be reducible to, or confounded with, any sort of sensible or physical expression. God is said to be everywhere, notes Boethius in his *De Trinitate*,

> not because he is in every place (for he is unable to be in a place at all) but because every place is present to him insofar as it holds him, although he himself is not contained in any place; and therefore he is said to be nowhere in place, for he is everywhere but not in any place.[5]

To be everywhere, but not in any place, synthesizes the paradox installed at the heart of the Christian theology of space. God has to be conceived of as being present – and able to intervene without limit – in every and any point of physical space.[6] But at the same time, that presence cannot correspond to any form of material spatiality. The Christian God has no dimensions, and his power cannot be taken as being spatially limited, contained or realized in any possible way, for as we are told, not even "the highest heaven" could contain him.

To understand the nature of this relation, Christian thinkers would need to transcend the very logic of the spatial as something restricted to its earthly, physical terms. The challenge implied nothing less than to de-spatialize the thought of God, and as a consequence, that of the essence and causes of the natural world too.

4.2 To Speak from Afar: Augustine's Theology of Space

In the midst of an investigation on beauty that would exert considerable influence on the fathers of the church, Plotinus describes the logic of transcendence as a form of distance that cannot be understood in spatial or physical terms:

> Our country from which we came is there, our Father is there. How shall we travel to it, where is our way of escape? We cannot get there on foot; our feet only carry us everywhere in this world, from one country to another. You must not get ready a carriage, either, or a boat. Let all these things go, and do not look. Shut your eyes, and change to and wake another way of seeing, which everyone has but few use.[7]

For Augustine of Hippo, this "different way of seeing" becomes a sort of theological premise to approach the relation between God and the world.[8] God is essentially unthinkable in terms of space. Grasping the transcendence of God requires conceiving the existence of a being that, though absolutely present, cannot be apprehended in terms of extension or physical spatiality. For that, it is necessary to purify first the very logic of human understanding, to de-spatialize our very categories of thought, lest our ideas of the divinity remain vain and essentially mistaken. Only then we can begin to intuit the structure of an ontological reality which was, before this operation, radically beyond the domain of the thinkable.

This process, Augustine explains, is of an extraordinary difficulty. The "mists of bodily images" take hold of human thought, they "obstruct the view and obscure the brightness."[9] Man "is space from head to foot" and cannot abstract himself easily from the spatial conception of things; even when he does, the doubt persists and remains, for things that are not in space could very well not have any form of real existence at all, they might be nothing more than phantoms of the imagination.[10] Truth itself might not exist, since it does not partake in the spatial nature of material things:

> And I said: Is truth then nothing at all,
> since it is not extended
> either through finite spaces or infinite?
> And Thou didst cry to me from afar:
> I am who I am.[11]

"I am who I am" means that God is beyond the very terms of Augustine's question, unattainable by its categories, ultimately unreachable by its logic (and yet, God replies "from afar," *de longinquo*, as if only through a radicalization of the very language of spatiality one could finally neutralize it).[12] God is a transcendent, spiritual substance, who is wholly everywhere and "in every place at once in the totality of his being."[13] God is present and able to intervene at any point and time in the physical world, yet nowhere limited by space or by any bodily shape or form.

From this conclusion, however, follow uneasy metaphysical consequences. The most apparent of them can be synthesized in simple terms: the infinite, non-spatial, spiritual power of God appears as the perfect cause of a finite, spatial, material world of creation, with which, however, it does not strictly coincide. The problem of cosmological mediation between the infinite and the finite – of nature as a realization of the transcendent principle of God – would linger for centuries in scholastic debates on the nature and properties of space. Despite Augustine's doctrinal efforts, this question would endlessly trouble the speculations of Christian philosophers of nature throughout the Middle Ages: how can a finite and imperfect world express the infinite greatness and perfection of God?

4.3 Imaginary Space and Divine Immensity

To denounce any form of limitation of the ineffable powers and capacities of God was precisely the object of a major theological document published by the Bishop of Paris in 1277. The "Paris Condemnation" denounced a variety of ways in which theologians restricted the powers of God by circumscribing them to the established principles of logic and natural philosophy. Among the articles condemned by the bishop were the denial of God's capacity to create other worlds, to move and displace the world from its place, to destroy the whole of creation, or to generate void spaces and *vacua* both in this world and outside of it.[14] Even an infinite, empty space could be imagined to exist; the only condition being that it must have been created by God.

In the wake of the Paris Condemnation, scholastic philosophers and theologians developed complex and systematic investigations on the relation between God and space, progressively leading to an identification of the idea of God's immensity with an infinite extension of space devoid of any sort of bounds or limitations. Of course, this identification is at the extreme opposite of the Augustinian de-spatialization of the thought of God. Indivisible and incorporeal, unbounded and unchanging, independent of thought or matter, space appeared as an expression of the power of God – and even as an image of the divinity itself.

Logically, the implications of such speculation were dangerous from a theological perspective. To identify God with a limitless space not only seemed to entail that the world of creation was infinite, but also led to the abhorrent conclusion that God could be understood as an extended being.[15] To confront the first problem, Christian scholastics adopted a Stoic-like image of the cosmos, according to which an infinite extent of empty space surrounded the finite sphere of the world. To confront the second, they posited the existence of such infinite space as "imaginary" (*spatium imaginarium*), not in the sense that it was a product of fiction or hypothesis, but that unlike the real space of the world, which is always occupied by bodies, the extra-cosmic space was characterized by the total absence of bodies and of physical reality as such.[16]

Distinct from the cosmic world of matter and earth, imaginary space could hence appear as the realm of infinite presence of the divinity, to the point that, according to Nicole Oresme, if asked about the vacuum outside the heaven, one should reply that it is "nothing but God Himself, Who is His own indivisible immensity and His own eternity as a whole and all at once."[17] Similarly, Thomas Bradwardine identified God's immensity with an infinite imaginary space in the corollaries of his *De causa Dei contra Pelagium*, which affirmed the following:

> First, that essentially and in presence, God is necessarily everywhere in the world and all its parts;
> And also beyond the real world in a place, or in an imaginary infinite void.
> And so truly can He be called immense and unlimited.

> And so a reply seems to emerge to the questions of the gentiles and heretics – "Where is your God?" And, "where was God before the [creation of the] world?"
> And it also seems obvious that a void can exist without body, but in no manner can it exist without God.[18]

In reason of his immensity, God must be said to be present in an imaginary void that extends infinitely beyond the boundaries of the cosmos. Making that imaginary space *real*, attributing actual physical extension to it, would still require tearing down the cosmic barrier of the Stoics, the ultimate shell that separated the world from an extra-cosmic space, totally devoid of matter and bodies, which had been now fully divinized. It would also require the workings of a cosmological imagination that no longer proceeds exclusively *via negativa*, equating the void with the imaginary absence of body, dimensionality, and reality, but positively asserts the physical existence of infinite space.[19]

On both counts, however, the universalist theology of Christianity produced and refined the conceptual framework that would allow for the transformation of imaginary space into an independent and objective empirical reality. Thus, the divinization of space (and, conversely, the spatialization of the infinite ubiquity of God) paved the way for the positive assertion of its absoluteness.

4.4 The World as an Infinite Sphere

In that process, a salient place is reserved to the eclectic work of another eminent theologian, Nicholas of Cusa, often credited with being the first thinker to fully reject the medieval conception of the cosmos.[20] The world, for Cusa, is an expression (*explicatio*) of God's perfection. In nature we experience as heterogeneity and individuation what in God is present in perfect unity and coherence (*complicatio*). To that unity nothing can be added or subtracted; in God all the determinations of being, from the incommensurable to the minuscule, are embraced and unified, to the point that the opposites can concur and coincide with one another in perfect harmony (*coincidentia oppositorum*).[21] The metaphysical infinity of God is beyond all relational capacities, beyond qualities and quantities, but includes and transcends them all.

The radicality of Cusa consists precisely in making the universe an *expression* of that infinite metaphysical essence. Borrowing a metaphor that was destined to a wealth of later appropriations and adaptations, Cusa describes the world as a sphere that "will *quasi* have its center everywhere and its circumference nowhere (*centrum ubique, circumferentia nullibi*), because the circumference and the center are God, who is everywhere and nowhere."[22] Unlike previous occurrences of this magnificent image, here we are not dealing only with an eloquent approximation to the theological immensity of God. Indeed, Cusa is using the metaphor to describe the "fabric of the world" (*machina mundi*), making "what is" a physical manifestation of the infinitely divine essence. The consequences for the cosmological imagination are shocking. The world in which we live has no circumference, Cusa explains,

> because if it had a center and a circumference, and thus had a beginning and an end in itself, the world would be limited in respect to something else, and outside the world there would be something other, and space, things that are wholly lacking in truth. Since, therefore, it is impossible to enclose the world between a corporeal *centrum* and a circumference, it is [impossible for] our reason to have a full understanding of the world, as it implies the comprehension of God who is the center and the circumference of it.[23]

In the absence of such full understanding, however, one thing still remains clear. Our universe must be understood as having no exteriority and no limits: there is no last boundary, no edge of the world, no extra-cosmic space on the other side of the line. Our world is rather an endless totality for which there are no fixed points of reference other than God, where everything is de-centered and, at the same time, every point is at once "beginning and end, foundation and limit" of the infinite universe.[24] With this image, Cusa demolishes any cosmic barrier or separation between the world and an infinite beyond, and breaks into pieces all the shells, vaults, and spheres that determined the spatial hierarchies and orders of classical cosmology and metaphysics.

As the success of the metaphor will demonstrate, Cusa's gesture anticipates the deep and sweeping transformation of European cosmology which has come to be identified with the epistemic origins of modernity. Many centuries after the early investigations of Anaximander and Heraclides Ponticus, the "promise" of an infinite universe – a universe whose center is everywhere and nowhere at once – would finally assert itself as the hegemonic logic of astronomical practice and imagination.[25] That promise, to be sure, was not without threats and challenges. In a delightful investigation that verses precisely on the philosophical history of the infinite sphere, Jorge Luis Borges recalls how Giordano Bruno experienced "the breaking of the stellar vaults as a liberation," while only seventy years later, Pascal lamented the fate of men now "lost in space and time," abandoned to fear and solitude in the "labyrinth" and the "abyss" of an absolute void.[26]

This emotional ambivalence expresses something essential about the early modern European imagination. As we shall see in the coming chapters, the resolution of the cosmological problems of modernity implied consequences that went far beyond the realms of physics and the philosophy of nature. Indeed, the logic of the infinite universe was ripe with ethical and political effects. That logic transformed not only the science and theories of the cosmos, but also the political discourses and practices of Western powers, precisely at the time in which they were about to extend their political dominion over the entirety of the known world. The "apotheosis of space" of the seventeenth century, which enunciated and advanced to the highest degree this early modern logic of universality, would have been unthinkable, nonetheless, without the long, intricate odyssey of space across the classical and medieval philosophical traditions. Without the ancient speculations on the principle of the unbounded; on the void and the positivity of nothingness; on an incorporeal dimension that would be distinct from matter and bodies; and on space as a *situs imaginarium* that is coincident with the immensity of a divine nature, the celestial spheres would have never been broken, and all those different practices, theoretical and political, that we now identify under the name of modernity, would have probably taken a different course.

Notes

1. Jammer signals that the word *makom*, "place," seems to have been used as a term for God in ancient Judaism (*Concepts of Space*, 28). Already in the first century BCE, Philo of Alexandria is reported to have identified God and space, or at least implied that God must be understood as implying a form of spatiality entirely of His own: "by reason of His containing things, and being contained by nothing whatever, and being a place for all to flee into, and because He is Himself the space which holds Him; for He is that which He Himself has occupied, and naught encloses Him but Himself. I, mark you, am not a place, but in a place; and each thing likewise that exists; for that which is contained is different from that which contains it, and the

Deity, being contained by nothing, is of necessity Itself Its own place" (cited in Grant, *Much Ado About Nothing*, 113).

2. Aristotle had famously rejected any kind of generation *ex-nihilo*; Averroes explained that if the world was created at all, there must have existed a previous void that it consequently occupied. Committed at the same time to the principle of divine genesis and to the Aristotelian refutation of the void, Christian scholastics would struggle for centuries to find a solution to this problem. Similar theological problems had to do with the issues of location (where is God with respect to the world?), limitation (if the world is finite and God's power is not, does creation restrict or limit the power of God?) and dimension (if God is ubiquitous, does it follow that He is extended and present in space?). See for instance Augustine: "Next, we must see what reply can be made to those who agree that God is the Creator of the world, but have difficulties about the time of its creation, and what reply, also, they can make to difficulties we might raise about the place of its creation. For, as they demand why the world was created then and no sooner, we may ask why it was created just here where it is, and not elsewhere. For if they imagine infinite spaces of time before the world, during which God could not have been idle, in like manner they may conceive outside the world infinite realms of space, in which, if any one says that the Omnipotent cannot hold His hand from working, will it not follow that they must adopt Epicurus's dream of innumerable worlds? with this difference only, that he asserts that they are formed and destroyed by the fortuitous movements of atoms, while they will hold that they are made by God's hand, if they maintain that, throughout the boundless immensity of space, stretching interminably in every direction round the world, God cannot rest, and that the worlds which they suppose Him to make cannot be destroyed," *The City of God*, XI, 5, ed. Marcus Dods (Edinburgh: 1871), 441.

3. Acts 17:28, New International Version. "Thou art the first cause, the place and space of things created, the basis of all things whatsoever they be" (Arnobius, *The Case against the Pagans*, ed. George Englert McCracken [Westminster: Newman Press, 1949], 80, cited in Grant, *Much Ado About Nothing*, 113).

4. For the biblical basis of ubiquity see Psalm 139:7–11: "Where can I go from your Spirit? Where can I flee from your presence? If I go up to the heavens, you are there; if I make my bed in the depths, you are there. If I rise on the wings of the dawn, if I settle on the far side of the sea, even there your hand will guide me, your right hand will hold me fast," and Jeremiah 23:28–29: "Do not I fill heaven and earth?" Newton mentions both verses in the General Scholium added to the second edition of the *Principia*. For the impossible containment of God in space see for instance 1 Kings 8:27: "But will God really

dwell on earth? The heavens, even the highest heaven, cannot contain you. How much less this temple I have built!"

5. Boethius, *On the Holy Trinity*, trans. Erik C Kenyon (2004), 179–82, 6.

6. See Psalm 33:13–14: "From heaven the Lord looks down and sees all mankind; from his dwelling place he watches all who live on earth"; and Genesis 28:16: "When Jacob awoke from his sleep, he thought, 'Surely the Lord is in this place, and I was not aware of it.'"

7. Plotinus, *Ennead, Volume I: Porphyry on the Life of Plotinus. Ennead I*, ed. Jeffrey Henderson (Cambridge: Harvard University Press, 1966), I 6.8.16, 257–9. On the influence of Plotinus on Christian theology see John Rist, "Plotinus and Christian Philosophy," in *The Cambridge Companion to Plotinus*, ed. Lloyd P. Gerson (Cambridge: Cambridge University Press, 1996), 386–414.

8. See for instance the following passage from *On Christian Teaching*: "Let us consider this process of cleansing as a trek, or a voyage, to our homeland; though progress towards the One who is ever present is not made through space, but through integrity of purpose and character" (trans. R. P. H. Green [Oxford: Oxford University Press, 1999], 13). See also *Confessions* 1.18.28: "It is not on our feet or by movement in space that we go from Thee or return to Thee" (trans. F. J. Sheed [Indianapolis: Hackett, 2006]).

9. Augustine, *On the Trinity*, 8.2.3, trans. Stephen McKenna [Cambridge: Cambridge University Press, 2002], 7.

10. "You are wholly everywhere, yet nowhere limited within space, nor are You on any bodily form. And yet you have made man in Your own image, and man is a space from head to foot" (*Confessions*, 6.3.4). In the seventh book of the *Confessions*, Augustine depicts in these terms the frustration generated by his first, unproductive efforts at producing a de-spatialized mental image of the divinity: "Whatever I tried to see as not in space seemed to me to be nothing, absolutely nothing, not even a void: for if a body were taken out of its place and the place remained without any body, whether of earth or water or air or sky, it would still be an empty place, a space – occupying nothingness" (7.1.1).

11. *Confessions*, 7.10.16.

12. After successfully de-spatializing his understanding of God, Augustine can look back and realize the magnitude of his previous errors: "how far [was] the reality of [God] from those empty imaginings of mine, imaginings of bodies which had no being whatever" (*Confessions*, 3.6.10). And still, he is constantly forced to remind the reader about the key according to which his use of spatial language must be understood (that is, in non-spatial terms). See, for example, the singular case in 12.7.7: "The less a thing resembles You, the further it is from You (I do not mean in space!)," and similar occurrences in 7.15.21 ("All things are in You in a different manner, being in You not as in a place, but ... held ... in the hand of Your truth") and 13.7.7 ("shall I say that we sink, and we rise again? But it is not in any space").

13. *Confessions*, 1.3.3. See also *The City of God*, XI, 5, where Augustine describes God as being "wholly though spiritually present everywhere."

14. See for instance Jean Buridan: "it must be believed on faith that God could form and create beyond this world other spheres and other worlds and any other finite bodies of whatever size He wishes" (*Questions on De Caelo*, cited in Grant, *Much Ado About Nothing*, 128). On the context of the condemnation of 1277 see Edward Grant, *The Foundations of Modern Science in the Middle Ages: Their Religious, Institutional and Intellectual Contexts*, Cambridge Studies in the History of Science (Cambridge: Cambridge University Press, 1996), 117–38.

15. Grant explains how the identification of God's immensity with space would have "made of God a divisible magnitude and destroyed His divine immutability" (*Much Ado About Nothing*, 180).

16. On the notion of imaginary space see Grant, *Much Ado About Nothing*, 150–6, where he retraces the genealogy of the concept in Aquinas (who denied the existence of extra-cosmic space), John Major (who affirmed that God is present in in an infinite imaginary space beyond the world), and Suárez, who describes empty spaces as imaginary to "preserve [their] nonpositive status" (ibid., 156). On the later influence of the concept of imaginary space see Cees Leijenhorst, "Jesuit Concepts of Spatium Imaginarium and Thomas Hobbes's Doctrine of Space," *Early Science and Medicine* 1, no. 3 (1996): 355–80.

17. Nicole Oresme, *Questiones super De celo*, translated by Claudia Kren (PhD diss., University of Wisconsin, 1965) and quoted by Edward Grant, "Medieval and Seventeenth-Century Conceptions of an Infinite Void Space beyond the Cosmos," *Isis* 60, no. 1 (1969): 48. Similarly, in his *Sentence Commentary* Jean de Ripa affirmed that "God is really present in an infinite imaginary vacuum beyond the world" (cited in Grant, *Much Ado About Nothing*, 129).

18. As translated in Grant, "Medieval and Seventeenth-Century Conceptions of an Infinite Void," 44.

19. An important step in the positivization of the infinite takes place in the work of Duns Scotus. Arguing against Aquinas, Scotus asserted that "if an entity is finite or infinite, it is so not by reason of something accidental to itself, but because it has its own intrinsic degree of finite or infinite perfection" (*Ordinatio* 1, cited in Thomas Williams, "John Duns Scotus," *The Stanford Encyclopedia of Philosophy*, ed. Edward N. Zalta [Metaphysics Research Lab, Stanford University, 2001]). Scotus's conception of a qualitative infinity is neither relative to something else, nor dependent on any form of negation. Rather, it has an affirmative character as an intrinsic property, and even, as the very mode of being of God Himself. The divinization of space that happened in the fourteenth and fifteenth centuries can be understood as a process of transference or projection of that affirmative character of divine infinity to the concept of absolute space, an equation, however, which would take a complex and winding path to resolve.

20. This is Alexandre Koyré's interpretation in *From the Closed World* (see, for instance, 6). Grant disagrees, claiming that from Cusa's metaphysical stipulations it does "not follow that [he] had enunciated a doctrine of real infinite space" (Grant, *Much Ado About Nothing*, 139). A similar interpretation is given by Lovejoy, for whom "the mind of Cusanus, however, was less concerned with astronomical questions than with a species of mystical theology"; for him, "the rejection of the notion of a finite universe bounded by the sphere of the fixed stars does not lead Cusanus to an entirely unequivocal assertion of an infinite physical world of other suns and planets beyond those imaginary limits, but only to the conviction of the unintelligibility of the whole conception of a physical and quantitative world and the necessity, once more, of passing from it to the conception of God" (*The Great Chain of Being*, 113). To be sure, Cusa did not explicitly proclaim the infinity of the world, which is for him *interminatum*; the infinite is a quality exclusively reserved to God. It is equally true that no precise theory of space is presented in *De Docta Ignorantia*. However, in what follows I coincide with Koyré's reading, according to which in Cusa occurs the "transference from God to the universe" of the notion of divine infinity. This reading is refined and elegantly expressed in Karsten Harries's "The Infinite Sphere: Comments on the History of a Metaphor", *Journal of the History of Philosophy* 13, no. 1 (1975): 5–15. A similar interpretation is offered in Michael H. Keefer, according to whom "Cusanus anticipates Pascal in making the Hermetic paradox express both the structure of the physical universe and the relation of this structure to the divine" ("The World Turned Inside Out: Revolutions of the Infinite Sphere from Hermes to Pascal," *Renaissance and Reformation*, 12, no. 4 [1988]: 305).

21. God's infinity is "a unity that embraces not only the different, but even the opposite, qualities or determinations of being" (Koyré, *From the Closed World to the Infinite Universe*, 8–9).

22. Nicholas of Cusa, *De Docta Ignorantia*, 1. II. 12, translated in Koyré, *From the Closed World*, 17. Long attributed to Cusa, the image of a sphere whose center is everywhere and its circumference nowhere (*sphaera cuis centrum ubique, circumferentia nullibi*) has itself a long history. Both Lovejoy and Grant retrace its origin in the pseudo-Hermetic treatise the Book of the XXIV Philosophers from the twelfth century, and find it formulated, in slightly diverging versions, in Bradwardine, Alexander Neckham, Bartholomew the Englishman, Alexander of Hales, St. Bonaventure, and Thomas Aquinas in the following years. Suárez, Ficino, Bruno, and Fludd also employed it before Pascal produced what is perhaps its most famous formulation (Grant, *Much Ado About Nothing*, 138 and 346–7; Lovejoy, *The Great Chain of Being*, 112). In what follows,

I rely on the reading of Karsten Harries, who not only believes that Cusa transferred the metaphor from God to the universe, but analyzes how the image itself presupposed "an understanding of God and man which had to lead men beyond the medieval cosmos" ("The Infinite Sphere: Comments on the History of a Metaphor", 6).

23. Ibid., 12.

24. Koyré, *From the Closed World*, 11. Jammer makes the case for identifying in the work of Cusa a "turning point in the history of astronomy" precisely in relation to this affirmation. The fact that the ontological structure of the world is everywhere the same, that "the universe presents the same aspect from every point," is the necessary condition for the repeatability of experiments and hence a premise for the conduct of modern science (*Concepts of Space*, 84).

25. See Couprie: "We had to wait centuries for Nicolaus Cusanus and Giordano Bruno to speculate again about an infinite universe, the center of which is everywhere and nowhere (. . .) 2,000 years after Heraclides Ponticus and the Infinite Universe Anaximander, the promise of an infinite universe that was contained in his notion of the apeiron was finally fulfilled" (*Heaven and Earth*, 228).

26. Jorge Luis Borges, "The Fearful Sphere of Pascal", in *Labyrinths: Selected Stories and Other Writings* (New York: New Directions Publishing, 1964), 191. With a certain freedom of interpretation, the text attempts at reconstructing the long genealogy of the metaphor of the infinite sphere: Borges mentions Xenophanes' attribution of the spherical form to God; Parmenides' comparison of being with "the mass of a well-rounded sphere, whose force is constant from the center in any direction"; the cosmogony of Empedocles of Agrigento, in which particles of earth, water, air and fire form an endless sphere, the *sphairos redondo*, which "rejoices in its circular solitude"; and finally Alain of Lille, who in the twelfth century allegedly found the hermetic manuscripts of Trismegistus and transcribed the maxim "God is an intelligible sphere, whose center is everywhere and whose circumference nowhere." Bruno uses the metaphor in the Fifth Dialogue of *De la Causa, Principio et Uno*: "Se il punto non differisce dal corpo, il centro da la circonferenza, il finito da l'infinito, il massimo dal minimo, sicuramente possiamo affermare che l'universo é tutto centro, o che il centro de l'universo é per tutto, e che la circunferenza non é in parte alcuna, per quanto é diferente dal centro; o pur che la circonferenza é per tutto, ma il centro non si trova in quanto che é diferente da quella" (translated in Robert de Lucca, *Giordano Bruno: Cause, Principle and Unity. And Essays on Magic* [Cambridge: Cambridge University Press, 1998], 89). Pascal applied the metaphor directly to nature: "Nature is an infinite sphere, the center of which is everywhere while its circumference is nowhere" (the original passage can be found in *Pensées*, 115–18. Apparently,

in the manuscript the erasure of an early inscription was still visible: Pascal would have added to nature the word *effrayable*, frightful, appalling. Borges gets from here the title of his essay: nature has become a frightening sphere).

PART 2

The Metaphysical Assertion of Space in Early Modern Natural Philosophy

Recurrently idolized as a radical severance from the past, the cosmological affirmation of modernity is intuitively associated with a form of historical discontinuity. The radical imagination of Renaissance and early modern natural philosophers, however, and the great quarrels on the nature of the world that paved the way for the assertion of the modern science of astronomy, were marked on the contrary by a renewed and pervasive presence of the past, by the resignification of traditional and classic sources, and by a passionate engagement with ancient testimonies and ideas.[1]

Much better than the idea of a clean break from the past, this notion of the genealogical ambivalence of antiquity, of a disruptive potential that emerges in the re-appropriation and expansion of the classical and medieval canons, allows an understanding of why Gassendi decided to unearth Epicurean atomism as a model for his revolutionary physics; why the cosmology of Aristotle was broadly recognized as both the canonical reference and the adversary to be debunked by the new astronomy; or why Euclid's geometry, which presupposed an empty and homogeneous space, became an object of renewed interest for those involved, from Galileo to Newton, in the titanic project of quantifying and mathematizing the very structure of the world. The metaphysical foundations of early modern science, borrowing the expression from Edwin Burtt's magnificent essay, extend deep into the philosophical past.[2]

What cosmologists and natural philosophers in the sixteenth and seventeenth centuries did, in fact, was not simply to abjure the ways and means of "tradition," embracing instead a radically new vision of the universe produced by a suddenly emancipated imagination.

Rather, those thinkers elaborated upon a series of thoughts that had been surfacing from the very beginnings of Greek metaphysics, had evolved through medieval theological speculations, and finally exploded in the Renaissance under a complete, systematic form. The philosophy of space is, in many respects, the very center of such transformation. Through space, early modern physicists, metaphysicians and natural philosophers re-signified the ancient ideas of the boundless, of emptiness, and of an incorporeal extension, unified under the monist structure of Christian theology, and made them at last coincident with the physical world. The four vectors of the infinity, emptiness, abstraction, and absoluteness of space define thus a universal logic – we might call it the logic of space – which would for at least 300 years inform the theory and practices of science, philosophy and, as we shall see, of modern politics too.

Notes

1. The rediscovery of Greek and Latin texts, especially the pre-Socratic fragments and the works of Epicurus, Lucretius, and the Stoics, inspired new creative and polemical manners in which those texts were immediately mobilized against the dominant traditions. As Panofsky puts it, "one antiquity is played against another, and the result is in all cases a new, third antiquity: the specifically 'modern'" (Erwin Panofsky, *Perspective as Symbolic Form*, 139).
2. Edwin A. Burtt, *The Metaphysical Foundations of Modern Physical Science* (New York: Humanities Press, 1932).

Chapter 5

Infinity: The Universe as One

The imagination of an open universe, so often taken as the *forma mentis* of early modernity, required and affirmed the existence of a positive infinite space.[1] The old thought of a boundless principle would no longer proceed by negation, under the form of a potential quantity, or in the guise of an imaginary form of extension. Rather, natural philosophers in the sixteenth and seventeenth centuries pronounced the identity of infinite space and our cosmological reality, their fusion in the idea of an actual infinity, which had been strictly forbidden by Aristotle.[2] The implications were extraordinary. Infinite space not only appeared as a real physical entity, a completed totality "containing at once an infinite number of simultaneously actualized parts."[3] Through space, the infinite itself became the very form and essence of the universe in which we live.

In this respect, the philosophy of infinite space offered precisely what was needed to sustain the early modern cosmological transition. Unbounded and unchanging, independent of thought or matter, space granted the empty, continuous and homogeneous regularity that could assume in Newton the status of an absolute framework, becoming thereby the logical and ontological foundation for a whole new system of knowledge and practice, that of modern universalism, whose import and consequences were to be nothing short of revolutionary.

5.1 Actual Infinities: The Identity of Metaphysics and Cosmology

In his *Nova de Universis Philosophia*, Francesco Patrizi posited the metaphysical kernel of the modern conception of space. Perhaps for the first time, space appears as a distinct entity that is both infinite and existent. Neither a substance nor an accident, space is said to be ontologically prior to the things that come to be in it, yet fully independent of them.[4] Space is also real: its infinity is not only conceived of as being imaginary or potential, but it is rather affirmed as an existing infinity, an *energeiai apeiron*, endowed with an independent ontological status and an unquestioned physical reality.

Despite the efforts to distance himself from the scholastic tradition, however, Patrizi still imagines the physical structure of that infinity along the lines of Stoic cosmology that were common for the likes of Buridan and Bradwardine. The world that we know – finite, spherical, and with the Earth at its center – is surrounded by an infinite void space full of nothing, in which no bodies or matter could be found. Such void space is infinite and real, but still has something like a lower limit – the limit of the world nothing less – which marks a fundamental asymmetry: the separation of what "materially is" and the infinite empty space that surrounds it.

It would take a courageous mind to erase for good that imaginary line, to tear down the last cosmic barrier, and, far from lamenting the loss, even extol its disappearance. That role belongs to Giordano Bruno, who described his endeavor with the most passionate, explicit words:

> Quindi l'ali sicure a l'aria porgo;
> Né temo intoppo di cristallo o vetro,
> Ma fendo i cieli e a l'infinito m'ergo.[5]

Bruno's cosmology can be quite precisely described as a work of demolition of cosmic limits. To assume the infinity of the world not just as a mere attribute of its divine creator, but rather as a true principle of its existence, makes for him the existence of any limit not only unnecessary, but even logically untenable. Why should we consider that God's power, Bruno wonders, "Be determined as the limit of the convexity of a sphere rather than he should be, as we may say, the undetermined limit of the boundless?"[6] But of course, even such formula implies a dead-end for the philosophical imagination. An undetermined limit (*termino interminato*) is already a problematic notion, but a limit of the boundless (*di cosa interminata*), that is, of that which has no limits, implies a straightforward contradiction. The very notion of limits, Bruno concludes, is repugnant to the conception of a truly infinite universe. To think the world from the standpoint of infinity implies subverting the very question on limits, to the point that we need to ask how the cosmos could be conceived of *as limited* in the first place.

As a metaphysical principle, infinity cancels the need to contain what is, by definition, unbounded. The image of a closed cosmos – with its concentric structure of homocentric spheres and planetary shells, as it had been conceived of in Aristotelian and Ptolemaic astronomy – gives way to the notion of an infinite universe extending limitlessly in all directions. Within that universe, the idea that there might exist a celestial vault, or any sort of ultimate boundary between a finite world of matter and an infinite space filled by nothing but God's presence, becomes meaningless too.[7] Rather, Bruno conceives of an infinite number of worlds free-roaming in infinite space; all of them are part of one and the same cosmic unit, the infinite universe that includes them all in a totality without exteriority, without limits, with no possible "beyond."

Bruno supports this extraordinary move by positing two further metaphysical premises at the heart of his cosmology. The first is a version of the principle of plenitude, inherited from classical and medieval metaphysics, which he enthusiastically endorses. If the universe is the effect of an infinite cause, Bruno asks, and if the perfection of that principle is better expressed by an infinite number of exemplars than by a limited one, then why should God have chosen the universe to be "scarce" and "sterile" when it could express his infinite power in the full range of its perfection?[8] For Bruno, there is no reason why the universe should fall short of its infinite possibilities: God is best glorified not in one, but in countless suns and an infinity of worlds. Thus, the thought of cosmic limits becomes not only unnecessary, but almost heretical. The infinity of worlds in the universe is the necessary expression of the perfection of its cause.

The second premise is a sort of identity of metaphysics and cosmology, a fundamental coincidence between the principle of infinity, on the one hand, and the physical reality of the universe, on the other. The Brunian universe is not created or derived from an infinite principle that would be somehow external to it. The universe rather *coincides* with the infinite, is co-eternal with it, at once the expression, embodiment, and reflection of the infinite principle (in a poignant metaphor, Bruno describes it as the "unrestricted mirror of the divine image").[9] But if that identity can hold, and moreover, if the infinity of the universe is actually accessible to our imagination and understanding, it is only because a third term sustains the equation and guarantees the unity and continuity of its terms:

> There is a single general space (*loco generale*), a single vast immensity (*spacio inmenso*) which we may freely call Void; in it are innumerable globes like this on which we live and grow; this space we declare to be infinite, since neither reason, convenience, sense perception nor nature assign to it a limit . . .[10]

Equal to itself and indifferent to everything else, space is one, general, and wholly unlimited; space is prior to, and distinct from, the infinite things and worlds that it receives, the "countless riches" that come to be and exist in it.[11] As the *loco generale* of everything that exists, space expresses and sustains at once the existence and materiality of the infinite universe. In space, the infinite is physically realized, and conversely, the universe becomes infinite at last.

5.2 The Loss of Cosmic Centers

The Brunian cosmology of the infinite implies an immediate problem of orientation. In an infinite universe with no fixed upper or downward limits, one that is moreover populated by uncountable stars and astronomical bodies, there seems to be no single criterion, no fundamental reference to discriminate between different regions of space and the compositions of matter that are scattered through it. It is not surprising that, to characterize that fact, Bruno made use of the old image of the infinite sphere:

> If the point does not differ from the body, nor the center from the circumference, nor the finite from the infinite, nor the maximum from the minimum, we may certainly affirm that the universe is entirely center, or that *the center of the universe is everywhere, and the circumference nowhere* insofar as it is different from the center; or else that the circumference is everywhere, but the center is nowhere insofar as it differs from the circumference.[12]

But here the metaphor is, more than ever, just an image of thought, and this for one simple reason: in the Brunian universe there can be no such thing as a sphere to begin with. In the absence of centers and limits, there are no forms that could express the immensity of what exists. There are no vantage points either, no central or privileged places, no fixed positions and directions. All there is in the universe is an infinite number of points, and these may all be regarded either as centers, or as points on the circumference, as poles, or zeniths, and so forth. Thus the earth is not in the centre of the Universe; it is central only to our surrounding space (*di questa nostra reggione*).[13]

The Earth, hence, becomes just one among the innumerable worlds scattered through infinite space at irregular distances. Its privileged uniqueness is lost to an exuberant cosmic multiplicity, of which our earthly world represents but an insignificant part. Metaphysically, everything is leveled in the undifferentiated, endless extent of a general infinite space that is everywhere equal to itself. The consequences of this ontological equation, as we shall see later, extended way beyond the realm of cosmology. For now, it is enough to underline the profound radicality of this vision, and the decisive role that it would play in the scientific explosion that was about to take place.

Unlike most thinkers of space in the sixteenth and seventeenth centuries, however, Bruno was not a skilled astronomer himself. Despite his efforts at pedagogy and illustration, many of his most striking speculations were of a strictly metaphysical nature. Still, in his mystical and poetic language Bruno anticipated some of the most ground-breaking scientific discoveries that were to come, including the dissolution of the orbs and the celestial spheres, and the existence of multiple suns and planetary systems like our own.[14] Perhaps more importantly, Bruno formulated in the clearest, most compelling manner the fundamental metaphysical principle – the actual infinity of the physical universe – that was destined to articulate those discoveries into a rational system of scientific practice and investigation.

5.3 Kepler's Nightmare: The Breaking of Spheres

Soon the Earth would lose its privileged cosmic position not only metaphysically, but scientifically as well. It would do so by way of an old problem, which had haunted for centuries the perfect harmony of medieval cosmology: the rotation of the outermost celestial spheres. A moving sphere – not contained by any contiguous body, with all its parts continuously changing place in their combined rotatory movement – could hardly be assumed as the stable limit of the entire cosmos, which as a consequence seemed to be literally *placeless*. To avoid that problem, as we have seen, Philoponus abandoned the Aristotelian notion of place altogether.

Other thinkers, such as Alexander Aphrodisiensis, posited the existence of an immobile outermost sphere, which thus contained all the revolving heavens. Christian theologians like Anselm and Campanus of Novara conceived likewise of an immobile sphere of light, named the Empyrean, which surrounded the outermost heaven and gave support and stability to the cosmos as a whole.[15]

The difficulty persisted, however, until Copernicus solved it by inverting the very terms of the problem: arresting the motion of the stars and making the Earth move instead, daily around its own axis and annually around the sun. To be sure, Copernicus preserved the existence of heavenly spheres (even if they no longer moved), as the material forms containing the planets in their motion.[16] He also maintained the notion of a cosmic center, which now corresponded to the center of the Earth's orbit.[17] The cosmos of Copernicus is still a finite, proportionate whole, expressing the harmony and nobility of creation and marked by its perfection and unicity.[18] But despite all these efforts, perhaps precisely because of them, the feeling of fragility created by this cosmic displacement becomes almost impossible to conceal. The framework of reference has shifted to the sun and the system of planets orbiting around it. The Earth has lost its position and its privileged role in the cosmic order, and appears now as a planet among other planets. The entire system of cosmic and theological hierarchies, which ordered the world and gave meaning to it, has been subverted, and the possibility of order and meaning itself seems to be now under threat.

Nowhere is that feeling more eloquently expressed than in the words of the great perfectioner of the Copernican system, Kepler. In a passage that deals precisely with the effects and implications of the imagination of an allegedly infinite world – which he emphatically rejects – Kepler affirms that the "very cogitation" of an actual infinity "carries with it I don't know what secret, hidden horror; indeed one finds oneself wandering in this immensity, to which are denied limits and center and therefore also all determinate places."[19] What is at stake for Kepler in the acceptance of the infinite universe is the loss of determinacy as such, of differentiation and order, the absence of any fixed system of reference, of any objective standpoint that would order and justify the sense and value of all cosmic movements and positions. The boundless universe threatens not only the qualitative specificity of the Earth; it jeopardizes the possibility of meaning and, potentially, the ultimate sense of human life. Hence the need to discover a new order of proportions behind the theory of celestial mechanics; the emphasis put on the absolute unicity of the solar system; the use of theology to justify how the central position of the sun, rather than diminishing the cosmic nobility of the system, actually elevates its perfection.[20] Kepler goes as far as to defend that the finite heliocentric system is meant to protect the Earth rather than displace it.

No matter how strenuous this effort, Kepler's nightmare of a "wandering immensity" was not to be easily dismissed. Soon, technological advances such as the invention of the telescope would not only multiply the number of stars and visible astronomical bodies, but also transform the way in which those bodies appeared, altering the form and meaning of the very things that were seen. If the tragic fate of Bruno did not encourage many open celebrations of the infinity of the universe, the triple conviction that there are no limits to this world, that the Earth does not occupy its center, and that no vault or shield contains the heavenly bodies, would become in the work of Galileo empirically irrefutable.[21]

Even earlier, two of Kepler's contemporaries had contributed to make the agony of the old cosmological imagination irreversible. Tycho Brahe had broken the material spheres of planets and stars, demonstrating that the celestial orbs do not exist. Another fellow astronomer, Thomas Digges, produced a graphic representation of the universe in which the stars were not placed at the same distance from the Earth but rather behind one another, all of them being dispersed at different and immense distances, in an infinite universe that was poetically compared to the "gloriouse court of ye great god."[22]

Digges's optimism would not dissipate the risk (we might call it the Brunian risk) that Kepler was so keen to avoid. In a de-centered infinite universe, populated by innumerable solar systems and worlds, the Earth becomes one planet among others erring through the inapprehensible immensity of space. The very rationality of that order, and hence the possibility to find any stable anchoring for truth and meaning in human life, was still very far from assured.

5.4 From Inertia to Gravitation: One Law for All

One concrete form under which that risk had been expressed from the very beginnings of cosmological thinking was the problem of falling. What could, in a universe without limits, prevent the heavens from collapsing upon the Earth? If the Earth was just one planet among countless others, scattered in the infinite fields of empty space, how could it not fall from its stance? Why does matter not disperse, what prevents the world from disaggregating into separate bits? The fear of falling demonstrated the need for a finite, centered universe.[23] Indeed, only in a bounded cosmos does everything find a place of its own, a position that is proper and stable, and a reason for its being *there*.

The pillars of the new astronomy had destroyed such an ideal of a stable cosmic organization. In a universe marked by the loss of centers and the breaking of spheres, in which the Earth now moved, and the sun did not, it was not clear what could keep the world together and prevent it from dismantling and falling apart. Indeed, the entire development of modern mechanics is based upon a principle that seems to aggravate the problem instead of solving it. In an extremely counterintuitive move, Galileo first, and then Gassendi and Descartes, established that in the absence of external impediments, things in the world would keep moving at constant speeds.[24] Motions are now ascribed to objects, not to places; there are no final destinations, no ultimate rest, only a universe composed of bodies endlessly moving in time and space. There is no longer this place or that place; the fundamental kinematics of the universe has been reduced to a straight line.

But how, then, do we explain the keeping together of the world? How is it possible that such perennial motion in straight lines does not produce precisely what was most feared in the idea of infinity, that is the disaggregation of matter and the dissolution of the world in the empty immensity of boundless space? The cause, once again, was not to be found in the limits of the cosmos, or in any inherent power of space that would keep things together and prevent their dispersion. Rather, it was matter what acted as a cause, exerting a reciprocal force of attraction upon matter itself.[25]

From here, only one more step was needed to cement the fundamental structure of the new astronomy: to link together the account of motion and the attraction of matter, to synthesize astronomy and mechanics within a single, coherent system of mathematical explanation. Newton's law of universal gravitation would achieve precisely that. The same mechanical principles explain the motions of objects in all regions of the universe, both the movements of celestial bodies and the fall of objects in the Earth.[26] Thus, the principles of the new astronomy do not pose any risks to the coherence and wholeness of the universe. On the contrary, they are precisely what dispels the fear of falling, explaining at once the fundamental structure of our world, its inner workings, and its keeping together in time and space.

Far from chaos and danger, hence, the new science expresses the logic of the universe with astonishing soundness and simplicity. Nature, Newton said, is "always simple and ever consonant with itself": there are no boundaries for its norms, no special domains, no realms of exception.[27] The same principles and laws govern all places of the cosmos; all are united under one law that is proved to hold universally, equally, and at once in all its localities and regions. Because it is everywhere one and the same, space grants the isotropic framework in which this monistic principle can be finally realized. But for that, all of its remaining qualities and powers had to disappear first. For the universe to be lawful, space needed to appear as being empty again.

Notes

1. Casey, *The Fate of Place*, 102.
2. Panofsky elaborates on the cosmological implications of this physical impossibility of the infinite: "Just as for Aristotle there is no 'quantum continuum' in which the quiddity of individual things would be dissolved, so there is for him also no *energiai apeiron* (actual infinite) which would extend beyond the Dasein of individual objects (for, in modern terms, even the sphere of fixed stars would be an 'individual object')" (*Perspective as Symbolic Form*, 44). In the early modern metaphysics of the universe, the infinite will become *natura naturata*, an *energiai apeiron* realized in, and coincident with, nature.
3. J. E. McGuire, "Space, Geometrical Objects and Infinity: Newton and Descartes on Extension," in W. R. Shea, *Nature Mathematized: Historical and Philosophical Case Studies in Classical Modern Natural Philosophy* (Dordrecht: Springer Science and Business Media, 2012), 74.
4. "For all things, whether corporeal or incorporeal, if they are not somewhere, are nowhere; and if they are nowhere they do not even exist. If they do not exist they are nothing" (Francesco Patrizi, "On Physical Space," *Nova de Universis Philosophia*, translation by Brickman cited in Grant, *Much Ado About Nothing*, 225). Unlike material things, which require space for their existence, space is itself in need of no other thing whatsoever. On the significance of Patrizi's conception of infinite space as being "ontologically and epistemologically the primary basis of all existence" and the "metaphysical foundation for the new physics" see Jammer, *Concepts of Space*, 87.
5. Giordano Bruno, *De l'Infinito, Universo e Mondi*, ed. Patrizio Sanasi, 1584, 12. For an English translation, see Jammer, *Concepts of Space*, 88: "I spread confident wings to space/ I fear no barrier of crystal or glass/I cleave the heavens and soar to the infinite."

6. Bruno, *De l'Infinito*, 18–19: "Come vuoi tu che Dio, e quanto alla potenza e quanto a l'operazione e quanto a l'effetto (che in lui son medesima cosa), sia determinato, e come termine della convessitudine di una sfera, più tosto che, come dir si può, termine interminato di cosa interminata? Termino, dico, senza termine, per esser differente la infinità dell'uno da l'infinità dell'altro: perché lui è tutto l'infinito complicatamente e totalmente, ma l'universo è tutto in tutto (se pur in modo alcuno si può dir totalità, dove non è parte né fine) explicatamente, e non totalmente; per il che l'uno ha raggion di termine, l'altro ha raggion di terminato, non per differenza di finito ed infinito, ma perché l'uno è infinito e l'altro è finiente secondo la raggione del totale e totalmente essere in tutto quello che, benché sia tutto infinito, non è però totalmente infinito; perché questo ripugna alla infinità dimensionale".

7. In Bruno, the imagination of a finite cosmos surrounded by infinite, imaginary space is finally overcome in the name of the principle of infinity itself. Speaking in the voice of Philoteo, in a famous passage from *De l'Infinito*, Bruno resuscitates some of the old arguments on the locality of the universe, reminiscent of Zeno's paradoxes and Archytas's metaphysics of place, to make precisely that point (*De l'Infinito*, first Dialogue, 14–5, my emphasis):

"PHILOTEO: Se il mondo è finito ed estra il mondo è nulla, vi dimando: ove è il mondo? ove è l'universo? Risponde Aristotele: è in se stesso. Il convesso del primo cielo è loco universale; e quello, come primo continente, non è in altro continente, perché il loco non è altro che superficie ed estremità di corpo continente; onde chi non ha corpo continente, non ha loco . . . Se tu dici che non v'è nulla; il cielo, il mondo, certo, non sarà in parte alcuna.

FRACASTORO: Nullibi ergo erit mundis. Omne erit in nihilo.

PHILOTEO: Il mondo sarà qualcosa che non si trova. Se dici (come certo mi par che vogli dir qualche cosa, per fuggir il vacuo ed il niente) che estra il mondo è uno ente intellettuale e divino, di sorte che Dio venga ad esser luogo di tutte le cose, tu medesimo sarai molto impacciato per farne intendere come una cosa incorporea, intelligibile e senza dimensione possa esser luogo di cosa dimensionata . . . E se tu vuoi escusare con dire, che dove è nulla e dove non è cosa alcuna, non è anco luogo, non è oltre, né extra, per questo non mi contentarai; perché queste sono paroli ed iscuse che non possono entrare in pensiero. Perché è a fatto impossibile che con qualche senso o fantasia (anco se si ritrovassero altri sensi ed altre fantasie) possi farmi affirmare, con vera intenzione, *che si trove tal superficie, tal margine, tal estremità, extra la quale non sia o corpo o vacuo*: anco essendovi Dio, perché la divinità non è per impire il vacuo, e per conseguenza non è in raggione di quella, in modo alcuno, di terminare il corpo; perché tutto lo che se dice terminare, o è forma esteriore, o è corpo continente."

8. This is the extraordinarily poignant passage in which Bruno celebrates the endless productivity of the divine infinite cause: "Perché vogliamo o possiamo noi pensare che la divina efficacia sia ociosa? perché vogliamo che la divina bontà la quale si può communicare alle cose infinite e si può infinitamente diffondere, voglia essere scarsa ed astrengersi in niente, atteso che ogni cosa finita al riguardo de l'infinito è niente? perché volete quel centro della divinità, che può infinitamente in una sfera (se cossì si potesse dire) infinita amplificarse, come invidioso, rimaner più tosto sterile che farsi comunicabile, padre fecondo, ornato e bello? voler più tosto comunicarsi diminutamente e, per dir meglio, non comunicarsi, che secondo la raggione della gloriosa potenza ed esser suo? *Perché deve esser frustrata la capacità infinita, defraudata la possibilità de infiniti mondi che possono essere, pregiudicata la eccellenza della divina imagine che deverebe più risplendere in uno specchio incontratto e secondo il suo modo di essere infinito, immenso?* (De l'Infinito, first dialogue, 18–19, my emphasis. Koyré comments on this passage in *From the Closed World*, 52ff. See also the classical commentary in Paul-Henri Michel, *The Cosmology of Giordano Bruno*, trans. R. E. W. Maddison [Ithaca: Cornell University Press, 1973]).

9. This is Koyré's translation in *From the Closed World*, 52. Lovejoy gives an alternative translation of the passage: "Why should the infinite capacity be frustrated, the possibility of the existence of infinite worlds be cheated, the perfection of the divine image be impaired – that image which ought rather to be reflected back in a mirror as immeasurable as itself?" (*The Great Chain of Being*, 118).

10. Once again, the passage from the fifth dialogue of *De l'Infinito* synthesizes with remarkable beauty and force the essential elements of the Brunian philosophy of space as the ontological structure of the infinite universe: "Non bisogna dunque cercare, se estra il cielo sia loco, vacuo o tempo; perché *uno è il loco generale, uno il spacio inmenso che chiamar possiamo liberamente vacuo*; in cui sono innumerabili ed infiniti globi, come vi è questo in cui vivemo e vegetamo noi. Cotal spacio lo diciamo infinito, perché non è raggione, convenienza, possibilità, senso o natura che debba finirlo: in esso sono infiniti mondi simili a questo, e non differenti in geno da questo; perché non è raggione né difetto di facultà naturale, dico tanto potenza passiva quanto attiva, per la quale, come in questo spacio circa noi ne sono, medesimamente non ne sieno in *tutto l'altro spacio che di natura non è differente ed altro da questo*" (De l'Infinito, 63, my emphasis).

11. "Di sorte che non è vana questa potenza d'intelletto, che sempre vuole e puote aggiungere spacio a spacio, mole a mole, unitade ad unitade, numero a numero, per quella scienza che ne discioglie da le catene di uno angustissimo, e ne promove alla libertà d'un augustissimo imperio, che ne toglie dall'opinata povertà ed angustia alle innumerevoli ricchezze di tanto spacio, di sì dignissimo campo, di tanti coltissimi mondi;

e non fa che circolo d'orizonte, mentito da l'occhio in terra e finto da la fantasia nell'etere spacioso, ne possa impriggionare il spirto sotto la custodia d'un Plutone e la mercé d'un Giove" (*De l'Infinito*, 10).

12. *Giordano Bruno: Cause, Principle and Unity*, 89, my emphasis.

13. *De l'Infinito*, 26–7. The translation is Koyré's, in *From the Closed World*, 41–2. Koyré mentions another passage from *La Cena de Le Ceneri* in which Bruno expresses how the concepts of center, periphery, and extremes, no less than the concept of limits, have lost their absolute value as cosmological representations: "the world is infinite and . . . there is no body in to which it would pertain *simpliciter* to be in the center, or on the center, or on the periphery, or between these two extremes of the world (which moreover do not exist)" (ibid.).

14. On Bruno's "truly revolutionary theses in cosmography" and their influence in the posterior developments of early modern astronomy and science, see Lovejoy, *The Great Chain of Being*, 108.

15. See P. Duhem, "The Empyrean as the Place of The Universe," in *The Concepts of Space and Time: Their Structure and Their Development*, ed. Milič Čapek (Dordrecht: Springer Netherlands, 1976), 43–5.

16. See Thomas S. Kuhn, *The Copernican Revolution, Planetary Astronomy in the Development of Western Thought* (Cambridge: Harvard University Press, 1966), 134–85.

17. "[Copernicus's theory] was not, of course, a heliocentric theory; the centre of the world was the centre of the earth's orbit. The sun, though nearest that position, did not occupy it, and the planes of the planetary orbits did not pass through the sun" (Lovejoy, *The Great Chain of Being*, 105).

18. In an effort perhaps to resist the effects of his own theory, Copernicus preserved the essential aspects of classical celestial dynamics. Motion, in fact, still functions as a cosmic differentiator between the celestial bodies that rotate, and hence are subject to the processes of change and becoming, and the immobile fixed stars, which remain at rest, selfsame, endowed with a greater degree of perfection. Both the sun and the fixed stars provide absolute, stable references for the distribution of the cosmic components and the government of their relations. Perhaps this conservative character of its cosmology explains the little influence that, according to Grant, the Copernican model played in the development of the early modern theories of space: "Despite occasional mention, the Copernican heliocentric system would play but a small and negligible role. Whether the earth turned around the sun or vice versa made no difference to those who sought to characterize the elusive nature of space or who were concerned with what, if anything, might lie beyond our world" (*Much Ado About Nothing*, 183).

19. Translated by Koyré, *From the Closed World*, 61. The original passage comes from *Joannis Keppleri . . . De Stella Nova in Pede Serpentarii*

(Prague: typis P. Sessli, impensis authoris, 1606), in which Kepler evaluates the hypothesis of the infinity of the universe in relation to the recent discovery of a new star. On Kepler's positions on the infinity of the universe see Miguel A. Granada, "Kepler and Bruno on the Infinity of the Universe and of Solar Systems," *Journal for the History of Astronomy* 39, no. 4 (2008): 469–95. For an interpretation of Kepler's program as the "true foundation of Copernicanism" see McGuire, *Tradition and Innovation: Newton's Metaphysics of Nature*, xiv.

20. On Kepler's "finitistic" affirmation of the unicity and singularity of the solar system, in which the sun becomes "the highest image of the divinity" and "the very cosmic embodiment of the first person of the Trinity," see Lovejoy, *The Great Chain of Being*, 105, and Koyré, *From the Closed World*, 62–7.

21. In the *Dialogue on the Great World Systems*, Galileo was cautious about stating the actual infinity of the world, inaugurating a prudent philosophical tradition of which Descartes would be the most famous exponent. Both, however, would be absolutely explicit about the impossibility to ascribe any limits to the universe or enclose it within any border, spherical or otherwise.

22. "And this may well be thought of vs to be the gloriouse court of ye great god, whose vnsercheable works invisible we may partly by these his visible conjecture, to whose infinit power and maiesty such an infinit place surmounting all other both in quantity and quality only is conuenient" (Digges, *A Perfit Description of the Caelestiall Orbes*, cited in Lovejoy, *The Great Chain of Being*, 116). See also Couprie, for whom Digges realizes the "promise of an infinite universe" formulated 2,000 years before by Heraclides Ponticus and Anaximander (*Heaven and Earth*, 228–9).

23. Aristotle had made it clear when denying the possibility that multiple worlds exist: the elements cannot have two centers, because then they would have two (or more) proper places to which they would tend, their natural motions would be contradictory, and matter would ultimate disperse (see *On the Heavens*, book 2, 13–14). That is why the natural motions of earth, water, fire, and air are confined to the terrestrial world, marked by the rhythms of change, of decay and becoming, and separated by the lunar orbs from the ethereal, immutable regions of selfsame being and circular motion. Between the two worlds everything was qualitatively different: space, matter, and motion responded to different principles and logics. According to Couprie, "the fear of falling that Aristotle so successfully had countered by proving that we do not have to be afraid that either the heaven will collapse or the that the celestial bodies will fall upon the earth, or even that the earth itself will fall, made a glorious comeback in the new world picture of an infinite universe and still haunts it until our days . . . [the return of] 'the fear of falling' is the price

we have paid for abandoning the Aristotelian conception of a safe but finite universe" (*Heaven and Earth in Ancient Greek Cosmology*, 228–30). The assertion of modern physics implied the constant effort to provide ever more counter-intuitive and abstract explanations to dispel such fear.

24. The philosophical sources of the concept of inertia are deep and manifold, but can be retraced to the problem of natural places and the abstraction of space. As we have seen, the Aristotelian cosmos could not explain the motion of the outermost spheres, which left the cosmos as such placeless. Facing those troubles, Philoponus had decided to abandon altogether the Aristotelian notion of place, and to replace it with the concept of space understood as abstract dimensionality. But how could the motion of objects and matter be explained without the physics of natural places? Philoponus replied that the motion of bodies in abstract space was not to be explained by any power or pull residing in places themselves, but rather by a natural impulse or tendency, an *impetus*, which directs them towards specific regions due to ultimately theological reasons. The origin of motion shifts hence from the powers of place, to bodies, only to fall back to the divinity itself. But the principle had been established: space does not act upon matter anymore, and it cannot explain by itself the motion of bodies (for an account of Philoponus's theory of movement and his rejection of natural places see "John Philoponus, Theologian and apologist," in Mark Edwards, *Aristotle and Early Christian Thought* [New York: Routledge, 2019]). Philoponus's concept of impetus was not met with immediate philosophical fortune. Several centuries had to pass until another heterodox thinker, Jean Buridan, illustrated the shortcomings of Aristotelian physics to explain the trajectory of projectiles. In order to overcome those difficulties, Buridan explained that bodies, and not places, had a certain circular impetus, that is, a tendency to maintain their motion unless prevented by the resistance of another, different force. That tendency is by nature permanent, without the need of any further force to intervene in order to maintain it. Impetus could thus explain the motions of the heavens without recurring to any natural property or quality of the matter that composed them: the same account and explanation, it follows, could explain both earthly and celestial motions. Buridan's idea was counter-intuitive, to say the least. Still, this insight was destined to play a decisive role in solving one of the main puzzles raised by the new astronomy, how to make sense of motion as a quantitative phenomenon in a world divested of qualitative substances, establishing thereby the fundamental pillars of modern universal mechanics. When in the *Two New Sciences*, Salviati expresses that an object has in itself "no inclination to move in any direction, nor yet any resistance to being moved," Galileo is not only anticipating the logic of

Descartes's first law of motion, but also elaborating on a long philo-sophical development that is fundamentally rooted in the philoso-phy of space (see Antonia LoLordo, *Pierre Gassendi and the Birth of Early Modern Philosophy* [New York: Cambridge University Press, 2007], 174–82; Nick Huggett, *Space from Zeno to Einstein*, 87–8; and Koyré, for whom the law of inertia is a necessary consequence of the "breaking of the circle" of Aristotelian-Ptolemaic cosmology, *From the Closed World*, 169).

25. Copernicus had already considered the hypothesis of a force of attraction that matter exerted upon itself. For Kepler, the concourse of such a force of attraction was necessary to explain the mainte-nance of the elliptical motion of planets. After Galileo exposed the laws governing the acceleration of bodies in free fall, the enquiry of its causes became the object of passionate exchanges and debates. Gassendi and Huygens identified in gravity the cause of such acceler-ation, paving the way for Newton's theoretical unification in the law of universal gravitation (see B. Brackenridge, *The Key to Newton's Dynamics: The Kepler Problem and the Principia* [Berkeley: Univer-sity of California Press, 1995], vii).

26. Celestial bodies, exactly like terrestrial ones, are now endowed with uniform motion in a straight line. If they do not disperse in the infinite space of the universe is because of the deflections from that motion caused by gravitational attraction of matter. That attraction fol-lows the same mathematical rule for any two bodies in the universe: they tend toward one another in direct proportion to the product of their masses and in inverse proportion to the square of the distance between their centers. "Newton's magnificent formulation of the law of gravitation," in the words of Edwin Burtt, "united astronomy and mechanics in one mathematical science of matter in motion ... the departure of the celestial masses from uniform motion in a straight line can be expressed by the same equation as the fall of terrestrial bodies to the earth" (Burtt, *The Metaphysical Foundations of Modern Physical Science*, 240).

27. Isaac Newton, "Rules for the Study of Natural Philosophy," *The Prin-cipia: Mathematical Principles of Natural Philosophy*, trans. Bernard Cohen and Anne Whitman (Berkeley: University of California Press, 1999), 795.

Chapter 6

Emptiness: Space as Void and Equal to Itself

Space plays a fundamental role in the realization of the metaphysics of infinity in early modern physics. After the dissolution of spheres, boundaries and limits, the universe appears to be governed by simple fundamental laws, which hold equally everywhere and for all its parts. The concept of space is precisely what guarantees that there is no resistance, no discontinuity, no interruption to the universal domain of the law. Indeed, space becomes the regular and homogeneous "thereness" of lawfulness as such: space is that which supports the rationality of the universe, what ensures its stability and the continuity of its order. But for that, space needs to be endowed first with its own, autonomous existence. It also needs to be emptied of any form of corporeality, of inherent attributes and qualities, of any power and capacity to act. The emptying of space, which will imply a very problematic relationship with matter, is in fact a necessary condition for the metaphysical assertion of universality on which the entire edifice of modern science depends.

6.1 Space as a Real and Independent Entity

The metaphysics of infinity transformed the very nature and being of space. Uncontained by any limits, everywhere equal to itself, space acquired within the new science a central and unique ontological status. This was not without theoretical difficulties: the conceptual tools inherited from the scholastic tradition, in fact, could hardly express the foundational role that was required of space in the new conceptions of the infinite universe.

Such was for instance the case of the Aristotelian doctrine of the categories, and particularly, of the logic of substance and accidents.[1] Space could not be considered an accident, for it was said to be prior to all the worldly things in which accidents take form, and to be completely unaffected by them. But at the same time space appeared hardly as a substance either. All qualities inhered in bodies and things, not in space itself, which had no accidents of any kind, presenting itself as a sort of universal term with no predication of individuals. The being of space appeared to be of a somewhat unique kind, as if it required a different logical and conceptual expression.

Breaking with the categories of scholasticism, Francesco Patrizi would characterize such uniqueness by evoking the move that Philoponus had made 1,000 years before. Drastically separating the dimensionality of space from the things that exist in it, Patrizi affirmed that space is a created thing, an *ens*, which is corporeal without being a body.[2] As dimensional extension, space is capable of receiving bodies and matter without offering any sort of resistance to them. Of course, bodies are dimensional too, but their dimensionality is determinate and concrete, impenetrable and resistant: they are always the attribute of a particular substance. Bodies are in space and move through space, but space is radically distinct from the things that come to be in it. Space is for Patrizi a pure form of dimensionality, a material opening that, through its aptitude to receive, allows for nothing less than the continuity of reality: without space, there would be no things in the physical universe at all.[3]

Following the footsteps of Patrizi, Pierre Gassendi develops to its ultimate consequences the metaphysical postulates of the reality and independence of space. In the second book of the *Physics*, Gassendi explains that when a body is removed from a certain place, the place that such body occupied, now devoid of matter, remains equal to itself.[4] Taking the argument to a suddenly grandiose level, he then imagines that God destroys all matter contained within the lunar sphere of the universe; all the bodies and things that exist in that space would immediately disappear, but the space of that sphere would remain, only empty of the matter that has been destroyed. If God was to repeat that operation for the entire universe, concludes Gassendi, the result would be nothing other than an infinite void of incorporeal space. Matter, hence, can be thought of as being annihilated and reduced to nothing; the room that such matter occupies, however, would still persist as an infinite vacuum of three-dimensional space.[5]

Several consequences follow from Gassendi's radical thought experiment. The first is, again, the reality of space and its independence from matter: we can conceive of matter as being subject to annihilation, but we cannot think the same of space. The second is the infinity of space: if space coincides with the extension of the world, and if that world is taken to be infinite, then space must be infinite too. The third is that space is equal to itself: everything can be removed from it, but space remains unaltered, immobile and at all times coincident with itself. The fourth is perhaps the most striking of all: if God could destroy everything there is in the world, but not space itself, it is because space appears to be uncreated (*improductum*). In quite a heretical manner, Gassendi asserts that God created all things that are in space, but did not create space itself; space is thus affirmed as being coeternal with the divinity, and even a condition of possibility for the creation of the world.[6] As such, space appears to be independent not only from matter, but even from God himself. Little wonder, then, if we cannot just think it away.

6.2 Space as Emptiness: The Return of Void Space

A paradox is inscribed at the heart of modern space: being closest to the divinity, space is also dangerously similar to nothingness. Divorced from corporeality, emancipated from matter, space appears in fact to be fundamentally empty. As proven by Gassendi's thought experiment of the destruction of the world, a portion of space can be occupied by a specific body, and then it is full; but when that body is moved to a different place, that same portion of space remains exactly as it was before, except that now it is empty, it contains no body at all.[7] Matter, moreover, is said to be discontinuous: it occupies only some parts of the space that contains it, so that at any given time, in a universe of infinite space and finite matter, there is plenty of room for empty space. When matter moves or is removed, the void is what remains, unaltered and equal to itself. Ultimately, this essential emptiness will make not only specific regions, but the whole of space as such indistinguishable from the void.

Of course, the concept of the void was not without a heavy philosophical charge. It is commonly accepted that the philosophy of the Middle Ages was deeply marked by the Aristotelian dictum on the plenary (and limited) character of the world, and consequently, by a general rejection of the void as an ontological principle. But the conviction that *natura abhorret vacuum* had been slowly eroded from various theological flanks and cosmological speculations.[8] Indeed, the adoption of Stoic cosmological models by many scholastics and heterodox thinkers had debilitated the conviction that no void could exist beyond the limits of the world. Philoponus, in his abstraction of a three-dimensional space that was by principle distinct and separated from matter, had posited the logical possibility of a void existing within those boundaries too, even if he immediately concluded that in our world that possibility is never realized as actual. The Persian thinker Muhammad ibn Zakariya al-Razi defended the existence of the void *in actu*, both within the material world and beyond it.[9] Still, not many thinkers would have echoed such claims in Europe before the seventeenth century, when the rediscovery of ancient texts and sources on the atomists, especially Lucretius, and the transformed cosmological imagination of the new astronomy, brought the old quarrels on the void back to the center of philosophical and scientific debates.

Intertwined with the discussion on the void at the time of Gassendi's writing was, in fact, a problem of essential importance to the new science. Both the principle of inertia, which was critical to the unification of mechanics, and the theories of gravitation, but also of magnetism and electricity, depended on the capacity to account for the various forms of resistances, alterations and deflections brought forth by factors external to the supposedly uniform action of physical forces. In his demonstration of the nonexistence of the void, Aristotle had affirmed that precisely because of the absence of any form of resistance, bodies moving in the void would do so with an infinite speed, which was obviously a logical aberration.[10] Now, the terms of that reasoning had been radically inverted: it was precisely the absence of resistance that granted the idealized, structural conditions in which, by abstraction, the subsequent findings of empirical science could be theoretically unified. It was not a coincidence that in the metaphysics of Patrizi, the nature of space was determined specifically by the fact that it "displays no resistance."[11]

To prove the existence and the actual nature of the void became hence a burning priority for those involved in the great scientific challenge of the time, the unification of Galileo's theories of motion and the explanations of the attraction of matter by physical forces which were as yet unknown. The great intellectual debate that took place in France in the 1640s, concerning the interpretation of the barometer experiments of Evangelista Torricelli and Blaise Pascal, was aimed precisely at proving that an actual void (and hence an ideal absence of matter and friction of any kind) could be artificially created in nature. At stake in the discussions was an association between the nature of space and the physics of resistance that was essential to the theoretical framework of the new science. It is not a coincidence that in his interpretation of the experiments, Pascal developed a definition of space as something that "occupies a midpoint between matter and nothingness."[12]

Inevitably, the great early modern debate on the nature of the void brings back the ancient association between the principle of nothingness and the being of space. Nowhere is that association more poetic and explicit than in the work of Otto von Guericke, another great scientist who was responsible for groundbreaking experiments on air pressure and the behavior of gases. For Guericke, space is the void affirmed universally, which means quite precisely that it is nothingness itself:

> everything is in Nothing (*nihilo*) and if God should reduce the fabric of the world (*machinam mundi*), which he created, into Nothing (*nihilum*), nothing would remain of its place other than Nothing (just as it was before the creation of the world), that is, the Uncreated (*Increatum*) . . . Nothing contains all things. It is more precious than gold, without beginning and end, more joyous than the perception of bountiful light, more noble than the blood of kings, comparable to the heavens, higher than the stars, more powerful than a stroke of lightning, perfect and blessed in every way. Nothing always inspires. Where Nothing is, there ceases the jurisdiction of all kings. Nothing is without any mischief. According to Job the earth is suspended over Nothing. Nothing is outside the world. Nothing is everywhere – They say the vacuum is Nothing; and they say that imaginary space – and space itself – is Nothing.[13]

Uncreated and independent, empty of all determination yet everywhere sovereign, void space is the great unifier, the universal medium that receives all existence and guarantees the rationality and coherence of the whole.

6.3 Not Fully Void: Subtle Matter and the Problem of Ether

The exorbitance of Guericke was not, however, quite the norm of the discussion. Famously, the conclusions from Torricelli's experiment

were met with disapproval by Descartes, perhaps the greatest oppo-
nent of the void among the natural philosophers of the seventeenth
century. Descartes radically denied the distinction between dimensionality and corporeality that sustained the entire metaphysics of
empty space. For him extension is the essence of body, and there
can simply be no extension without body, no space that is devoid of
corporeal substance. From here it follows that the notion of a void of
empty space is contradictory and logically impossible. Indeed, there
is no real difference between space and corporeal substance: matter
and space are for Descartes not distinct, "except in our thought."[14]

This total identification of the dimensionality of space and the
extension of bodies raises once again the question of how motion
is possible in a universe that is materially saturated, where the fullness of bodies leaves by definition no empty space whatsoever for
them to move into. Descartes's ingenious solution consists in devel-
oping a theory of vortices, currents of revolving particles that carry
bodies and planets through purely mechanical displacements of
adjacent matter.[15] Those small particles constitute what Descartes
names "subtle matter," which is according to him the most basic
element of the universe. Agitated by a series of motions that they
communicate by impacting against each other, the small particles of
subtle matter fill the space that we believe to be vacant between the
different perceptible bodies. Invisible but real, subtle matter thus
allows for the continuity of the material chain of causes and effects
in the world. In Descartes's physics, subtle matter accounts for the
basic facts of Copernican astronomy (but also of the mechanics of
air circulation, light transmission, optical perception, magnetism,
and, most interestingly, also gravity itself), making it unnecessary to introduce further hypothesis, or to explain the motion and
attraction of bodies through occult qualities or mysterious properties of objects, which seemed inescapable in the new philosophies
of the void.[16]

Descartes's theory of subtle matter connected him with a long
philosophical tradition, but nor was it without a footing in the contemporary scientific debate. Indeed, the definition of the void as a
radical form of emptiness where there is strictly nothing, a position
defended by Gassendi and Guericke, was minoritarian even among
the modern atomists. Patrizi, from whom Gassendi adopted much of
his philosophical framework, had filled the void with light (not unlike
Proclus had done with his sphere a thousand years before). Even a
man like Giordano Bruno, despite his grand definition of a *spacio
immenso che chiamar possiamo liberamente vacuo*, conceived of a

divine ether covering this universal openness.[17] But why should the void be invested with anything else? Was not the point of recuperating the ancient notion of the void precisely to prescind from the need to fill up the radical emptiness of space? Patrizi's light and Bruno's ether are incorporeal and show no resistance; as such, they do not seem to add any fundamental capacity to the infinite space that they had just liberated from matter.

There were, of course, theological reasons for that insertion. To explain why God would leave empty such a significant part of creation was obviously not easy to answer (unless one decided, as did Gassendi or von Guericke, to separate space from God altogether, which implied, however, a whole set of different theological problems). Bruno, for instance, was deeply committed to the principle of plenitude, which required the actual realization of all the possibilities and potentialities of being. Perhaps ether was a means to avoid any possible deficiency in that cosmic picture, to dispel the idea of any want or lack in creation, to guarantee the fulness and continuity of the world. Perhaps, in the manner of Plato's *chora*, a third term was needed to mediate between the two elements that had been so drastically split off, space and matter, and thus provide a foothold for divine intelligence in the actual physicality of the world.[18]

There were scientific reasons too for the filling of the void. Galileo and Descartes had very clearly expressed the difficulties involved in assuming the existence of forces that could act upon matter at a distance. That implied accepting mysterious, occult principles that seemed to work in an almost magical manner, breaking the material continuity of causal chains and jeopardizing the very rationality of the natural order. Such distress was only increased by contemporary developments in the fields of optics, magnetism, chemistry, and very soon, of electricity too. The radical emptiness of space, by which there was supposed to be absolutely nothing between material bodies in the world, posited an obvious problem in that respect. For how could phenomena such as the transmission of light, the forces of gravity, or the attraction of magnets, be explained without a mediational term? In the absence of any material contact, there seemed to be no rational way of justifying the interaction of matter over an extension of pure nothingness, that is, of empty space.[19]

Variously conceived of and declined, the concept of ether soon became common in the explanation of apparently extra-mechanical physical phenomena. Ether served to unify the action of forces across regions of space. It provided a homogenous medium that could transmit, propagate and materialize forces across distances of seemingly empty space. Most importantly, it assured the uninterrupted materiality of physical events, dispelling the threat that emptiness represented for the lawfulness and continuity of the world.

6.4 The Spatial Contradiction of Early Modern Science

For some, however, the difference between vacuum and ethereal matter was still not quite clear. Hobbes, for instance, interestingly linked together the notions of vacuum, ether and subtle matter in a conversation with Samuel Sorbière:

> I did not think that Epicurus' theory was absurd, in the sense in which I think he understood the vacuum. For I believe that he called "vacuum" what Descartes called "subtle matter", and what I call "extremely pure ethereal substance", of which no part is an atom, and each part is divisible . . . into further divisible parts.[20]

This conflation of the vacuum and divisible matter, empty space and corporeal substance, shows a deep tension that animates the early modern physics and metaphysics of the void. If ether is to be conceived as being material, as Hobbes seems to be doing in his letter, then we are back to a plenist conception of the world and, following Cartesian logic, ultimately the concept of the "void" ceases to make sense. If, on the other hand, ether is conceived of as immaterial, and offers for instance no resistance to the mechanics of motion, attraction and transmission, then one wonders how we can investigate its existence, and even why that existence is necessary at all. Perhaps the clearest expression of that tension is to be found in the work of Isaac Newton, who accepted both principles at different times, before famously concluding, in the General Scholium of the *Principia*, that God is present everywhere not virtually only, "but also *substantially* . . . In him are all things contained and moved; yet neither affects the other: God suffers nothing from the motion of bodies; bodies find no resistance from the omnipresence of God."[21]

The problem of ether, a result of the radical separation of space from matter and of the emptying of space brought forth by the logic of the new astronomy, shows the emergence of a spatial contradiction in the early modern metaphysics of science. The apparently manifold workings of nature, acting through a variety of recently discovered forces and physical principles, needed to be synthesized into a single coherent whole and a unitary system of rational explanation. Radically distinguished from matter, voided of all contents, powers, and inherent qualities, empty space is precisely what guarantees this unification of physical phenomena across the universe. The emptiness of space sustains the generality, continuity, and homogeneity of the world. On the condition of being void, space coincides with the realm of validity of laws, it guarantees their universality and the rationality of the all.

At the same time, however, that same emptiness of space appears as a threat to the causal continuity of the world. Because it interrupts the mechanic chains of materiality, the void jeopardizes the rational coherence of the whole; it requires the adoption of occult or extravagant hypothesis to explain the action of forces and motions in the absence of direct contact between the particles of matter. Covering the void with ether, or investing it with a mediational or transitional element, is an attempt to bridge that material gap and save the lawful continuity of reality. But such a move implies getting space back to matter again, undoing their separation, finding new forms in which matter and space are associated again, rather than fundamentally distinct.

This contradiction would not be easily resolved. On the contrary, it inspired the development of drastically divergent conceptions of space (infinite or finite, empty or full, objective or subjective, absolute or relative) which marked scientific and philosophical debates well into the Enlightenment, and still resonate in our own day. Despite all his hesitations, however, Newton was forced to take a clear position in the debate. The framework of his new physics required the postulation of empty space as the neutral, homogenous medium for the totality of physical processes in the universe.[22] The Newtonian universe is thus composed of discontinuous matter in an infinite, independent, real, and continuous empty space. Space receives and contains all the bodies in the universe, but is ultimately indifferent to them: it remains unaltered, immobile, and indivisible, everywhere equal to itself. The empty space of modern physics becomes at once foundation and reference of all our knowledge and of the structure of reality itself.

Notes

1. For the role of Italian natural philosophy in overcoming the categorial logic of scholasticism see Jammer, *Concepts of Space*, 90.
2. Francesco Patrizi, *Nova de Universis Philosophia*, 61–5. I am following here the translations and interpretive framework of LoLordo in *Pierre Gassendi and the Birth of Early Modern Philosophy*, 104–5.

3. That is why space, the first thing created by God, is the logical and ontological condition for all other things to exist: "for it is necessary that what exists before all other things is that thing by which, when supposed, all other things can be supposed and by which, when taken away, all other things are destroyed" (*Nova de Universis Philosophia*, 61a, in LoLordo, *Pierre Gassendi and the Birth of Early Modern Philosophy*, 104). The influence of Patrizi's mentor, Bernardino Telesio, who affirmed space as "the great receptor of all being whatever" is especially significant here (on the significance of Telesio's *De Rerum Natura*, see Jammer, *Concepts of Space*, 85–6).

4. Pierre Gassendi, "De loco et tempore seu spatio et duratione," in G. S. Bertt, *The Philosophy Of Gassendi* (Macmillan, 1908), 35ff.

5. The hypothesis of the divine annihilation of the world was a speculative tool widely employed in medieval scholastic philosophy. After Gassendi, it would play an important role too in early modern speculations about the nature of space and reality, most notably in Descartes, Locke, and Newton. The image was not devoid of political implications either, as we will see in Chapter 11.1. At any rate, we should bear in mind that, for Gassendi, space and time are independent of thought and observation: they "must be considered real things, or actual entities, for although they are not the same sort of things as substance and accident are commonly considered, they still actually exist and do not depend upon the mind like a chimera since space endures steadfastly and time flows on whether the mind thinks of them or not" (*Exercitationes*, 1.182a, in LoLordo, *Pierre Gassendi and the Birth of Early Modern Philosophy*, 107).

6. Grant reconstruct in this respect the arguments through which Walter Charleton, who shared with Gassendi the identification of space as uncreated and independent of God, tried to defuse the accusation of impiety: "though we concede them [i.e., spatial dimensions] to be improduct by, and independent upon God, yet cannot our Adversaries therefore impeach us of impiety, or distort it to the disparagement of our theory" (*Physiologia Epicuro-Gassendo-Charltoniana: or a Fabrick of Science Natural Upon the Hypothesis of Atoms*, article 16, cited in Grant, *Much Ado About Nothing*, 393). On Charleton's role in the early modern resurgence of atomism and its influence on Newton see Robert Rynasiewicz, "Newton's Views on Space, Time, and Motion," *The Stanford Encyclopedia of Philosophy*, ed. Edward N. Zalta, Summer 2014 edition.

7. Against the warning of Aristotle, matter and space can once again coexist in the same place. Patrizi had expressed this argument in the clearest terms: "When [Space] is filled with a body, it is locus; without a body, it is a vacuum. And on this account this vacuum, like locus, must have the three common dimensions – length, width and depth. And the vacuum itself is nothing other than three-dimensional Space" (*Nova de Universis Philosophia*, as translated in Casey, *The Fate of*

Place, 127. See also: "A vacuum is certainly prior to locus . . . But it is an essential attribute of Space to be a vacuum, hence Space is prior to locus both in nature and in time" [ibid., 129]).

8. The expression is used by Rabelais in *Gargantua and his Son Pantagruel* (trans. Thomas Urquhart, 1653, chapter V). In *Much Ado About Nothing*, Grant thoroughly reconstructs the overcoming of the "almost universal conviction that nature abhorred a vacuum" in scholasticism and medieval thought (see 67–100, 260, and "Medieval and Seventeenth-Century Conceptions of an Infinite Void Space beyond the Cosmos," 39–60). In a similar vein, LoLordo describes the process through which "late medievals tended to abandon the claim that the void was altogether impossible . . . so it became more or less taken for granted that a void is conceptually and logically possible, if not naturally possible . . . Eustachius, for instance, states that no vacuum occurs naturally in this universe, although God could create a vacuum" (LoLordo, *Pierre Gassendi and the Birth of Early Modern Philosophy*, 101–2).

9. See Max Jammer, *Concepts of Space*, 92.

10. *Physics*, 215a26ff.

11. "[Space] is not a body, because it displays no resistance, nor is it ever an object of, or subject to, vision, touch, or any other sense. On the other hand, it is not incorporeal, being three-dimensional. It has length, breadth, and depth – not just one, two, or several of these dimensions, but all of them" (Francesco Patrizi, "On Physical Space", *Nova de Universis Philosophia*, 61b–3a; cited in Casey, *The Fate of Place*, 126). The notion of the void corresponds then quite naturally to the ideal conditions of absence of resistance that are posited by the principles of modern kinematics. In this sense, LoLordo reproduces an entry from Beeckman's journal according to which, in 1629, he transmitted to Gassendi his conviction that "in a vacuum all things that were once moved are always moved" (*Pierre Gassendi and the Birth of Early Modern Philosophy*, 45).

12. "Space is something that possesses three dimensions, is immobile, is penetrable by bodies, and occupies a midpoint between matter and nothingness" (Pascal, *Experiences Nouvelles Touchant le Vide*, cited in LoLordo, *Pierre Gassendi and the Birth of Early Modern Philosophy*, 115). Even though in his interpretation of the barometer experiment he diverged from Pascal, Gassendi made essentially that same association. For an interpretation of the role of experiments on the vacuum in seventeenth-century science and epistemology see the classic work by Steven Shapin and Simon Schaffer, *Leviathan and the Air-Pump* (Princeton: Princeton University Press, 2011), which reconstructs the debate between Hobbes and Boyle in relation to the experimental method of the latter.

13. Otto von Guericke, *Experimenta Nova*, cited in Grant, *Much Ado About Nothing*, 216–17. Again, the absence of resistance is a decisive

property of space for Von Guericke: space is for him the "container of all things, in which all things exist, live, and are moved and which supports no variation, alteration or mutation" (ibid.).

14. For Descartes, all forms of dimensionality belong to a material substance, which excludes the conception of space as a container of the corporeal objects that are located in it. See for instance Principles 11 ("The extension constituting the nature of a body is exactly the same as the extension constituting the nature of a space") and 12 ("The difference between space and corporeal substance lies in our way of conceiving them") in the *Principles of Philosophy* (*Descartes: Selected Philosophical Writings*, Part 2, 1–18, ed. John Cottingham [Cambridge: Cambridge University Press, 1988], 189–98). One may wonder, consequently, whether we can still talk of space as a category. According to Descartes, it is *us* who attribute "generic unity" (Principle 10) to the extension of space, by abstracting it from the bodies that are ultimately identical to it. Logically, this view makes the existence of the void *impossible*. See for instance Principle 16: "It is a contradiction to suppose there is such a thing as a vacuum, i.e. that in which there is nothing whatsoever . . . it is a complete contradiction that a particular extension should belong to nothing; and the same conclusion must be drawn with respect to a space that is supposed to be a vacuum, namely that since there is extension in it, there must necessarily be substance in it as well." In Principle 18, Descartes responds to Gassendi's interrogation on "what would happen if God were to take away every single body contained in a vessel." For Descartes, there would be no void whatsoever: "the sides of the vessel would, in that case, have to be in contact." Interestingly, however, Descartes asserts that we cannot posit limits to the material world, so that space must be considered as indefinite in itself (see Principle 26, Part I: "We should never enter into arguments about the infinite. Things in which we observe no limits – such as the extension of the world, the division of the parts of matter, the number of the stars, and so on – should instead be regarded as indefinite," ibid., 168). On Descartes's metaphysical distinction of the concepts of the infinite and indefinite, their origins in the scholastic tradition, and the relevance of this distinction for his geometry and physics, see Dmitri Nikulin, *Matter, Imagination, and Geometry: Ontology, Natural Philosophy, and Mathematics in Plotinus, Proclus, and Descartes* (Farnham: Ashgate, 2002), 52ff and 107–9. On the political and theological motivation of Descartes's argument for the indefiniteness of the world see Chapter 8.2.

15. See *Principles of Philosophy*, Part III, 24–30. On the relation of Descartes's vortex theory, the indefinite character of the world, and religious censorship, see Andrew Janiak, "Space and Motion in Nature and Scripture: Galileo, Descartes, Newton," *Studies in History and Philosophy of Science* 51 (2015): 89–99.

16. See Hylarie Kochiras, "Subtle Matter," in Lawrence Nolan, ed., *The Cambridge Descartes Lexicon* (Cambridge: Cambridge University Press, 2015), 708–9.

17. As Koyré points out, Bruno alternatively depicts space as a radical void or as filled with ether (not unlike "ethereal medium" that, likened to the Holy Spirit, moved according to Kepler the orbits planets around the sun. See *From the Closed World*, 40, 47–8). See also Casey, *The Fate of Place*, 126.

18. See for instance Panofsky's reading of ether as an attempt to invest the coldness of the infinite universe, "along with the infinite extension of the Democritan *kenon*, with the infinite dynamic of the neoplatonic world-soul" (*Perspective as Symbolic Form*, 66. See also Grant, *Much Ado About Nothing*, 188). For the importance of Henry More on the elaboration of this theological filling of the void, see note 196 and Chapter 8.2 below.

19. In his groundbreaking exploration of magnetism, William Gilbert confronted precisely this problem. The earth, according to Gilbert, works as an enormous magnet, generating an attractive force that emanates from its center and is thus "felt" by bodies on the surface of earth. That force reaches out to bodies though "magnetic effluvia," a kind of breath or vapor that is said to be extremely light and thin, but that still manages to generate a series of pressures and reciprocal contacts through empty space. Thus, the ethereal vapors explain mechanically both the transmission of magnetism and the continuity of the force (see Edwin Burtt, *The Metaphysical Foundations of Modern Physical Science*, 156–8, 184–5).

20. Cited in LoLordo, *Pierre Gassendi and the Birth of Early Modern Philosophy*, 105–6.

21. Isaac Newton, "General Scholium," in *Mathematical Principles of Natural Philosophy*, vol. 2, London, 1729. In the *Queries* added to the Latin edition of the *Optiks* in 1706, Newton had posited the existence of an ethereal medium through which forces of attraction and repulsion of matter could be propagated: "And is not this Medium exceedingly more rare and subtile than the Air, and exceedingly more elastick and active? And doth it not readily pervade all Bodies? And is it not (by its elastick force) expanded through all the Heavens?" (*Opticks: Or, A Treatise of the Reflections, Refractions, Inflexions and Colours of Light. The Second Edition, with Additions*, London, 1718, Query 18). Ether works as a transmitter of forces and a mechanical unifier, and consequently solves the problem of propagation and action at a distance. Such ether, however, only occupied parts, not all, of space; empty space was to be found within ether itself and in the regions of space beyond our solar system, where ether is not to be found at all (see Koyré, *From the Closed World*, 171, 207; and Burtt, *The Metaphysical Foundations of Modern Physical Science*, 242).

In the General Scholium, however, Newton famously acknowledges his incapacity to provide an exhaustive causal explanation of the causes of gravity or electricity. A purely materialistic explanation of natural philosophy seems then insufficient (Koyré, ibid., 213), and Newton falls back instead into a theological conception of an immaterial ether, in which God would offer no resistance to the motion of bodies in space. Both the influence of Henry More, for whom a divine immaterial spirit fills the entirety of infinite space and determines the action and movement of matter, and the re-elaboration of early themes that Newton had dealt with, for instance in *De Gravitatione*, are salient here. Grant cites evidence by Westfall according to which, in his unpublished papers, Newton had already affirmed the existence of an "infinite and omnipresent spirit in which matter is moved according to mathematical laws" (Richard S. Westfall, *Force in Newton's Physics: The Science of Dynamics in the Seventeenth Century* [New York: American Elsevier, 1971], 399, cited in Grant, *Much Ado About Nothing*, 247. See also J. A. Ruffner, "Newton's De Gravitatione: A Review and Reassessment," *Archive for History of Exact Sciences* 66, no. 3 (2012): 241–64). To make matters more complex, in the fourth reply to Leibniz, Samuel Clarke formulates a hypothesis according to which substances other than matter might in fact fill up void space. These substances, Clarke affirms, are not "tangible," but he explains nothing more about their ontological and physical status: "Void space, is not an attribute without a subject; because, by void space, we never mean space void of every thing, but void of body only. In all void space, God is certainly present, and possibly many other substances which are not matter; being neither tangible nor objects of any of our senses" (Samuel Clarke, *The Leibniz–Clarke Correspondence, Together with Extracts from Newton's Principia and Opticks*, ed. Henry Gavin Alexander [New York: Philosophical Library, 1956], 47).

22. Jammer describes how space becomes the "necessary substratum" that serves as "precondition" and as "metaphysical foundation for the new physics" (*Concepts of Space*, 87–93). See also Huggett, *Space from Zeno to Einstein*, 89.

Chapter 7

Abstraction: Rational Mechanics

Modern science finds before itself an open world, emptied of all qualities and purposive features. The logic of sameness guarantees that the same exact rules apply everywhere and at every time; the real has no other bounds than a system of universal laws that are accessible as such to human reason. Nature is stripped of its fabric of hierarchies, substances, and relations; the correspondence of places and values, of positions and potencies, collapses in a world that excludes the anomalies, rejects the exceptions, and forbids everything that is incommensurable. Instead, science affirms a world where all places are now projected onto a single, isotropic plane. In the absence of qualities and final causes, all positions become mere points in the single geometrical matrix of infinite space; all are endowed with the same dignity and value, obey the same rules, and are expressed by the same universal language. The great ontological unification of early modern science, as we shall see now, finds in the abstraction of space both its fundamental premise and its clearest expression.

7.1 Mathematics as the Logic of Nature

Among the ruins of the old cosmos, Copernicus and Kepler found a series of mathematical proportions. Knowing the universe was equivalent to unveiling the mathematical harmony that governed the disposition and the apparent motion of its elements; in those numbers appeared a divine mark, the trace through which men could not only discover the logic of nature and its workings, but also appreciate the coherence and beauty of creation. Science and the disclosure of truth appeared hence as grandiose mathematical endeavors.[1] In itself, this notion was hardly new or revolutionary: the Pythagorean and Platonic cosmologies had already posited the fundamental equivalence of physical and mathematical realities, developed the idea of astronomy as a "geometry of the heavens," and set the task for natural scientists of revealing the numeric harmonies governing the facts of nature as a principle.[2] The blowing up of the celestial spheres, however, and the realization that all cosmic motions follow the same principles and laws, which were reducible to (and expressible by) precise mathematical functions, elevated that identity into a general premise for the new science, which posited as a fact that the structure of the infinite universe was unequivocally mathematical.

Such identification found its most fortunate expression in Galileo's famous metaphor of a "great book of nature" written in geometrical forms and mathematical language.[3] Mathematics constitutes our way of access to the knowledge of the world, and conversely, the world can be reduced to, and understood by, mathematical principles expressing its most fundamental relations. Science conveys the structure of reality in abstract and exact laws; all physical processes proceed in accordance with strict mathematical principles and measurable logical determinations. The study of those determinations constitutes our knowledge of the physical world, which must also proceed, in all its ramifications, according to applied geometry and the postulates of mathematical logic.

Perhaps no one expressed more clearly the faith in the new methodology than Descartes, who in a letter addressed to Mersenne in 1649, affirmed his resolve to explain by means of it "all the phenomena of Nature, i.e. Physics."[4] This exuberant ambition – but also his characterization of nature as an *automaton* of matter and motion – rests on the general principle of the mathematization of the world that was previously formalized by Galileo. The whole of nature appears then as a mechanical structure, governed by relations of efficient causality; bodies move in space and time according to quantifiable proportions, which can be measured, calculated, and deduced in their full mathematical precision.[5] Nature works with the regularity of a mechanism because it follows strict apodictic laws. Mathematics and geometry grant us access to the rational engine of the world; the duty of the natural philosopher, via a refined logic of deductions and demonstrations, is to formalize and extend their principles to the entirety of reality and to human life too.[6] In a fully mathematized world, indeed, even the passions of the soul proceed *more geometrico*.

In the epistemology of Isaac Newton, this program would find both its grandiose accomplishment and a sobering contention. Unified under the universal laws of motion and gravitation, the world is for Newton an essentially mathematical system: a sum of masses moving in space and time, acted upon by forces according to exact and regular relations.[7] The task of physics is precisely to investigate those forces, to measure their quantities and their effects on natural phenomena, to deduce the propositions that explain the relations between them, to verify and demonstrate those propositions so as to confirm their universality. But if science explains how the world works, it is no less true that we can never depart too far from its observation, from the art of measurement, from careful verification. More dramatically, even as our knowledge progresses we realize that there is much that escapes us regarding the origin and qualities of the very things that are explained, not to mention the purposes and ultimate ends of reality.[8] The mathematical principles of natural philosophy allow us access to the universal structure of the physical world, but that structure is never entirely transparent, and many things of the world, including its causes, simply cannot be mathematically explained.

7.2 The Geometrization of Space

Those reservations were not easy to accommodate from the standpoint of the philosophy of science. As Galileo anticipated, the world appears to the new physics as an entirely geometrical reality. Science abstracts ideal figures and relations from the natural world; life itself is objectified into metrical determinations. Nature is thus constructed as an abstract and ideal structure, a system of pure forms interconnected by logical relations, which expresses the fundamentally mathematical and geometrical character of reality and, ultimately, of the nature of being itself. Any exception or limit to that logic seems to contradict a basic metaphysical premise of modern science: the fundamental commensurability of reason and nature that is expressed by the universal principles of geometry and mathematics. By that premise, geometry is the language of nature and nature, geometry "made real" in the physical world.[9] It is no wonder, hence, that such world has little room for contradictions.

Obviously, the geometrization of being has a number of quite direct implications for the conception of space. If the order of nature is geometrical in character, it follows by necessity that the space in which things are must be compatible with the fundamental principles of geometry, that is of reality itself. Space is the where of mathematical principles becoming real in the physical world; it is the pure geometrical entity that guarantees the continuity between the mathematical logic expressed by numbers and their dimensional unfolding in reality. Space, moreover, is not only the container of things; it is also a real entity, an existing and independent thing. But if the being of reality is geometrical through and through, then the essence of space must be geometrical too, it must be consonant, precisely *qua ens*, with the being of nature itself. The abstract space of Euclidean geometry is thus taken to define and represent the real space of the world. Abstract space becomes an objective feature of reality itself, at once an instance and a premise of the general geometrization of the world.[10]

Indeed, the abstract space of geometry would couple seamlessly with the metaphysical framework of the new science.[11] Euclidean space matches essentially the openness of an infinite universe. Such space is indefinite by definition, logically in defiance of any bounds: there is no outside and no beyond, no a priori conceivable limits, which allows the expansion of the scientific potential to a virtually infinite domain of problems.[12] The space of geometry is also empty of qualities and local particularities, of any regional property or differentiation. Voided of all values and determinations, the uniform plane of pure geometry is a space without metaphysical depth, a space of points and surfaces, of lines and solids, which extends without limits in all directions at once. All possible stations and positions within it are reduced to the status of qualitatively indistinguishable points. All are equalized within a single frame of reference that guarantees their uniqueness, but also their ontological uniformity and indifference.

Unified only by a series of essential postulates and operational principles, the space of geometry provides the homogenous and isotropic background that is required to sustain, without any qualitative hindrances, the continuity and lawfulness of the mathematical principles of physics. Fully geometrized, space sustains hence the rationality of the world; it embodies its logico-mathematical structure and dispels the abyssal threats of meaninglessness and disorder. As such, the infinite space of the world is idealized and abstracted to the point of becoming not only compatible with mathematics, but an essential condition for the realization of mathematics in nature as such.

7.3 Relative Space and the Problem of Motion

The identification of geometrical space with the real space of the world did certainly not go uncontested. Interestingly, a salient form of opposition would come from mechanicist philosophers who adopted with enthusiasm the geometrical method to explain the structure of the natural world, but nonetheless rejected categorically the objective existence of space. Descartes, as we have seen, equated space with extension, and extension with bodies and matter; his world is a corporeal plenum from which no real dimensions can be detached. Going even further, Hobbes denounces that space is nothing but a phantasm, a fiction, a byproduct of the imagination.[13] Both conceive of the world as a machinery of matter and motion that functions according to strict mathematical rules, but do not believe that there is such thing as a real space endowed with independent existence. Both explain what exists according to the basic principles of geometry, but do not confer to space a nature of its own.[14]

For Descartes, we can only say that things occupy space by virtue of a certain abstraction. Each point in space can be distinguished, as separate from the body "occupying" it, only by an intellection that expresses, however, no correlate in the actual physical world. Such is the space defined by Euclidean geometry, which correctly describes the functioning of nature but has no real, objective existence in the bodily realm of extension. In other words, we can make use of abstract space in order to measure and understand the way in which the world works, but we cannot mistake that use for an assertion of its existence. Things do not exist in a space that would be separate from them; rather, a thing is spatially extended in the sense that it has a three-dimensional volume, a size, and a position with which it coincides.[15]

The world can hence be analyzed and described geometrically, but space is nothing apart from the relation of concrete, extended bodies to other equally concrete and extended bodies. Of course, we can measure with exactitude and precision the position of objects, model their relations according to geometrical determinations, calculate their trajectories following mathematical laws. But all those abstract measurements and calculations only have a real correspondence, a grip on physical reality, by virtue of the concrete relations that exist between bodies in the natural world. Indeed, measurements are only meaningful in relation to specific and tangible points of reference from which spatial relations can be determined; all geometrical determinations for an object are hence relative to, and dependent on, the reference point that has been adopted for the measurement. And while there might be good reasons to select a particular reference point for the determination of a particular relation or measure, that choice will always be ultimately subjective, conventional, or pragmatic. All abstract points on a geometrical plane are fundamentally equal, and there is no ultimate reason, besides convention or convenience, to establish one instead of another.

This is the novelty and paradox of Cartesian geometry as applied to the study of physics: as determinate and precise as they are, all systems of coordinates are ultimately arbitrarily chosen. There are necessary reasons for this, but also quite significant consequences. For instance: in a universe without limits, marked by a pervasive ontological flatness, by the essential equality of all its regions and points, there can be no ultimate center, no fixed point, no absolute reference from which to set and determine for good the order of nature. "Nothing in our world," says Descartes, "has a permanent place, except as determined by our thought."[16] Things in themselves have no final positions, and there are no places other than the actual positions of things.

The relativity of geometrical values, however, would soon prove quite troublesome for the development of mechanics. For if the motion of a body cannot be measured in relation to a permanent, objective system of reference, but only as the change of position in relation to a referential point that is arbitrarily established, then it follows that depending on the system of reference that is assumed, a single thing, set in the same exact relations with other surrounding bodies, can have at the same time different positions and motions; the same thing can even be moving and not moving in relation to two different referential frames. This posits an obvious problem precisely for one of Descartes's greatest achievements: the formulation of the law of inertia, according to which bodies tend to maintain their state of rest or rectilinear motion at a constant velocity unless acted upon by an external force. By its definition, the principle of inertia establishes a fundamental difference between forced motions (the velocity of which depends on the action of external forces) and inertial ones (which tend to maintain a constant velocity of motion or rest). But if acceleration and velocity are relative notions, and depend on the reference frame that is chosen each time for the measurement, then there is ultimately no way to make sense of this distinction. The same object can at the same time be moving uniformly in one frame and in an accelerated motion in another. The law of inertia seems to require the existence of a frame that is not relative, or otherwise put, of an absolute reference. For Newton, that reference is given precisely by the nature of space.[17]

7.4 The Abstraction of Space in Newtonian Mechanics

In the Scholium on space and time that opens the *Mathematical Principles of Natural Philosophy*, Newton discards all definitions of space that are derived from our relations to sensible objects.[18] Those definitions are based on nothing but "prejudices": since in our "common life" we are surrounded by things, but we do not see space itself, we assume that the nature of space, like our concrete measurements of spatial relations, must be defined in reference to those same things that we see around us. Thus, we determine what space is in relation to "sensible measures", and

> From the positions and distances of things from any body considered as immovable, we define all places; and then with respect to such places, we estimate all motions, considering bodies as transferred from some of those places into others.[19]

Of course, in the conduct of our "common affairs" this manner of proceeding generally creates no inconvenience. In philosophical disquisitions, however, such as the investigation of nature and the fundamental laws of the universe, "we ought to abstract from our senses and consider things themselves," that is, things as they are in the world independently from the relation that they bear to us.[20] It is hence by abstraction that we can posit and demonstrate the existence of an absolute space that is unchanging and independent of the bodies that are in it, and hence distinct from the relative spaces that we habitually measure as a sensible determination of the relation of things:

> Absolute space, in its own nature, without relation to anything external, remains always similar and immovable. Relative space is some movable dimension or measure of the absolute spaces; which our senses determine by its position to bodies; and which is commonly taken for immovable space; such is the dimension of a subterraneous, an aerial, or celestial space, determined by its position in respect of the earth. Absolute and relative space are the same in figure and magnitude; but they do not remain always numerically the same.[21]

Newton acknowledges that it is extremely difficult to distinguish absolute space, because its parts, invisible and undifferentiated, are not immediately perceived or otherwise accessible to us. Indeed, in our common practice we specify the location and motion of concrete objects simply by means of relative measurements. Absolute space does not alter such practice, nor our general experience of space. What absolute space proves is that a framework exists that is independent of any sensible body, and hence that our systems of reference are not ultimately arbitrary, that there is a permanent, objective, inalterable background that holds at once for each and every one of them. Indeed, while things can have many relative positions depending on the framework of reference that is adopted to measure them, they only have one position in absolute space. When that position changes, a thing must be said to move absolutely, that is, not in reference to any other body or system of relations, but simply in relation to absolute space. And although "it is a matter of great difficulty," again, to distinguish those true motions in absolute space from the apparent and relative ones, Newton proves that we can do so by a consideration of their causes and their effects:

> The causes by which true and relative motions are distinguished, one from the other, are the forces impressed upon bodies to generate motion. True motion is neither generated nor altered, but by some force impressed upon the body moved; but relative motion may be generated or altered without any force impressed upon the body. For it is sufficient only to impress some force on other bodies with which the former is compared, that by their giving way, that relation may be changed, in which the relative rest or motion of this other body did consist . . . And therefore any relative motion may be changed when the true motion remains unaltered, and the relative may be preserved when the true suffers some change. Thus, true motion by no means consists in such relations.[22]

This distinction is precisely what Descartes's model of mechanics could not afford. Relative space might "move" with the system of material relations that it denotes, but absolute space provides the fixed, unchanging framework against which forced and inertial motions can be distinguished and made sense of, without reference to any other system of material bodies.[23] Absolute motion implies the existence of absolute space, and conversely, absolute space is what allows us to verify the absolute, true, and mathematical character of the fundamental laws of motion and mechanics.

The abstraction of absolute space in Newton's system of mechanics produces a number of important consequences. First, it confirms that space is wholly *incorporeal* and distinct from matter. For if absolute and relative space can be discriminated, then it follows that space is distinct from everything that is in space and moves through it.[24] Second, space is a wholly *independent* entity: each point of space exists before it is occupied by a body, and subsists when the body that occupies it moves elsewhere or disappears (in other words, there can be space without objects, but there cannot be objects that are not in space). Third, space is *real*, for its existence as the inertial framework for matter is verified by empirical demonstration. Fourth, space is *continuous, homogenous,* and *isotropic*, for all existing bodies in the world are affected by it in the same manner in each and every one of its points. Fifth, space is *selfsame* and *immobile*; for the order of its parts cannot be changed, and *infinite*, because so are the points that compose it and no a priori limits can be set to it in any possible direction. Finally, space is *mathematical*, for it acts according to the fundamental laws of mechanics, independently of any particular choice of a system of reference; and it is *geometrical*, for space is the sum of all possible locations in the universe measurable in perfect determination. Precisely as a geometrical object, each of the infinite points in space is at the same time unique and equal to every other: each of them represents a singular position, not relative to any other body or spatial region; in their complete lack of differentiation, however, nothing can tell them apart.[25] Unified in the laws of mechanics and gravitation, fully abstracted and geometrized, set to coincide with the boundless extension of an infinite world, in Newton's metaphysics space becomes the absolute foundation of a world that no longer had one.

Notes

1. In the "mathematico-aesthetic" conception of causality of early modern science, "not only is it true that we can discover mathematical relations in all objects presented to the senses; all certain knowledge must be knowledge of their quantitative characteristics, perfect knowledge is always mathematical" (Burtt, *The Metaphysical Foundations of Modern Physical Science,* 57). According to Casey, this process of abstraction raised "absolute mathematical continua . . . to the rank of ultimate metaphysical notions" (*The Fate of Place,* 84). Arguably, the logic of mathematics becomes a sort of natural ontology, driving

at once the epistemological concerns of natural philosophers and the fundamental postulates of metaphysicians.

2. On the potential and limits of Greek mathematics, its early application to the study of physics, and its legacy for early modern natural philosophy see Eduard Jan Dijksterhuis, *The Mechanization of the World Picture: Pythagoras to Newton* (Princeton: Princeton University Press, 1986), 50–68, and Dmitri Nikulin, *Matter, Imagination, and Geometry*, 82–4.

3. "La filosofia [della natura] è scritta in questo grandissimo libro che continuamente ci sta aperto dinanzi a gli occhi (io dico l'universo), ma non si può intendere se prima non s'impara a intender la lingua, e conoscere i caratteri ne' quali è scritto. Egli è scritto in lingua matematica, e i caratteri son triangoli, cerchi, ed altre figure geometriche, senza i quali mezi [sic] è impossibile a intenderne umanamente parola; senza questi è un aggirarsi vanamente per un oscuro laberinto" ("Il Saggiatore," in *Opere* vol. VI, ed. A. Favaro, Giunti-Barbera [Florence: Edizione Nazionale, 1966], 232). Husserl famously interpreted the process of mathematization of the natural world that ensued from Galileo's program as the transformation of nature into a mathematical multiplicity, that is, an ensemble of pure ideal forms that is accessible, through the system of their causal connections and relations, via the precise method of mathematics (*The Crisis of European Sciences and Transcendental Phenomenology: An Introduction to Phenomenological Philosophy* [Evanston: Northwestern University Press, 1970]). The ideal subsumption of the immediate experience of the world to the abstract, objective language of mathematics expressed the rationality of the order of physics and thus granted a secure hold for truth in a universe desperately threatened by the dangers of relativity. The price to pay was the sacrifice of any ambition on the part of science to have a say in the explanation of the reasons or purposes of nature. The benefit was an immensely powerful epistemic technology, which could capture in mathematical terms the manifold expressions of natural causality in a seemingly unending accumulation of knowledge and experimentation. See for instance the interpretation of James Dodd: "By means of pure mathematics and the practical art of measuring, one can produce, for everything in the world of bodies which is extended in this way [as a collocation of bodies in relative positions to one another], a completely new kind of inductive prediction; namely, one can "calculate" with compelling necessity, on the basis of given and measured events involving shapes, events which are unknown and were never accessible to direct measurement. Thus ideal geometry, estranged from the world, becomes "applied" geometry and thus becomes in a certain respect a general method for knowing the real (*Crisis and Reflection: An Essay on Husserl's Crisis of the European Sciences* [Dordrecht:

Springer Netherlands, 2005], 91). Ultimately, this logic of inductive prediction would take in Laplace the most radical expression of the mathematical metaphysics: given a certain arrangement of matter in the universe, and the inexorable mathematical laws of physics, we should be able not only to know all possible states of the universe in the future too.

4. "Instead of explaining only one phenomenon, I have resolved to explain all the phenomena of Nature, i.e. Physics" (Rene Descartes, "Letter to Mersenne," cited in Robert Stoothoff, translator's preface to "The World", *The Philosophical Writings of Descartes*, vol. I [Cambridge: Cambridge University Press, 2007], 80. In the *Principles*, Descartes presents the following description of his method: "The only principles which I accept, or require, in physics are those of geometry and pure mathematics; these principles explain all natural phenomena, and enable us to provide quite certain demonstrations regarding them . . . I recognize no matter in corporeal things apart from that which the geometers call quantity, and take as the object of their demonstrations, i.e. that to which every kind of division, shape and motion is applicable . . . And since all natural phenomena can be explained in this way, as will become clear in what follows, I do not think that any other principles are either admissible or desirable in physics" (Principle 64, Part II, cited in Nikulin, *Matter, Imagination and Geometry*, 125). On the distinction between "*mathesis*" and mathematics, the role of the latter in the formation of the Cartesian method, and the broader relation between arithmetic, geometry and epistemology in Descartes, Nikulin writes: "In a sense, mathesis universalis for Descartes is a (or even the) method of discursive overcoming of human finitude, which appears in the unavoidable discursiveness of thinking. Mathesis mediates between metaphysics, which has to reveal the necessity of existence of the infinite thinking substance, and physics, which refers to the finite (or indefinite) extended substance. If this is the case, then if one also takes into consideration that mathematics is considered detached from its contents, then mathematics qua discursive method of reasoning may be applicable to every extended entity without discrimination, be it physical or geometrical" (ibid., 120).

5. "I have described this earth and indeed the whole visible universe as if it were a machine: I have considered only the various shapes and movements of its parts" (Principle 188, *Selected Philosophical Writings*, 200). In another beautiful passage of the *Discourse on Method*, Descartes describes the human body "as a machine which, having been made by the hand of God, is incomparably better ordered than any machine that can be devised by man, and contains in itself movements more wonderful than those in any such machine" (ibid., 44). The philosophy of natural mechanicism, which found in the introduction to the

Leviathan its most celebrated expression ("For what is the heart, but a spring; and the nerves, but so many strings; and the joints, but so many wheels?") and figured prominently in the philosophy of Bacon, Boyle, or Leibniz, rests on the premise of the rational-ideal mathematization of nature. The "geometrico-mechanical" qualities of the real, explains Dijksterhuis, "were considered to be really inherent" and "objectively present" in a physical body as such (*The Mechanization of the World Picture*, 431). All further secondary qualities could then be reduced to the features of the first, and hence be mechanized and quantified too. This general "mechanization of qualities" generated the feeling that "in mathematics and mechanics it was possible to arrive, apparently without any recourse to sense-experience and yet with a sense of being supported by sufficient evidence, at an extensive knowledge of the geometrico-mechanical qualities, inevitably gave these sciences a place apart" (ibid.).

6. In the preface to the French edition of the *Principles of Philosophy*, Descartes ascribes an ultimate moral end to the task of philosophy and the natural sciences: "Thus the whole of philosophy is like a tree. The roots are metaphysics, the trunk is physics, and the branches emerging from the trunk are all the other sciences, which may be reduced to three principal ones, namely medicine, mechanics and morals. By 'morals' I understand the highest and most perfect moral system, which presupposes a complete knowledge of the other sciences and is the ultimate level of wisdom" (*Selected Writings*, 188). On the metaphysical, epistemological and political implications of the metaphor see Pablo Bustinduy, "Two or Three Battles: Organicity and Temporality in Cartesian Ethics," *Ramon Llull Journal of Applied Ethics* 4 (2013): 9–29.

7. The Newtonian concept of mass fits perfectly within the mathematic/mechanistic view of nature: "the idea of mass had been incorporated into the Cartesian geometrical machine; and its substitution for the fanciful vortices only made the world-system seem all the more rigidly mechanical" (Burtt, *The Metaphysical Foundations of Modern Physical Science*, 243). In his famous critique of the metaphysics of time, Henri Bergson analyzed this modern operation as an adaptation of time to the requirements of space. The space-centric view of time makes both into homogenous and measurable dimensions, maximizing their scientific-practical potential but losing along the way something essential about our experience of space and time (see especially *Creative Evolution*, translated by Mitchell Abidor [New York: New York Review Books, 2019]).

8. In Newton's mathematical-empirical methodology, deduction from observation and demonstration are essential to the scientific process; natural philosophy has no say in establishing the non-demonstrable, hidden causes of the nature of things. See for instance the famous

passages from the preface to the *Principia*: "the basic problem of philosophy seems to be to discover the forces of nature from the phenomena of motions and then to demonstrate the other phenomena from these forces . . . by means of propositions demonstrated mathematically . . . we derive from celestial phenomena the gravitational forces . . . then the motions of the planets, the comets, the moon, and the sea . . . If only we could derive the other phenomena of nature from mechanical principles by the same kind of reasoning! For many things lead me to have a suspicion that all phenomena may depend on certain forces by which the particles of bodies, by causes not yet known, either are impelled . . . or are repelled . . . Since these forces are unknown, philosophers have hitherto made trial of nature in vain. But I hope that the principles set down here will shed some light on either this mode of philosophizing or some truer one ("Newton's Preface to the First Edition", *The Principia*, 382–3). For a discussion of the General Scholium, the different interpretations of "*hypothesis non fingo*," and Newton's positions on the limits of mechanical philosophy, see Bernard Cohen, "The Concluding General Scholium," in *A Guide to Newton's Principia*, ibid., 274–93.

9. See Koyré, *From the Closed World*, 100–1. James Dodd's analysis of the *style of the world* as entailed by Galilean science may also be of relevance here. According to Dodd, the problem for early modern science "is not how to coordinate a Platonic mathematical realm with the nonmathematical physical world using a sophisticated application of hypothetical methods (as was the project of Ptolemaic astronomy), but to rediscover the concrete in light of its deep, hidden connection to mathematical structures, leading to the conviction that nature itself, in its concreteness and not just in its being-thought, is intrinsically mathematical . . . [the world] behaves mathematically" (*Crisis and Reflection*, 88). For the analysis of the *verum factum* principle, by which "subjectivity knows its object to the extent that, and only insofar as, it produces this very object and the means for knowing it," and the importance of modern subjectivity for the project of "applying exact mathematical reasoning to [the] overtly inexact and fluent physical things," see Nikulin, *Matter, Imagination and Geometry*, 223.

10. Was this purely geometrical space, as formalized by the abstract coordinate system, taken as a real, objective feature of the world? Or was it merely a convention or a "useful fiction," adopted for the sake of scientific practice only? For Patrizi and Newton, geometrical solids and figures seem to exist as real features of the world. In a famous passage from *De Gravitatione*, Newton asserts the existence of invisible geometrical figures everywhere around us ("De Gravitatione," in *Unpublished Scientific Paper of Isaac Newton* [Cambridge: Cambridge University Press, 1962], 99–101, 110).

According to McGuire, space for Newton is full of "inherent figures" that act as a sort of "place-holders" for sensory experience
within a theological theory of perception and reality: space "is so
structured that God, in virtue of his creative power, can 'pick out'
and condition various of space's inherent figures so that they in
turn can cause the mind, via sensory experience, to form representations of material phenomena . . . in Newton's view, for anything
that can be said consistently of space, there must exist a real and
corresponding ground in the nature of space itself" (*Tradition and
Innovation: Newton's Metaphysics of Nature*, 183–4. See also Max
Jammer, *Concepts of Space*, 17–26, 101, and Grant, *Much Ado
About Nothing*, 232–43). Without necessarily going as far as positing the invisible existence of geometrical objects, the ontological
equation that binds together geometry and nature seems to imply
the necessity of adopting some form of spatial realism. For the con-
testation of this view and an alternative conception of the relation
between geometry, space and physical reality see next section, "Relative Space and the Problem of Motion."

11. The importance of the process of geometrization of space in early
    modern developments of the philosophy of science has been the object
    of intense philosophical discussion. In the opening passages of *From
    the Closed World to the Infinite Universe*, Koyré describes the gen-
    eral cosmological transition of modernity as "the replacement of the
    Aristotelian conception of space – a differentiated set of innerworldly
    places – by that of Euclidean geometry – an essentially infinite and
    homogeneous extension – from now on considered as identical with
    the real space of the world" (*From the Closed World*, viii). Counter-
    ing that narrative, Edward Grant has argued that the assertion of an
    infinite, three-dimensional void space coinciding with the real space
    of the universe was the result of a gradual process of divinization of
    space in theological and cosmological debates, in which mathemat-
    ics and geometry played no essential part ("The infinite space that
    surrounded the world was the product of cosmological and physical
    controversy and had nothing to do with any alleged application of
    Euclidean geometric space to the physical world," *Much Ado About
    Nothing*, 107, see also 232–3). For Burtt, such assimilation of geo-
    metric and physical space was not a novelty at all, since "the space
    of geometry appears to have been the space of the real universe to
    all ancient and medieval thinkers who give any clear clue to their
    notion of the matter. In the case of the Pythagoreans and Platonists
    the identity of the two was an important metaphysical doctrine"
    (*The Metaphysical Foundations of Modern Physical Science*, 33). All
    qualifications aside, it seems impossible to deny the significance of
    the rationalization and geometrization of space as a premise for the
    metaphysical assertion of the new science.

12. How could Euclidean space, "with its homogenous and infinite lines and planes, possibly fit into the finite and anisotropic Aristotelian universe?" (Max Jammer, *Concepts of Space*, 26. See also Nick Huggett, *Space from Zeno to Einstein*, 24). On geometry and the infinite set of mathematical problems see for example Matias Osta-Velez: "mientras que para los griegos a la geometría euclidiana le correspondía un a priori finito y cerrado, dentro de la concepción galileana a la geometría le correspondían tareas infinitas. La matematización se nos presenta como un método de tareas infinitas pero virtualmente asequibles; un método que a través de la deducción precisa nos permite alcanzar el mundo de todas las formas idealmente inscribibles en un espacio . . . Nuestro pensamiento apodíctico, progresando por etapas hasta el infinito según conceptos, proposiciones, consecuencias, demostraciones, sólo 'descubre' lo que ya de antemano, lo que en sí ya es verdad" ("La matematización galileana de la naturaleza según Husserl," in *La Filosofía y su Enseñanza* [Montevideo: ANEP, 2017], 89).

13. In the *Elements of Philosophy*, Hobbes famously explains how our mental perception of space does not correspond to any form of objective reality, and consequently describes space as "the phantasm of a thing existing without the mind simply" (Thomas Hobbes, *The English Works of Thomas Hobbes. Elements of Philosophy*, part 2, chapter VII "Of Place and Time" [Charlottesville: InteLex Corporation, 1995], 93). Hobbes reaches this conclusion by making use again of the rhetorical device of the destruction of the world, from which he obtains, however, a conclusion radically opposite to Gassendi's. Like Descartes, Hobbes distinguishes the purely imaginary or intellectual construction of space from the objective existence and reality of bodies and matter: "If therefore we remember, or have a phantasm of any thing that was in the world before the supposed annihilation of the same; and consider, not that the thing was such or such, but only that it had a being without the mind, we have presently a conception of that we call *space*: an imaginary space indeed, because a mere phantasm, yet that very thing which all men call so. For no man calls it space for being already filled, but because it may be filled; nor does any man think bodies carry their places away with them, but that the same space contains sometimes one, sometimes another body; which could not be if space should always accompany the body which is once in it . . . I define *space* thus: SPACE is *the phantasm of a thing existing without the mind simply* . . . that phantasm, in which we consider no other accident, but only that it appears without us."

14. Descartes's metaphysics implied a doubling or scission of mechanical reality that was not present in Hobbes's treatment of geometrical space. His physics, however, are built on the premise that the entire world of extension can be analyzed and understood according to the logic of geometry.

15. See for instance *Principles*, Part 2, 13: "The terms 'place' and 'space', then. Do not signify anything different from the body which is said to be in a place; they merely refer to its size, shape and position relative to other bodies" (*Selected Philosophical Writings*, 194). For Descartes's conception of space as a "mode of material extension" in counterposition to Newton's, see McGuire, *Tradition and Innovation: Newton's Metaphysics of Nature*, 184. On the complex issue of geometrical realism in Descartes, see Nikulin, *Matter, Imagination and Geometry*, 128–30: "Geometrical objects do not merely substitute physical objects and adequately express their properties – geometrical entities are even better and more preferable objects of study. Indeed, if physical things are to be treated as 'the objects of geometry made real', then physical things have the same essence, although they differ in their existence, insofar as the existence of geometricals is only possible, even if necessary, whereas the existence of the physicals is real, even if contingent." Obviously, for Descartes extension is the key element to grasp that essential coincidence of the physical and the geometrical: "both physical and mathematical objects (the latter being adequately represented as, and in, geometricals) are put into one and the same extension or space. Therefore, both are considered co-substantial – so, first, geometrical entities can adequately represent physical objects and, second, both are studied exactly in the same way, by the same procedures of reason supported by imagination. Since the world is *res extensa*, it can be conceived as substituted, and adequately represented, in its entirety and in each of its extended parts by geometrical figures" (ibid., 222).

16. Ibid., Principle 13 implies that "places might be made of matter in some sense, but really they are relative locations ... things are not located in a matter-independent space, but in various relations to one another"; indeed, by its metaphysical principles Cartesian relationism appears committed to the "complete equality of all reference bodies" (Huggett, *Space from Zeno to Einstein*, 101–2). This relativity of places and measures, and with it the threat of an absence of final anchoring, extended to the entire spectrum of human knowledge: "Our earth was no exception – it, too, was essentially geometrical in nature – therefore the principle of relativity of mathematical values applied to man's domain just as to any other part of the astronomical realm" (Burtt, *The Metaphysical Foundations of Modern Physical Science*, 44). To dispel the metaphysical danger implied by this general relativism was the goal, in the *Meditations*, of the quest for a "fixed point" that could act as foundation and basis for our knowledge – but also for the meaningfulness of the human experience as such. See for instance this beautiful passage by Richard Bernstein: "Reading the Meditations as a journey of the soul helps us to appreciate that Descartes' search for a foundation or Archimedean point is more than a device to solve metaphysical

or epistemological problems. It is the quest for some fixed point; some stable rock upon which we can secure our lives against the vicissitudes that constantly threaten us. The specter that hovers in the background of this journey is not just radical epistemological skepticism but the dread of madness and chaos where nothing is fixed, where we can neither touch bottom nor support ourselves in the surface. With a chilling clarity Descartes leads us with an apparent and ineluctable necessity to a grand and seductive Either/Or. *Either* there is some support for our being, a fixed foundation for our knowledge, *Or* we cannot escape the forces of darkness that envelop us with madness, with intellectual and moral chaos" (Richard J. Bernstein, *Beyond Objectivism and Relativism: Science, Hermeneutics, and Praxis* [Philadelphia: University of Pennsylvania Press, 1983], 18).

17. Of course, this problem was originally acknowledged by Descartes himself ("To determine the position, we have to look at various other bodies which we regard as immobile; and in relation to different bodies we may say that the same thing is both changing and not changing its place at the same time," *Principles*, II, 13). What Newton proved is that we can distinguish uniform and accelerated motions absolutely, that is that not all systems of reference are equivalent in mechanics. Newton demonstrated that we can measure the effects of forces on the motion of bodies: different bodies are accelerated differently by the action of the same external force, so that we can calculate the change of velocity for each body and express it in exact mathematical terms (as in the constantly accelerated motion of rotating bodies). That acceleration is thus an absolute mathematical measure: we cannot make sense of it as being relative to any particular frame. From here it follows that the law of inertia requires and implies the existence of an absolute frame, which for Newton was provided by space itself.

18. "I do not define time, space, place, and motion, as being well known to all. Only I must observe, that the common people conceive those quantities under no other notions but from the relation they bear to sensible objects. And thence arise certain prejudices, for the removing of which it will be convenient to distinguish them into absolute and relative, true and apparent, mathematical and common" ("Newton's Scholium on Time, Space, Place and Motion," translated by Andrew Motte, revised by Florian Cajori [Berkeley: University of California Press, 1934], 6–12).

19. *Scholium on Time, Space, Place and Motion*, VII.

20. Ibid., my emphasis: "But because the parts of space cannot be seen, or distinguished from one another by our senses, therefore in their stead we use sensible measures of them. For; but in philosophical disquisitions, we ought to *abstract* from our senses, and consider things themselves, distinct from what are only sensible measures of them.

For it may be that there is no body really at rest, to which the places and motions of others may be referred."

21. Ibid., I.

22. *Scholium on Time, Space, Place and Motion*, XI. In XIV, Newton speaks again of the "great difficulty to discover and effectually to distinguish the true motions of particular bodies from the apparent; because the parts of that immovable space, in which those motions are performed, do by no means come under the observation of our senses. Yet the thing is not altogether desperate; for we have some arguments to guide us, partly from the apparent motions, which are the differences of the true motions; partly from the forces, which are the causes and effects of the true motions."

23. The distinction of relative and absolute space is what Newton needed to make sense of the differences of acceleration generated by the application of the same force to different material bodies, such as the tendency to recede of rotating bodies. Those measures now appear as absolute, independent of any arbitrary system of reference. See Koyré, *From the Closed World*, 168–9, and Jammer, *Concepts of Space*, 101. Huggett provides a clear and succinct reconstruction of Newton's overhaul of Cartesian mechanics, emphasizing the significance for that purpose of Newton's empirical experiments: "it would amount to a virtual *petitio principii* were Newton to rest a case for absolute motion on the existence of absolute space. Hence, one would expect him to appeal to various physical phenomena that might provide independent warrant. Now it is well known that Newton's laws satisfy the principle of Galilean relativity, according to which there can be no experimental test to determine whether a system is at rest or in a state of uniform rectilinear motion. However, Newton's laws *do* support a distinction between inertial and non-inertial motion in that they predict, in non-inertial frames, the appearance of so-called "fictitious forces," for instance, centrifugal forces in rotating frames, resulting in a tendency for bodies to recede from the axis of rotation. Since this is exactly the effect involved in the rotating bucket experiment, it is tempting to interpret Newton as marshaling it as a case in which this phenomenon suggests independent warrant for the existence of absolute motion" (*Space from Zeno to Einstein*, 104–39). On the different interpretations of the Newtonian experiments see Stanford Robert Rynasiewicz, "Newton's Views on Space, Time, and Motion," in *The Stanford Encyclopedia of Philosophy*.

24. Indeed, space acts as the inertial framework for matter, but matter does not act in any manner on space, which remains always unaffected and equal to itself. See Huggett, *Space from Zeno to Einstein*, 140. See also the introduction to the next chapter "Absoluteness: The Logic of Space."

25. "All points are identical, and absolute space is Euclidean: utterly flat and featureless. There is no way to distinguish experimentally one absolute place from any other" (Huggett, *Space from Zeno to Einstein*, 161).

Chapter 8

Absoluteness: The Logic of Space

In a text written in 1953, Albert Einstein described in the following terms the role that space came to play in Newton's physics:

> Space is not only introduced as an independent thing apart from material objects, but also is assigned an absolute role in the whole causal structure of the theory. This role is absolute in the sense that space (as an inertial system) acts on all material objects, while these do not in turn exert any reaction to space.[1]

The absoluteness of space, an expression of its logical and ontological independence, links together a universal system of causes and the order of objects in the physical world. Space fixes what was in motion and anchors what was decentered. At once, it secures the empirical system of science and the order and stability of the new image of the physical world. The rationality of the universe depends on the absoluteness of space; absolute space, in turn, is not dependent on anything else.

8.1 Space as Absolute: On Metaphysical Necessity in the *Principia*

As it emerges from Newtonian mechanics, space is first of all absolute in a logical sense. Among the infinite possible relational systems, absolute space denotes the fixed, independent framework that is required to make sense of the first law of motion, and thus to guarantee the theoretical coherence of mechanics. Absolute space provides the logical architecture in which those laws can be asserted and verified, but in turn its existence is not deduced from them. This is the sense in which absolute space sustains the "causal structure of the theory" as Einstein puts it: the logical architecture of physics (and of cosmology too) rests on the foundation of absolute space, while space itself is logically independent of it.

But space is certainly more than a logical structure. Absolute space is endowed too with ontological existence, which Newton believed could be both geometrically deduced and experimentally proven.[2] That existence is absolute in the sense that space is completely independent, that it does not require anything else for its subsistence. Space is not affected by any of the material objects that come to be and move in it; space can receive anything and everything in itself, but it remains indifferent to what is thus received, unaffected by any relation or phenomena; it is quite literally unmovable.[3] Space also has no limits whatsoever. It extends endlessly "from infinity to infinity" as the general medium of existence, the "universal container of all things," a condition for the presence of everything that exists except itself.[4]

Independent of any relation to external objects, space is also absolute in relation to itself. The order of its parts is immutable, and any change in that order is unthinkable and contrary to the very essence of space, for it would imply that its parts move "out of themselves," that places stop being what they are, that they abandon the "place of place."[5] Apart from their permanent and unchangeable order, however, not much can distinguish those parts of space between them: they are neutral, mathematical points, subsumed in a homogenous infinite structure that remains forever equal to itself (as Euclid had defined them, indeed, "a point in space is that which has no parts").[6] The parts of absolute space have thus no differential qualities or properties; there is nothing about their being that can be properly called their own. In any of its given points, space persists hence without alteration: absolutely continuous, self-sufficient, forever equal to itself.[7] Uncreated, unchangeable and liberated from any contingency, the mode of being of space is that of an absolute entity: space is fully independent, not in relation to anything; nothing can act upon it, and it is in need of nothing else.

Finally, space appears as an absolute metaphysical condition. Certainly, we cannot see or touch space; by no means can it be accessed by our senses. But we can come to know that without space, nothing sensible would ever come to existence. Absolute space appears then as a condition for the being of everything else, to the point that nothing exists or can exist "unless it is related to space in some way."[8] Remarkably, this metaphysical condition for the things that exist coincides with the extension of the infinite universe; it is at once the physical space of the world and the condition for everything that comes to be in it.[9] A logical, ontological, and metaphysical necessity, absolute space appears as a ground not only for the practices of science, but for the entire system of physical reality.

8.2 Two Infinities: Theology of Space in More and Newton

Obviously, such a conception of absolute space resonates with theological undertones. In the case of space, it is particularly difficult to leave aside speculations on transcendent and invisible causes, which for Newton is a necessary condition for the scientific investigation of nature. To be sure, through physics we come to know the order of the world, and hence the perfection of the supreme being that created it.[10] But such access appears to be, at least formally, of an indirect nature. Strictly speaking, the principles and proceedings of science are mathematical and empirical, and one must take good care of avoiding the use of any occult or transcendent hypothesis in all matters related to the advancement of natural philosophy.

In the case of space, however, that exercise becomes quite problematic. The reason is that God and space – and as a consequence, physics and theology – appear to be bound by a complex, ambiguous relation. The essential traits of absolute space – which is said to be infinite, uncreated, immaterial, invisible, self-same, and independent – coincide with the traditional attributes of divinity. Precisely as absolute, the notion of space seems to imply thus something threatening or challenging: the simultaneous existence of two absolute, infinite, and independent entities becomes difficult to reconcile in theological terms.[11] What relation does absolute space entertain with the perfect infinity of God? Is it to be thought of as a second absolute entity, wholly independent of the first? Is it perhaps its attribute or its expression? Already in *De Gravitatione*, these problems figure prominently in Newton's thinking; his answers, however, would not cease to create problems and misunderstandings up until the very end of his life.[12]

The import of this discussion was, as we have seen, certainly not new. From the early identification of God and space in Palestinian Judaism, the problem of space had been prominent in theological debates since the origins of Christianity; theologians and cosmologists had been speculating for centuries on the problematic relation between the imaginary infinity of space and the divine immensity of God. Now, however, the issue had become more urgent than ever: there was a pressing need for natural philosophers, especially for Christian thinkers, to eliminate any discordances between the essential postulates of religion and the conception of the universe asserted by the new science. Kepler had likened the sun to an image of God the father, and saw in the world a divine mathematical expression – but rejected that such world could extend to infinity, and made the presence of the divinity felt through the perfection of the world's design rather than in its actual embodiment. Bruno and Spinoza paid a high price for the radical gesture of identifying the divinity with the immanent extension the world. Warned by their examples, Descartes famously refused to assert the infinity of the extended world to avoid political risks in the formulation of his cosmology and natural philosophy, but he then struggled to justify the "general concourse" of God in the functioning of nature – a futile attempt at avoiding the ostracism of the divinity in a mechanical universe that did not seem to require one.[13] Indeed, the metaphysical consequences of his mechanical philosophy would soon be taken to the extreme: if nature proceeds with the regularity of a perfect machine, according to the necessity of mathematical laws, there seems to be no significant task at all that is left for its designer.

To counter the threat of mechanism, Henry More made the radical choice of declaring that God is an extended spirit, which pervades the entirety of nature and becomes materially present in all the spaces of the universe. In the *Enchiridion Metaphysicum*, he consequently ascribes to both space and God twenty common titles or qualities of being, among them those of being "one, eternal, complete and all-pervasive."[14] Although More falls short of completely identifying the two, specifying that space is only a representation of the divine essence, and must not be identified with the life and activity of God himself, the result is that the two become somewhat indistinguishable. God is omnipresent in the physical dimensionality of space, and space is divinized as the form of God's infinite extension. Space is thus not only infinite and positive, but everywhere filled by the powerful presence of the deity.[15]

Newton would express a similar view on the relation between God and space in the unpublished text of *De Gravitatione*.[16] Something about that relation, however, strikes immediately as problematic. Indeed, Newton takes great pains to distinguish the infinity of space, which refers only to duration and magnitude, from the infinite perfection that is exclusively reserved to God.[17] At the same time, however, he ratifies the uncreated nature of infinite space, which is moreover a sort of condition for everything that exists: to exist is to be in space (and in time), so that all actual forms of being, including the *ens realissimum* that is the divinity, require necessarily the existence of space. Therefore, it would seem that the two infinities of God and space coexist from eternity, one exceeding the other in perfection, the other in turn being necessary for God's existence and presence in all the infinite spaces of creation. Infinite space seems to be at the same time an uncreated condition and an essential expression of divine immensity, without which, however, it becomes utterly unthinkable. One infinity refers to the other; both appear to be distinct and inseparable at once.

8.3 The Theological Reduction of Absolute Space

Newton never published the text on *De Gravitatione* and in the first edition of the *Principia*, which came out in 1687, did not say much of the relation between God and space. To the early reader of the book, the Newtonian universe might have seemed a hostile place indeed for the presence of God. Although much was still unknown about the forces operating in the physical world, there was sufficient clarity about the fact that the presence and action of the divinity was not required to explain the inner functioning of nature. The machine, so it seemed, could perfectly work without its creator. In theological terms, to such reader the infinity and self-sufficiency of absolute space might have even appeared as a dangerous, if not a straightforwardly heretical idea.

Perhaps Newton was addressing such fears when he published the Latin edition of the *Optiks* in 1706. There, he famously describes God's mode of presence in the world with a formula that raised the astonishment of his contemporaries, for it apparently asserted the existence of the divinity as a *sentient* being in infinite space:

> does it not appear from Phænomena that there is *a Being incorporeal*, living, intelligent, omnipresent, *who in infinite Space, as it were in his Sensory, sees the things themselves* intimately, and throughly perceives them, and comprehends them wholly by their immediate presence to himself: Of which things the Images only carried through the Organs of Sense into our little Sensoriums, are there seen and beheld by that which in us perceives and thinks.[18]

Even if the argument is presented as a sort of analogy, perhaps little more than an effect of poetic license, the notion of a God who sees, perceives and comprehends all things *through his presence* in infinite space certainly alters the way in which the Newtonian universe presents itself. The presence of God, for instance, is now almost indistinguishable from the mode of being of space itself: God appears as a living, all-powerful presence that is spatially extended throughout the existing world. Of course, Newton immediately warns us that we must not consider "the World as the Body of God," for the divinity has no parts and is in no need of any "Organs": the things themselves are immediately present to Him without the concourse of any mediation.[19] But as the "sensory of God", one could then wonder, what could space become other than the very manner of presence of God himself in the world, and as such, something completely inseparable, proper and inherent in Him? Far from being a threat, space seems to be the very mode in which God "returns" to the world.

Such seems to be the conclusion towards which Newton points in the *General Scholium* added to the second edition of the *Principia* in 1713. In this fabulous text we are told that God's mode of presence in the world is not merely virtual, but rather that God is present in space substantially: quite literally, bodies are said to be "contained and moved" in God, who is present everywhere from infinity to infinity.[20] The identification seems so strong that Newton immediately needs to clarify that God is not to be confounded with space. Rather, by existing always and everywhere, God is said to constitute through his presence space itself:

> He is Eternal and Infinite, Omnipotent and Omniscient; that is, his duration reaches from Eternity to Eternity; his presence from Infinity to Infinity; he governs all things, and knows all things that are or can be done. He is not Eternity or Infinity, but Eternal and Infinite; he is not Duration or Space, but he endures and is present. He endures for ever, and is every where present; and by existing always and every where, he constitutes Duration and Space.[21]

Here, space is no longer a condition or a medium for the presence of God in the world. Rather, space appears to be a consequence of divine power, an effect of the power of God in the mode of omnipresence.[22] The uncreated absoluteness of space is obviously curtailed, reduced to an expression of the omnipotence of God through his infinite presence in creation. That presence might have acquired an essentially spatial character, it might even be contaminated by the logic of a space that is infinite, everywhere empty and equal to itself, abstract and mathematical in nature. But as an expression of divine power, as being constituted by the presence of God, space is now clearly subsumed under an undisputed theological absolute.

Some contemporary readers, however, found Newton's solution far from satisfactory. Only two years after the publication of the *General Scholium*, Leibniz denounced in a letter to Caroline of Wales the conception of space as a "Sensory of God," which he harshly portrayed as an example of the decay of "natural religion" in England, and even as a likely source of atheism.[23] In the famous epistolary exchange that ensued with Samuel Clarke, Leibniz launches a systematic attack on Newton's conception of space, specifically addressing the theological ambivalence of the status of space as an absolute entity. Indeed, the existence of an uncreated infinite reality implies a sort of duplication of the absolute, and consequently, a major theological threat. For if space is real and absolute, Leibniz writes in his fourth letter to Clarke,

> God cannot destroy it, nor even change it in any respect. It will be not only immense in the whole, but also immutable and eternal in every part. There will be an infinite number of eternal things besides God.[24]

The only way to avoid such a conclusion, as Leibniz had said in his third letter, is either to affirm that space and God are the same thing, or to make space an attribute of God. But as he rightly points out, Newton's own premises do not seem to allow for either of those alternatives.[25] As a result, Leibniz believes that the attempt to reconcile absolute space with the Christian God is destined to failure. In the absence of such reconciliation, the absolute space of Newtonian physics will continue to appear as an "an attribute without a subject" and an "extension without anything extended," a sort of unanchored absolute that is both disquieting and ungranted.

Clarke, of course, denies all of Leibniz's charges. He takes great care in explaining that God is not in need of any organs, and to reject any accusation of impiety, not to mention atheism.[26] Most importantly, he tries to expand and clarify the argument expounded by Newton in the *General Scholium* according to which space and God are not the same thing, but rather space is constituted as a consequence of God's existence:

> Space is not a being, an eternal and infinite being, but a *property*, or a consequence of the existence of a being infinite and eternal. Infinite space, is immensity: but immensity is not God, and therefore infinite space is not God.[27]

But under Leibniz's pressure, Clarke has already conceded to one of his major demands. Space appears not only as a consequence, but also as a property of God's existence.[28] Space and God are not the same thing, but the two are different in the same manner that an attribute differs from its substance: space is nothing but God's extension, his omnipresence in the physical world. The theological tension of absolute space is thereby resolved. Space is not an alternative absolute threatening the first, but simply a property or an attribute of the all-powerful God, the very form of his presence in the mechanical world, in which all things are and through which he knows all things. The two infinities are thus brought together under one single theological form: God, the absolute ruler of the infinite universe, is now also the master of absolute space.

8.4 Emancipation of Absolute Space: Abstract Universalism

The theological reduction of absolute space was the price to pay for the reconciliation of religion and the new physics. The threatening character of space, and with it the potential scission that had been opened at the very foundation of the new cosmology, disappears in the confident words of Dr Clarke, who in the dedicatory letter that opens the published version of the correspondence, even asserts his faith in the usefulness of physics to "confirm natural religion" and give proof, from the rigorous analysis of phenomena, of God's "continual government of the world."[29] Far from contradicting the foundations of Christian doctrine, the science of physics is presented as a ratification of its worldview.

When Clarke speaks of God's "continual government" of the world, he is not using the terms as a mere metaphor. In fact, the reduction of absolute space depended on what Leibniz called "a very odd" opinion on the part of Newton, according to which God is not only present throughout the physical world but is also said to keep an active control and dominion of it.[30] To be sure, the world functions according to mathematical principles and laws; still, God's intervention is required to preserve that order and uphold those laws. God, hence, is master and ruler of the world not in an abstract, figurative way, but in a direct and immediate one: God is present in the world "as a governor," acting upon all things, acted upon by nothing.[31] Far from being exiled from the natural world, then, in the Newtonian universe God cannot be set aside. On the contrary, God becomes more present and active than ever:

> If a King had a Kingdom wherein all things would continually go on without his Government or interposition, or without his attending to and Ordering what is done therein; it would be to him, *merely a nominal kingdom*; nor would he in reality deserve at all the title of King or Governor. And as those Men who pretend that in an Earthly Government things may go on perfectly well without the king himself ordering or disposing any thing, may reasonably be suspected that they would like very well to *set the king aside*.[32]

But that, Clarke claims, is precisely what Leibniz and the mechanicists do when they portray the world as a self-sufficient machine, which would be set once and for all and exclude any further action from God in its proceedings. In the eyes of Clarke, that exclusion was doubled by Leibniz's understanding of space not as the universal medium of things, but merely as an order, the lattice of ideal relations between things in the world: God is not only set aside, but also divested of his spatial attributes, of his omnipresence throughout space, of his very being among things in the world. Space is no longer the nowhere where everything happens, the opening where all things become immediate to the divine presence, but rather an order that refers only to things and to the relations of things in the world. Such is, according to Clarke, "the notion of materialism and fate" that Leibniz defends: the world of an absent and demeaned God, one that restricts his power and capacity and excludes his providence from the government of reality.[33] Instead, in the theology of Newtonianism, God governs the world actively and entirely, and through that government brings about the unity of reason and mechanism, spirit and matter, freedom and nature. Exactly like absolute space sustained the new physics in the first edition of the *Principia*, now God, who has taken such space as his attribute, is the ultimate principle and foundation of all.

No matter how strenuously Leibniz alerted to the shortcomings of this voluntarist theology, Newton and Clarke were on a favorable historical tide. For all its brilliance, the criticism of absolute space could not do much against the seemingly unending advancement made possible by Newton's achievements in science. Absolute space, which laid the metaphysical foundation of that scientific framework, would thus reign almost undisputedly over physics for the next two centuries. As science progressed, however, the irregularities that Newton could still not account for were gradually solved, and the hypothesis of an interventionist God lost most of its traction.[34] Physicists and philosophers verified that the Newtonian world, in fact, worked perfectly well without such "unnecessary hypothesis." In the end, the charges that Leibniz had brought against Newton seemed hence to be verified: the physics of absolute space did indeed open a path towards atheism.

Absolute space would thus ultimately overturn its reduction. Along the way, space preserved all the properties inherent in the absolute substance – it remained infinite and uncreated, real and equal to itself, independent and unchanging – except that now it was free from the divinity too.[35] With no theological garments clothing the concept, space could now appear unimpeded as the universal background and container of all things, as the condition and medium for everything that exists and even for the universe itself. Space is the last absolute standing; it is the framework of frameworks, the metaphysical foundation not only of science, but also of our possible ways of making sense of the world.

In such space resonate the classical principles of the unbounded, the void, the incorporeal and the immense; the shattering of the cosmic spheres, and the Brunian flight of metaphysics over a unified infinite universe. It is the space emancipated from all substances conceived by Patrizi and Gassendi, an empty space that is everywhere equal to itself and has no qualities and no differentiations. It is a Galilean space in its mathematical nature; a space geometrized after Descartes, and abstracted from all relations in the experiments of Newtonian mechanics. Still standing after its attempted theological reduction, space now reigns undisputedly as the ultimate absolute, at once foundation and background, universal container and concrete form. Infinite, empty, abstract, and absolute, this space is not simply a concept of physics. Space implies a logic of the world, a metaphysics of knowledge and practice, which was about to define the experience of modern politics too.

Notes

1. Albert Einstein, "Foreword," *Concepts of Space*, 1953, xvi.
2. On Newton's spatial realism, see Chapter 7.2. On the importance of the experimental dimension for the abstraction of absolute space see *supra*, notes 217, 220. In the words of Jammer, "motion is the means and medium though which space can be explored," and Newton "succeeds in convincing himself that he has proved the reality of the concept by physical experiment" (*Concepts of Space*, 110). Grant describes the sequence in a particularly eloquent form: "Where all other advocates of absolute infinite space were content to argue for it theologically, metaphysically, or by appeal to the impossibility

of conceiving an end to space, Newton, the great experimentalist, sought to verify its existence experimentally by means of the rotation of a pail of water" (*Much Ado About Nothing*, 244).

3. In a passage reminiscent of Gassendi, the young Newton presents space in *De Gravitatione* as a "disposition of all being" that is somehow independent of every concrete form of existence. In fact, space is a sort of condition for the existence of all beings, to the point that we can think away the existence of all existing matter and bodies in the world, but we cannot imagine that space would not exist. Space is hence absolute in the sense that it is not dependent on anything else for its existence, which excludes any form of external determination (see Grant, *Much Ado About Nothing*, 242; J. A. Ruffner, "Newton's De Gravitatione: A Review and Reassessment," *Archive for History of Exact Sciences* 66, no. 3 (2012): 241–64; and McGuire, *Tradition and Innovation: Newton's Metaphysics of Nature*, 4: "Time and space . . . By nature they are independent of all finite things which exist in them, whereas finite things depend on space and time for existence").

4. *Scholium on Time, Space, Place and Motion*, X: "Now no other places are immovable but those that, from infinity to infinity, do all retain the same given position one to another; and upon this account must ever remain unmoved; and do thereby constitute immovable (*immobile*) space."

5. Absolute places, as Newton says, are "the places as well of themselves as if all other things." The age-old dilemma on the locality of place is thus resolved in the realist metaphysics of absolute space. See *Scholium on Time, Space, Place and Motion*, VI: "As the order of the parts of time is immutable, so also is the order of the parts of space. Suppose those parts to be moved out of their places, and they will be moved (if the expression may be allowed) out of themselves. For times and spaces are, as it were, the places as well of themselves as of all other things. All things are placed in time as to order of succession; and in space as to order of situation. It is from their essence or nature that they are places; and that the primary places of things should be movable, is absurd. These are therefore the absolute places; and translations out of those places, are the only absolute motions."

6. Euclid, *Elements* I, definition 1, cited in Nikulin, *Matter, Imagination and Geometry*, 105 ("In a sense, the point may be taken as infinite, because it has no limit by itself or is limitless," ibid.).

7. Any part of absolute space is "quite indistinguishable from any other equal part; any position in them is identical with any position; for wherever that part or position may be it is surrounded by an infinite stretch of similar room in all directions" (Burtt, *The Metaphysical Foundations of Modern Physical Science*, 255). See also Edward Casey's powerful description of the being of parts of Newtonian space as "a mere portion

of what is always already there as Absolute, universally given" (*The Fate of Place*, 144).

8. See Arnold Koslow, "Ontological and Ideological Issues of the Classical Theory of Space and Time," in Peter K. Machamer and Robert G. Turnbull, *Motion and Time, Space and Matter: Interrelations in the History of Philosophy and Science* (Cleveland: Ohio State University Press, 1976), 224. The original passage from Newton is from *De Gravitatione*: "Space is an affection of being in so far as it is being. No being exists, or can exist, which is not related to space in some way. God is everywhere, created minds are somewhere, and body is in the space that it occupies; and what is neither everywhere nor anywhere does not exist. Hence it follows that space is an emanative effect of the primarily existing being, because when any being is posited, space is posited" (*Unpublished Scientific Papers of Isaac Newton*, 136).

9. According to Jammer, Newton drew a "clear line between science and metaphysics . . . but for one exception, namely, his theory of space" (*Concepts of Space*, 98). Quite literally, the metaphysical condition of the physical world is also supposed to "give it a center": the "universal center of gravity of the world," which is at rest in a universe marked by endless motion, is the "reference point for the determination of unique absolute space" (ibid., 103).

10. The knowledge of nature, i.e. physics, is a way of accessing the supreme goodness of God as creator of the world: "God was not detached from the world that science seeks to know; indeed, every true step in natural philosophy brings us nearer to a knowledge of the first cause" (Burtt, *The Metaphysical Foundations of Modern Physical Science*, 281). The God of Newton, according to McGuire, "is the pantokrator, or the lord of the universe, the supreme being who exercises direct dominion over the constitution of creation. It is God's actions, emanating from a free and omnipresent will, that are manifest in the natural world, not the transcendent perfection of divine nature. Newton insists that God is best known from the design of creation, a structure that reveals the power and wisdom of divine action" (McGuire, *Tradition and Innovation: Newton's Metaphysics of Nature*, xv).

11. In his enlightening discussion of the theological problem of absolute space in Newton's physics, Jammer quotes Berkeley's defense of the relational character of space, "or else there is something beside God which is eternal, uncreated, infinite, indivisible, immutable" (*Principles of Human Knowledge*, cited in *Concepts of Space*, 112).

12. Jammer affirms that the theological problem only preoccupied Newton in a late stage of his career, by the time he added the Queries to the Latin edition of the *Optiks* and added the General Scholium to the second edition of the *Principia*. I agree with Grant and McGuire,

however, in their reading of the genealogy of the theological principles in the early unpublished papers of Newton, especially in *De Gravitatione*, where the problem of the absoluteness of space and its theological implications figure already in a prominent way. It is quite clear, at any rate, that the philosophical and conceptual framework through which absolute space is conceived derive from the traditional logic of theology.

13. In a letter to Henry More written in 1649, Descartes asserted that "It conflicts with my conception, or, what is the same, I think it involves a contradiction, that the world should be finite or bounded; because I cannot but conceive a space beyond whatever bounds you assign to the world." Famously, in the Principles he explains that the notion of infinity should be reserved to the concept of the divinity alone (Principle 27) right after having asserted, in an uncharacteristically mysterious tone, that we "should never enter into arguments about the infinite" (Principle 26). For a reconstruction of the context of this problem, see McGuire, *Tradition and Innovation: Newton's Metaphysics of Nature*, 167–73, and Andrew Janiak, "Space and Motion in Nature and Scripture: Galileo, Descartes, Newton," 89–99. See also notes 188 and 189.

14. Henry More, *Enchiridion Metaphysicum*, VIII, in *Philosophical Writings of Henry More* (London: Oxford University Press, 1925), 294. See also Aharon Lichtenstein, *Henry More: The Rational Theology of a Cambridge Platonist* (Cambridge: Harvard University Press, 1962), 170.

15. According to Koyré, More posits an essential identity between God and space (see *From the Closed World*, 147–53). McGuire harshly criticizes this view, affirming that "it must not be concluded that More's position entails that the defining attributes of God and space are one," because space "does not possess any of the defining perfections of Divine nature" (*Tradition and Innovation: Newton's Metaphysics of Nature*, 7). McGuire goes on to describe More's metaphysics as "a form of pantheism, combined with an emanationist conception of causality" (ibid., 15). In the *Enchiridion*, More defines space as "a representation of the Divine essence or essential presence, in so far as it is distinguished from his life and activities" (Part 1, ch. VIII). Only a few years later, that complete identification would be achieved by Joseph Raphson, who in his *De spatio reali* described space as a divine attribute through which the essence of God becomes present "everywhere through the whole world and beyond the world through an immense vacuum" (cited in Grant, *Much Ado About Nothing*, 113).

16. For a critical reconstruction of the composition and significance of *De Gravitatione*, generally taken as an early work written between 1684 and 1685, see Ruffner, "Newton's De Gravitatione: a review

and reassessment" and Zvi Biener, "De Gravitatione Reconsidered: The Changing Significance of Experimental Evidence for Newton's Metaphysics of Space," *Journal of the History of Philosophy* 55, no. 4 (2017): 583–608.

17. *De Gravitatione*, in *Unpublished Scientific Papers of Isaac Newton*, 104. For McGuire, this essential distinction of the perfections of space and God is the main difference between More's conception of space as "an intrinsic attribute which defines the essence of Divine omnipresence" and Newton's understanding of space and time as "consequences of God's infinite existence, where existence is not a perfection identical with God's defining nature" (*Tradition and Innovation: Newton's Metaphysics of Nature*, 17–20). For a different interpretation of *De Gravitatione*, according to which Newton understands space as an attribute of God, see Grant, *Much Ado About Nothing*, 243.

18. Isaac Newton, *Opticks: Or, A Treatise of the Reflections, Refractions, Inflexions and Colours of Light*, Query 28, my emphasis. I am following both the text and the numbering of the Second English Edition of 1718. For a reconstruction of the context of publication of the Queries and the theological significance of this passage, see Stephen David Snobelen, "God and Natural Philosophy in Isaac Newton's Opticks," *Estudios De Filosofía* 35 (2007): 42.

19. *Opticks*, Query 31.

20. "God is the same God, always and every where. He is omnipresent, not *virtually* only, but also *substantially*; for virtue cannot subsist without substance. In him are all things contained and moved; yet neither affects the other: God suffers nothing from the motion of bodies; bodies find no resistance from the omnipresence of God," *General Scholium*, 389.

21. Ibid., 389–90.

22. There is obviously something paradoxical about Newton's solution, which has to do precisely with the unresolved tension between the two absolute entities. For how could God "constitute" a space that is said to be uncreated, which was even presented in *De Gravitatione* almost as a condition for the existence of God himself? See McGuire's interpretation of the passage: "Newton distinguishes between the nature of Divine substance, and the space and time of his existence. In other words, he states that space and time are not real attributes of God's nature. On the contrary they themselves are, as Newton rather oddly puts it, constituted by God's eternal and omnipresent existence. This way of phrasing the point is odd because it implies that space and time are 'ingredients' of God's nature. But Newton explicitly states that God is 'not duration and space'; rather they themselves exist because God exists. In characterising God as existing and enduring with respect to space and time, we are not saying that God is identical with infinite space and time" (McGuire, *Tradition and Innovation: Newton's Metaphysics of Nature*, 13).

23. "Sir Isaac Newton says, that space is an organ, which God makes use of to perceive things by. But if God stands in need of any organ to perceive things by, it will follow that they do not depend altogether upon him, nor were produced by him" ("Mr. Leibniz's First Paper, being An Extract of a Letter Written in November, 1715," in Samuel Clarke, *The Leibniz–Clarke Correspondence, Together with Extracts from Newton's Principia and Opticks*, ed. Henry Gavin Alexander [New York: Philosophical Library, 1956], 11). Leibniz would go on to adjudicate to Newton "a very mean notion of the wisdom and power of God" (ibid., 12).

24. *The Leibniz–Clarke Correspondence*, "Mr Leibniz's Fourth Paper," 37.

25. "Such being [i.e. space] must needs be eternal and infinite. Hence some have believed it to be God himself, or, one of his attributes, his immensity. But since space consists of parts, it is not a thing which can belong to God (*The Leibniz–Clarke Correspondence*, "Mr Leibniz's Third Paper," 25). Clarke would contest that space consists of parts, but Leibniz's general point is much deeper: as established in the *General Scholium*, Newton *does not want* to make neither of these conclusions. In his Fourth Paper, in fact, Leibniz makes this tension even more clear and explicit: "Space is the place of things, and not the place of God's ideas: unless we look upon space as something that makes a union between God and things" (*The Leibniz–Clarke Correspondence*, "Mr. Leibniz's Fourth Paper," 37).

26. In his first reply, Clarke had already established that "Being omnipresent, [God] perceives all things by his immediate presence to them, in all space wherever they are, without the intervention or assistance of any organ whatsoever" (*The Leibniz–Clarke Correspondence*, "Dr Clarke's First Reply", 13). Against the charge of atheism, Clarke's tone would grow increasingly pious, as in this passage from his second reply: "He is not far from every one of us, for in him we (and all things) live and move and have our beings" (*The Leibniz–Clarke Correspondence*, "Dr Clarke's Second Reply," 24.)

27. *The Leibniz–Clarke Correspondence*, "Dr Clarke's Third Reply," 31, my emphasis.

28. In his fourth reply, Clarke would be even more explicit in his description of space as a property of God: "Space is not a substance, but a property; and if it be a property of that which is necessary, it will consequently (. . .) exist more necessarily" (*The Leibniz–Clarke Correspondence*, "Dr Clarke's Fourth Reply," 47). Perhaps inadvertently, Clarke then refers to space as an *attribute* of God's extension. "Void space is not an attribute without a subject, because, by void space, we never mean space void of every thing, but void of body only. In all void space, God is certainly present, and possibly many other substances which are not matter; being neither tangible nor objects of any of our senses" (ibid.). The tension between the two absolutes has been here completely reduced to the characterization of space as an

attribute of the divinity. On this point see Grant, *Much Ado About Nothing*, 248–9.

29. *The Leibniz–Clarke Correspondence*, "To Her Royal Highness the Princess of Wales," 6.

30. *The Leibniz–Clarke Correspondence*, "Mr Leibniz's First Paper," 11. Leibniz is referring to an argument advanced by Newton in the Queries to the *Opticks*, according to which God intervenes in the world so as to amend and reform any irregularities that the laws of mechanics cannot account for, including the conservation of motion. As a creator and designer of the universe, God established its fundamental principles of laws, but his actions, which are not subject to them, are still necessary to maintain those laws, and can at any given point make and remake the universe following exclusively his unrestrained will. For Leibniz, this amounts to recognizing that God needs to "wind up his watch from time to time," which to him is an unacceptable and even blasphemous premise. The status of those "exceptional interventions" of the deity, hence, will be the object of a stark polemical exchange with Dr Clarke.

31. *The Leibniz–Clarke Correspondence*, "Dr Clarke's Second Reply," 24.

32. *The Leibniz–Clarke Correspondence*, "Dr Clarke's First Reply," 14.

33. Ibid.

34. I am following here the very illuminating reading of Burtt, which reconstructs the philosophical transition from the secularization of the Newtonian world to the foundations of modern critical philosophy: "Newton's successors accounted one by one for the irregularities that to his mind had appeared essential and increasing if the machine were left to itself. This process of eliminating the providential elements in the world-order reached its climax in the work of the great Laplace, who believed himself to have demonstrated the inherent stability of the universe by showing that all its irregularities are periodical, and subject to an eternal law which prevents them from ever exceeding a stated amount . . . But with the farewell of the Deity, the epistemological difficulties of the situation could hardly fail to offer an overwhelming challenge. How could intelligence grasp an inaccessible world in which there was no answering or controlling intelligence? It was by no means an accident that Hume and Kant, the first pair who really banished God from metaphysical philosophy, likewise destroyed by a skeptical critique the current overweening faith in the metaphysical competence of reason. They perceived that the Newtonian world without God must be a world in which the reach and certainty of knowledge is decidedly and closely limited, if indeed the very existence of knowledge at all is possible" (Burtt, *The Metaphysical Foundations of Modern Physical Science*, 295–8). Ultimately for Burtt, absolute space and time would be left standing in the absence of any ultimate logical or theological grounding: "in the

eighteenth century, Newton's conception of the world was gradually shorn of its religious relations, the ultimate justification for absolute space and time as he had portrayed them disappeared, and the entities were left empty, but still absolute ... divested of both logical and theological excuse, but yet unquestioningly assumed as an infinite theatre in which, and an unchangeable entity against which, the world-machine continued its clock-like movements" (ibid., 260–1). As I will try to prove in what follows, this philosophical transition, by which space persists as an abstract and empty absolute, was of an extraordinary political significance.

35. "The infinite universe of the new cosmology, infinite in duration as well as in extension, in which eternal matter in accordance with eternal and necessary laws moves endlessly and aimlessly in eternal space, inherited all the ontological attributes of divinity. Yet only those – all the others the departed God took away with him" (Koyré, *From the Closed World*, 276; see also Grant, *Much Ado About Nothing*, 255).

PART 3

The Physico-political Logic of Modern Space

The transformation of the spatial imagination that took place at the advent of the modern age was not merely a matter of theoretical significance. Indeed, the ancient cosmological order was built upon a physics and a metaphysics – we might call it a "logic of place" – which had remarkable political effects. Centered, hierarchical and finite, the classical cosmos was an utterly solid world, where everything was, or at least could be, in its "proper place," where the harmony of the whole, whether that whole be the cosmos, the city or the soul, depended on the good emplacement and arrangement of its parts, on a balance that could only be reached by disposing each of its elements in its most proper and natural position. Like smoke goes up in the air and stones fall down toward the center of the Earth, each in search of the places that are natural to them, in such world there are also political places that are proper to each kind of being: the virtue of politics consists precisely of arranging the political whole in the manner that is most consonant to its nature.

It is not a surprise, then, that the demise of that order had a specific political significance. In the open, infinite universe, things seem to be out of joint, separated from their places, lacking a foundation and an anchorage in firm ground. All positions seem to be leveled, all relations equalized; hierarchies appear to be unjustified, and orders are suddenly in need of new reasons. Paradoxically, however, this essential voiding will be the source of a new kind of political power: one which, exactly like space, is now abstract and universal, absolute in its vocation, and ready to reshape the world according to its own image.

Chapter 9

Freedom in an Infinite Universe

Because it had no limits, modern space seemed no longer able to contain the old world. In its infinite openness, the empty materiality of space could preserve none of the powers previously attributed to place as the limiting container or the surrounding vessel of physical bodies. Space, moreover, had no room for heterogeneity, for finality, for specificity. The new physics brought the vision of a world without qualities, without ends and teleologies, a universe reduced to the ostensibly purposeless mechanics of masses of matter in motion.

Separated from the whole, each thing now seems to be placeless, decentered, estranged from the purposive hierarchy of forms that gave sense and meaning to reality. In the vastness of infinite space, human beings feel placeless too, surrounded by things that are out of proportion, by idols and beliefs now lost.[1] In a world without places, every order must be made anew. But it is precisely this capacity to begin what now seems to make human beings what they are: in a sense, their freedom also consists in having no limits at all.

9.1 The Logic of Place: Order, Position, and Limit

For Aristotle, proper emplacement is indeed a sign of perfection. Each thing moves to its own place, where it fits naturally to the point that the "limit coincides with that which is limited".[2] Place is not merely a passive recipient but has an active role in determining what a body is capable of as contained in and by that place: in its limiting, the place makes room for everything that the body that it limits can do. Places, therefore, are not simply formal or quantitative demarcations. They are essential for the ordering of the world: there are proper and improper places, perfect and imperfect dispositions of the relations of things, and reasons why things should be placed in some ways rather than in others.

Indeed, place has a certain power to attract and direct the movement of bodies.[3] In the absence of hindrance or resistance, bodies move in determinate directions to their natural places, which have a certain power of attraction, a certain capacity to draw. Heavy bodies move downward, light bodies move upward, all of them following their own natural movement toward the place that is their own. In their proper place, elements and bodies find rest; far from it, they are pulled by a potentiality that calls for fulfillment, by an affinity that aims at being satisfied. Things find in their natural place the most perfect of their dispositions, an accordance with the order of nature, which is not unlike the bond that exists between a part and the whole of which it is a part. Properly emplaced, things come to a standstill: there, they are held and supported in their most stable and authentic form.

If the world is not petrified, however, if what exists keeps moving and changing over time, it is because things are often forced out of their places. There are violent, unnatural movements that can displace a body far from where it belongs; there are external causes that can dislocate things and keep them apart from their places.[4] A spatial tension animates the movement of things: fighting powerful resistances, bodies move until they are disposed in the places that are proper to them. Those places are, in their turn, naturally ordered between themselves. From the center of the Earth to the inner surface of the lunar orbs, there is a general disposition of places within the world, an order of places that disposes them in the most perfect and stable arrangement, like parts are disposed in relation to the whole.[5]

The logic of place, hence, orders the physical world at least in a double sense. First, things move until they are disposed in their natural places, and only there do they find rest. Second, those places are in a certain arrangement between themselves, since there is a general disposition of places within the world as a whole. The concern with order and position, with the proper placement of things in the wider scheme of the world, becomes hence the first occupation of the cosmologist, but also of the physicist and the metaphysician. The place of a thing, in this respect, has nothing to do with an act of measurement. Rather, place refers to a certain arrangement of things within the order of the cosmos. There are countless possible dispositions of things in the world, but only one that, being entirely natural, corresponds with its true order and makes it perfect as a whole.

According to Aristotle's successor, Theofrastus, such order must be understood as a certain relation of "the natures and powers" of things.[6] Originally, the nature of a thing denoted that into which a thing grows, the character that it has when it has grown, when it looks and acts as the kind of thing that it is.[7] The principle of growth governs the development of the capacities of beings; when properly followed, this principle produces a certain harmony in the thing itself and in its relation to the whole. A world ordered according to the "natures and powers" of things, hence, implies a general relation between their capacities and dispositions. In that order, all beings are placed according to their potentialities, ranging from the nutritive power of plants (which in their biological growth are said to follow a natural movement, that is, a movement towards the place that is proper to them), to the rational ability of humans, in a gradual succession where each level includes the capacities of all the precedent ones.[8] The wealth of forms that populate the physical world can thus appear as an ordered scale, in which each step corresponds to a certain degree of value and perfection, all of them linked in perfect fullness and continuity. The potentialities of being are limited for all physical forms: the natural place of each thing, the position that each occupies within the general order of nature, corresponds to a specific arrangement of its capacities and possibilities, to what kind of thing it is capable of doing. Ultimately, its value depends on such arrangements too.[9]

The limits of a thing, hence, define its place within the apparently inexhaustible multiplicity of nature. Limits discriminate between kinds: they distinguish things from what they are not; they express the dignity and possibilities of the forms that they limit. Consequently, limits should not be conceived of as a sort of abstract determination, which would be somehow independent of the things that are limited by them. Limits, as Aristotle reminded us constantly in the *Physics*, "are together with what is limited."[10] Iambilichus, for instance, thinks of them as a sort of living environment, the "alive boundaries" of beings that are "ensouled" within them:

> One must not conceive of place as a mere limit (*peras*) in the way that we conceive the mathematical surfaces as limits of mathematical bodies, but as the physical limits (*horoi*) of physical bodies, and as the alive boundaries of ensouled living beings.[11]

Places are not static, lifeless boundaries, but are rather fundamentally implied in the constitution of things. Places express their possibilities of action, their potentiality and perfection, the horizon of what they are capable of in the world. Places and things, hence, are not separate and independent realities. Rather, they are bound by an essential relation, by a principle according to which for each thing that exists there is a natural position, one that is proper to it and expresses its dignity and potentiality within the general distribution of being.

When Damascius identified the perfection of the world with the natural order of positions of things, he was formulating a general logic that can perhaps be expressed in a simple statement: when each thing is in its proper place, in the place where the kind of thing that each is belongs, then the whole is well disposed too.[12] When they are not, when things transgress their limits and come to be out of their bounds, the result is violence and disorder, a dislocation of the order of the world that calls for its restoration.

9.2 Beautiful Wholes: Place in Christian Metaphysics

This conception of the order of things would offer a fertile ground for the development of natural theology. Of course, the world of Christian creation is affected by a constitutive tension; the material world, which is the object of study of physics and cosmology, is the world of the fall, a passing valley of tears ultimately destined to be "destroyed by fire."[13] But even in its transience, the world is endowed with a natural order expressing the goodness and perfection of its maker. The Christian God is "not a God of confusion."[14] The disposition of nature expresses the divine spirit; God set an order of ends in nature, and remains present in the world of creation as the guarantor of those ends and the ultimate reason of every form of life.

Already in Genesis, God gives form to an Earth that was without any, "appoints places" to the mountains and valleys, "sets bounds which shall not be passed."[15] God then populates the Earth with all its living creatures, "each according to its kind".[16] But things are not simply thrown into a flat surface of existence, and all are certainly not equal between themselves. Of those kinds of things, according to Augustine, there are "first and second and so on, down to the creatures of the lowest grades."[17] Each thing is thus marked by a differential degree of perfection: the nobility of their purposes determines a hierarchical teleology, by which to each being corresponds a place within the natural order of creation. Each form of life, Augustine explains in the *Confessions*, possesses something like a "weight," and it tends by its weight towards the place proper to it – weight does not necessarily tend towards the lowest place but towards its proper place . . . by their weight they are moved and seek their proper place . . . things out of their place are in motion: they come to their place and are at rest.[18]

The logic of place, according to which each being instinctively seeks the place that is proper to it in the hierarchical order of nature, becomes thus a pillar of Christian metaphysics and natural philosophy. From the celestial bodies to the lowest organic forms, an order of goodness, beauty and intelligence governs the world and holds it together.[19] And it is precisely in that "wondrous connection of things" (*mirabilis rerum connexio*), in the harmonious order and hierarchy of all the unequal things existing in nature, where we find the supreme beauty (*summus decor*) of the world.[20] The world is a beautiful whole, ordered by God and animated by a metaphysical dynamic through which each kind of being strives to return to the place that is proper to it.

Perhaps no work can portray better the Christian logic of place than Dante's *Divine Comedy*, in which we are presented with something like a metaphysical topology of human places and trajectories: each person that the poet encounters in his journey has been ranked and "re-placed," by the works of a divinely retributive justice, exactly where the kind of being that it is most properly belongs. Thus, towards the end of the opening canto of *Paradiso*, Beatrice describes the divine order of the world to the poet:

Le cose tutte quante
hanno ordine tra loro, e questo è forma
che l'universo a Dio fa simigliante.

Qui veggion l'alte creature l'orma
de l'etterno valore, il qual è fine
al quale è fatta la toccata norma.

Ne l'ordine ch'io dico sono accline
tutte nature, per diverse sorti,
più al principio loro e men vicine;

onde si muovono a diversi porti
per lo gran mar de l'essere, e ciascuna
con istinto a lei dato che la porti.[21]

The form given by God to the universe is a mutual order observed by all things. Things are placed in that order according to the impress of worth that they have received from God; their *diverse sorti* define how they relate to their divine principle, and consequently to other things too, within the great *scala naturae* that links together and orders the totality of the forms of existence, from the lowest of minerals to the purest essence of souls.[22] Ultimately, Dante's image expresses with sublime clarity the same logic of place expressed by the pagan philosophers of antiquity: the good arrangement of things (*euthetoi kai eutopoi*) makes the harmony of the world; within the beautiful order of nature, things need to be disposed in the places that are proper to them.[23]

9.3 Infinite Space and the Metaphysics of Openness

Modern space threatens the solidity of a world where everything was, or at least could be, in a "proper" place. In a space that is fundamentally indifferent and undistinguishable, where every place is by definition equal to every other, each standing against the vastness of a neutral and homogeneous background, the preoccupation for the proper placement of things within the general order of being becomes in itself something problematic. For space is devoid of qualitative distinctions and meaningful differentiations. Lacking values, ends, and any sort of purposive structure, space appears at first to be incompatible with the metaphysical presuppositions of a perfectly ordered world.[24]

Indeed, in the empty and unlimited space of modern physics qualities and hierarchies can no longer explain the motion of objects. From the standpoint of modern mechanics there are no destinations, no final positions for the movement of things, in the double sense that objects will keep moving if unimpeded by external forces, and that there is no ultimate destination, no "natural place" where they will ever find rest.[25] Places, moreover, are now incapable of any action. They no longer contain anything; they do not pull, hold, or keep bodies at rest.

The logic of place tied beings and forms to the particularity and distinctiveness of meaningful, concrete locations: places situated things, determined their horizons and their capacities, their movements and possibilities. Now, in a space where every place is equal to every other, where each appears as a part among parts of the same unrestrained sameness, places present themselves as mere interchangeable points, indistinguishable from one another except by a metric determination. Koyré reconstructs a beautiful image by Raphson: in the open fields of infinite space, there is no longer "here" nor "there"; one could endlessly walk and yet remain in the exact same place.[26] The modern universe is devoid of places; places, conversely, seem to have lost all their powers, to no longer have strength.[27]

With its solid system of concentric spheres, its upper and lower limits, its stable center and proportional dimensions and forms, the ordered classical cosmos was a finite unity, perfectly closed upon itself.[28] The logic of place supported a physics of containment that now dissipates in infinite space. All the bounds and limits that guaranteed the proportion and order of the world disappear without trace, they are lost in an unending extension that is only unified by a series of abstract, invisible laws. The modern universe has no exteriority: there is no last boundary, no edge of the world, no extra-cosmic space on the other side of the line. Our world is rather an endless totality where there are no fixed points of reference, where everything is de-centered, where each point becomes at once "beginning and end, foundation and limit" of the totality itself.[29]

The essential metaphysical presupposition of modern space is the sheer openness of the world, the absence of all forms of limitation, of cosmic barriers, of every stable form of distinction and separation. In the celebratory tone of the likes of Giordano Bruno, the infinitely open character of the universe becomes the symbol and expression of the unrestricted power of creation, which now shines in the unfathomable greatness of the physical world. But even the most cautious assessments of the nature of the universe, those that for theological or political reasons refused to term it infinite as such and defended instead its indefinite character, recognized thereby the same essential metaphysical premise: its negative character as undelimited, the undeniable fact of its un-containment.

Soon, the radical openness of the universe became, however, a source of scientific and philosophical anxiety. The old problems associated with the physics of the unbounded re-emerged then under new forms.[30] Those fears did not only concern the specific workings of mechanics; with the dissolution of natural places in the radical openness of the universe comes the disappearance of an entire topology of being based on the correspondence between the physical cosmos and the natural order and position of things. In a world that is no longer emplaced, where each being has lost its natural anchoring and seems to float instead in an endless, potentially meaningless nowhere, coming to know the nature of things, discerning their value and perfection, becomes indeed a problematic task. The abstract voice of mathematics, in fact, could reduce the world to quantifiable relations of matter in space, but science could not explain much about the finality of things, and had almost nothing to say about questions of order, authority or moral necessity.[31]

Something fundamental had been lost in the transition, something like a "sense of place" which held fast objects and their qualities, the how and the why of things, their purposes and their arrangement within a general order of existence.[32] Gone is the sense of limit, of boundaries and proportions; now the center is truly everywhere and nowhere at all. In that infinitely open universe, one can feel at once liberated and lost, unchained and diminished, ecstatic and terrified. Indeed, one can feel as the king of infinite space, and still be tormented by very bad dreams.[33]

9.4 Disproportion of Man: Pascal's Problem

In a text that bears the appropriate title "Disproportion of Man", Pascal famously links together the infinite vastness of space, the minuscule presence of man in its regard, and the impact of this discrepancy on the value and dignity of all human enterprises.[34] Pascal's tribulation – *what is a man in the midst of infinity?* – has precisely to do with issues of measure and proportion, or rather with the lack thereof. More precisely, it is a matter of the position in which human beings find themselves after the explosion of the universe into infinity, of the dislocation of their standing within the very order of being.

In the ancient cosmos, man occupied the "central place" of all; everything in that world seemed so arranged as to give him "a high sense of his own importance and dignity."[35] Now, that whole economy of value seems to be completely gone. Against the unfathomable vastness of space, man's place on Earth is felt as "insignificant and precarious"; everything that is cherished by him appears "buried in a universe of ruins."[36] In the open universe of the new physics, the Earth and all its living creatures, including human beings and all the activities to which they devote their passions and their talents, are fundamentally displaced, if not disjoined from the overall scheme of things. Everything of which man is a measure – and paradoxically, in the great dissolution of cosmic references and frames, man will end up becoming the basis and measure of all things – seems marked by a cosmic lack that threatens its solidity and dignity: around him, there seems to be no longer a purpose, no higher orders, no whole to which he must conform.

The fall of the classical cosmos brings with it the menace of chaos and disorder. The bursting of the cosmic spheres makes the world feel as a city that has been broken into, vulnerable and exposed, no longer protected by walls (or, in the Cartesian metaphor of the *Discourse on the Method*, as a house in which one can no longer live).[37] The search for new foundations, for solid frameworks of reference and orientation, for "firm and immoveable" points upon which to erect new structures of knowledge and experience, becomes hence paradigmatic both of the requirements of the new science and of the quest for practical and moral guidance for the conduct of life in the world.[38] On both counts, however, the solution could no longer be found in any sort of cosmological projection. There is no cosmic structure protecting the disposition of beings and things, governing their growth and their movements, ordering their qualities and their capacities, giving to each a place of their own. Simply put, there will be no undoing of the dislocation of the world, which will remain unanchored and exposed to the radical openness of infinite space.

Given that openness, any horizon of certainty, of stability and security, would now have to be found by turning "inside," in the realm of human rationality as such, or perhaps more precisely, in the encounter of human reason and the invisible logic of reality, in the coincidence of rationality and the mathematical structure of the world. But even in its geometrical regularity, the world remains somehow foreign to this discovery. Inert and devoid of purpose, the universe appears as a "dead infinity" that has little to say about who we are or what we should do in it.[39] Only in our thoughts, hence, we find restored the possibility of order and regularity in the world; only there, severed from the cosmos, we find a foundation for our knowledge, for the stability of our experience, and even for the possibility of overcoming our feeling of fragility in relation to the unqualified vastness around us. In our capacity to think the universe, in fact, to encompass the whole in an idea – however abstract and imperfect – we raise ourselves beyond the very greatness that generates our insignificance.[40] In the realm of reason, human beings overturn their sense of disproportion and the apparent precarity of their stance in the world.

The radical openness of the world will hence come to be signified not only as a threat, but also as a source of greatness and freedom. For human beings, there is now no external order to which they must conform. Nothing else is there to determine them; they have no standard or foundation, no principle of growth other than the use of their own reason. The nature of human beings consists precisely in their capacity not to be determined and contained, but rather to determine themselves, to be free. This is precisely the mission that God himself had set for the human kind in Pico della Mirandola's *Oratio de hominis dignitate*:

> We have given you, O Adam, no visage proper to yourself, nor endowment properly your own, in order that *whatever place*, whatever form, whatever gifts you may, with premeditation, select, these same you may have and possess through your own judgement and decision. The nature of all other creatures is defined and restricted within laws which We have laid down; you, by contrast, impeded by no such restrictions, may, by your own free will, to whose custody We have assigned you, trace for yourself the lineaments of your own nature. *I have placed you at the very center of the world*, so that from that vantage point you may with greater ease glance round about you on all that the world contains. We have made you a creature neither of heaven nor of earth, neither mortal nor immortal, in order that you may, as the free and proud shaper of your own being, fashion yourself in the form you may prefer. It will be in your power to descend to the lower, brutish forms of life; you will be able, through your own decision, to rise again to the superior orders whose life is divine.[41]

The dislocation inherent in the new cosmology is thus turned into an ontological privilege of the human being. In a world without places, not having a place becomes what is most proper to them. The dignity of men consists precisely in the capacity to select whatever place they may wish, to trace the lineaments of their own nature, to become shapers of their own being. In a universe that knows no limits, man's nature is open-ended too. As Kant would put it several centuries later, their nature is an "empty place."[42] It is now up to them to shape and determine that place in new and powerful ways.

Notes

1. By announcing that "perfection" was among the *idola tribus* to be dismantled by the new rational imagination, Bacon was certainly declaring war on the qualitative uniqueness of the Aristotelian world as a natural whole, that is a coherent order of well-disposed natural places. But is interesting to note that Bacon, realizing that "the human understanding is of its own nature prone to suppose the existence of more order and regularity in the world than it finds," also included among such excesses the fictions of the "perfect motions of celestial

bodies," and other "fancies" and similar "dreams" derived from classic astronomy (*The Philosophical Works of Francis Bacon: Reprinted from the Texts and Translations* [Abingdon: Routledge, 2011), XLV).

2. *Physics*, 212a30-1.

3. See *Physics*, 208b1-212b29, 255b13–7, and *On the Heavens*, 268b11ff. For an alternative rendition of Aristotle's theory of natural places, which rejects that they can be presented as a cause for motion, see Peter K. Machamer, "Aristotle on Natural Place and Natural Motion," *Isis* 69, no. 3 (1978): 377–87.

4. On the transient character of the subversions of nature see Duhem's comment of *On The Heavens*: "tout ce que la violence engendre contrairement a la nature doit, tot au tard, prendre fin, en sorte que la nature reprenne son cours normal, une chose qui subsiste par violence et contre nature ne peut pas être éternelle, car l'ordre du monde est éternel" (*Le Système du monde*, 227).

5. This is the famous tension between *topos koinos*, the world as single common place for all the things that are, and *topos idios*, the proper place for each single body, enunciated in *Physics*, 209a33-4 (see also *Physics*, 212b18-20, my emphasis: "It is true, then, to say – 'all things are in heaven' . . . but what constitutes the *place-universal* is not the whole rotating aetherial mass but the inner surface of that mass, which is at rest and is in contact with the world of modifiable substances"; and *supra*, note 109). The place of the world is hence a vessel for all the places that it contains and surrounds, a place for all places, the internal limit of everything that exists within it.

6. "Perhaps place is not a substance in itself, but is predicated in relation to the order (*taxis*) and position (*thesis*) of bodies according to their natures and powers, equally in the case of animal and plants and, generally, of the things composed of different elements, whether animate or inanimate, that have a natural shape. The order and position of these parts is relative to the whole being. Therefore each is said to be in its own space (*chora*) through having its proper order (*taxis*) since each of the parts of a body would deserve and demand its own space (*chora*) and position (*thesis*)" (cited in J. O. Urmson, *Simplicius: Corollaries on Place and Time* [London: Bloomsbury, 2014], 639, 19–23, and Casey, *The Fate of Place*, 96). For Theofrastus, hence, the relation of place is not simply twofold but threefold: it concerns the internal disposition of each thing (the place of each part, *chora*), its relation to the place that is proper to it (its position, *thesis*), and the general arrangement of places within the world as a whole (the order of that world, *taxis*). On this point see also the introduction by Richard Sorajbi in ibid., 5.

7. I am following the account of Leo Strauss, *Natural Right and History* (Chicago: University of Chicago Press), ch. 3, "The Origin of the Idea of Natural Right."

8. *De Anima*, 415a24, 423a20ff, and *De Generatione Animalium*, 736b13 (see also Christopher Shields, "Aristotle's Psychology", in *The Stanford Encyclopedia of Philosophy*). Lovejoy takes the Aristotelian "hierarchical arrangement of all organisms," based on the different powers of the soul, as a decisive moment in the conformation of the view of nature as a scale in which "each higher order [possesses] all the powers of those below it . . . and an additional differentiating one of its own" (*The Great Chain of Being*, 58–9). The metaphysical image of a "great chain of being," hence, would appear to the medieval interpreters of Aristotle as a most perfect unity, composed of an "immense, or – by the strict but seldom rigorously applied logic of the principle of continuity – of an infinite, number of links ranging in hierarchical order from the meagerest kind of existents, which barely escape non-existence, through 'every possible' grade up to the *ens perfectissimum* – or, in a somewhat more orthodox version, to the highest possible kind of creature, between which and the Absolute Being the disparity was assumed to be infinite, everyone of them differing from that immediately above and that immediately below it by the 'least possible' degree of difference" (ibid.). Everything, from the simplest elements of matter to the purest forms of intellectual life, is thus disposed in an "ascending scale . . . in dignity and value" that also corresponds to "actual spatial relations" (Burtt, *The Metaphysical Foundations of Modern Physical Science*, 24).

9. What defines, in the apparently inexhaustible multiplicity of things, the extent to which each of them participates in the goodness and perfection of the world? *Privation* plays according to Lovejoy a decisive role within the logic of taxonomy, as it establishes a fundamental connection between the capacity and moral dignity of beings, that is with the "scheme of values implicit in the principle of plenitude," understood as the "the fullness of the realization of conceptual possibility in actuality" (*The Great Chain of Being*, 50–2, 85, 121). As he presents the argument, within the scale of being the position of things is defined by their potentialities, by what each of them can and cannot do: "everything, except God, has in it some measure of 'privation'. There are, in the first place, in its generic 'nature' or essence, 'potentialities' which, in a given state of its existence, are not realized; and there are superior levels of being, which, by virtue of the specific degree of privation characteristic of it, it is constitutionally incapable of attaining. Thus 'all individual things may be graded according to the degree to which they are infected with [mere] potentiality'" (ibid., 59). The ascending fullness of potentiality corresponds hence to diminishing degrees of privation in the scale of nature (here too, privation arguably appears as an "absence of being . . . not an active act but a lack, a shadow that happens to 'be,' or rather not be, there where the light does not penetrate" [Dmitri Nikulin, *Neoplatonism in*

Late Antiquity, 190]). As we shall see soon, this graduality of privation is essential, within an organic, hierarchical vision of the cosmos,
for the articulation of the ethical and political implications of the logic
of place.

10. *Physics*, 212a30-1. As Casey expresses, "the limit of a place is specified
by what a body can do in that place" (*The Fate of Place*, 78).

11. Simplicius, *In Aristotelis Categorias Commentarium* (cited in Casey,
The Fate of Place, 375).

12. As Simplicius recounts in the *Corollaries on Place and Time*, for
Damascius position (*thesis*) is the inseparable attribute of a thing (see
Corollary on Place, 625,28; 627,2; 627,14). Position refers both to
the internal arrangement of the parts of a thing and to its external
disposition within the cosmos, which in turn has one most perfect
and natural form that all its elements strive to achieve: "ce lieu essentiel, cet ordre naturel du monde, c'est donc la forme qui conférerait
au Monde sa perfection, celle qu'il tend à reconquérir lorsqu'il en a
été écarte par violence; le lieu essentiel est ainsi la cause finale de tous
les mouvements naturels qui se remarquent dans l'Univers" (Duhem,
Le Système du monde, 349).

13. "The heavens will disappear with a roar; the elements will be
destroyed by fire, and the earth and everything done in it will be laid
bare . . . That day will bring about the destruction of the heavens by
fire, and the elements will melt in the heat" (2 Peter 3, 10–12, New
International Version).

14. 1 Corinthians 14:33.

15. See Genesis 1:1–31, Psalm 104. In the *Confessions*, Augustine presents
a fascinating reading of Genesis as an ordering of the world that neutralizes the chaotic and destructive tendencies of an already existent
matter, imprinting goodness and beauty against the abyss of darkness
that drew matter into "disorder and unlikeness" to God (*Confessions*, 13.2.2). For a reconstruction of the early Christian cosmological imagination see Mircea Eliade, *Cosmos and History. The Myth of
the Eternal Return* (New York: Harper and Brothers), 14: "for Christians, Golgotha was situated at the center of the world, since it was the
summit of the cosmic mountain and at the same time the place where
Adam had been created and buried. Thus the blood of the Saviour
falls upon Adam's skull, buried precisely at the foot of the Cross, and
redeems him. The belief that Golgotha is situated at the center of the
world is preserved in the folklore of the Eastern Christians."

16. "And God said, 'Let the earth bring forth living creatures according
to their kinds – livestock and creeping things and beasts of the earth
according to their kinds'. And it was so. And God made the beasts of
the earth according to their kinds and the livestock according to their
kinds, and everything that creeps on the ground according to its kind.
And God saw that it was good" (Genesis 1: 24–5).

17. "Non essent omnia, si essent aequalia" (Augustine, *De diuersis questionibus octoginta tribus*, 41, 3, cited in Lovejoy, *The Great Chain of Being*, 67). Here too, the influence of Plotinus is clearly observable. *Enneads* III.2.8, for example, provides a clear rendition of the principle of gradation of things in the cosmos according to their excellency (my emphasis): "So it remains to enquire in what way these are *excellently arranged*, and how they have a *share in order*, and in what way not. Certainly they are not arranged badly. The upper parts of every living thing, the face and head, are more beautiful, and the middle and lower parts are not equal to them; *but men are in the middle and below*, and above are heaven and the gods in it; and the greatest part of the universe is gods and all the heaven round about it; but the earth is like a central point even in comparison with only one of the stars" (Plotinus, trans. A. H. Armstrong, *Ennead, Volume III* [Cambridge: Harvard University Press, 1967], 67–8).

18. *Confessions*, 13.9.10. See also *De Civitate Dei*, XI, 28, where Augustine explains that beings "possess a kind of attraction towards our own proper position and natural order."

19. From the most insignificant material forms to the perfect arrangement of heaven itself, the entire cosmos is disposed according to relations of order and proportion. In the bottom of the scale, even inanimate objects in nature possess a "master element" which "rules and holds together all of its component parts, controls its movement, and propels it *towards its own rightful place* in the world"; in the top, angels are ranked according to "*leurs offices et degrez*" and each accepts its place in "perfect charity and love" (Stephen H. Rigby, "The Body Politic in the Social and Political Thought of Christine de Pizan. Reciprocity, Hierarchy and Political Authority," *Cahiers de Recherches Médiévales et Humanistes. Journal of Medieval and Humanistic Studies* 24 (2012): 14, my emphasis).

20. Following Augustine, in the *Consolation of Philosophy* Boethius described how God, shaping and ordering the parts of a "beautiful universe," calls back on each form of life to return to the place that is proper to it (Boethius, *Theological Tractates. The Consolation of Philosophy*, trans. H. F. Stewart, E. K. Rand, and S. J. Tester [Cambridge: Harvard University Press, 1918], III, 9, 18–25). Aquinas, who in the *Summa Theologiae* affirmed that "it is ridiculous" to assert that there are natural places for spiritual substances, immediately qualifies that claim to admit that "some particular place may have a certain fitness in regard to spiritual substances," and famously praised the highest beauty of a world that resides precisely in the inequality of things: "Moreover, perfect goodness would not be found in created things unless there were an order of goodness in them, in the sense that some of them are better than others. Otherwise, all possible grades of goodness would not be realized, nor would any

creature be like God by virtue of holding a higher place than another. The highest beauty would be taken away from things, too, if the order of distinct and unequal things were removed" (*Summa Theologiae* 1, question 102, reply to objection 2, cited in Joseph Anthony Mazzeo, "Dante's Conception of Love," *Journal of the History of Ideas* 18, no. 2 (1957): 147–60; and *Summa Contra Gentiles*, 3.71.3; see also Lovejoy, *The Great Chain of Being*, 76–9). On the theological importance of the aspect of *ordo* and the multiplicity and inequality of things, see Oscar James Brown, *Natural Rectitude and Divine Law in Aquinas: An Approach to an Integral Interpretation of the Thomistic Doctrine of Law* (Toronto: Pontifical Institute of Mediaeval Studies, 1981), 77.

21. *Divina Commedia*, Paradiso, Canto I, 103–14. Lovejoy provides a translation in *The Great Chain of Being*, 117: "All things whatsoever observe a *mutual order*; and this the form that maketh the universe like unto God. Herein the exalted creatures trace the impress of the Eternal Worth, which is the goal whereto was made the norm now spoken of. In the order of which I speak *all things incline, by diverse lots, more near and less unto their principle*; Wherefore they move to diverse ports o'er the great sea of being, and each one with instinct given it to bear it on.

22. In the *Convivio*, Dante had expressed the logic of possibility and hierarchy that orders the world in terms of a theory of *love*, understood as a cosmic principle that governs the natural movement of things towards their proper places in the general order of being. See Joseph Anthony Mazzeo, "Dante's Conception of Love," 150: "Every level in the order of creation has its own kind of love or desire. Simple bodies have a natural love for their own proper place. Thus earth always tends downwards to the centre while fire has a natural love to ascend to the circumference adjoining the heaven of the moon. The primary composite bodies, such as minerals, have a natural love for that place which is suitable for their generation. Such is the place in which they grow and acquire vigor and power. Plants, which are the first of all creatures endowed with soul, i.e., the vegetative functions, more obviously manifest this love. They display a preference to grow in places adapted to the requirements of their natures, e.g., some plants grow well by water, others at the foot of mountains, and if they are transplanted either die or love, so to speak, sadly, like separated lovers. Animals not only more obviously love their own particular place but love one another; man, possessing a portion of the nature of every one of these lower creatures, can and does experience all of these kinds of love as well as his own specific love for all perfect and noble things, a kind of love he possesses by being the noblest of created things under the heavens." See also Patrick Boyde: "The natural love of being declares itself in a natural movement towards the natural *place* where the subject's being will be conserved; and

the love, the movement and the place are all determined by its level on the Scale of Being. As one ascends from one *grado generale* to the next, the place becomes ever more particularized, and the power of movement ever greater" (Patrick Boyde, *Dante Philomythes and Philosopher: Man in the Cosmos* [Cambridge University Press, 1983], 257).

23. Simplicius, *In Aristotelis physicorum libros quattuor priores commentaria*, cited in Casey, *The Fate of Place*, 99.

24. This the core of the philosophical narrative that describes the transition from the classical cosmos, a "closed world" where the "spatial structure embodied a hierarchy of perfection and value," to an infinite universe that is "no longer united by natural subordination, but unified only by the identity of its ultimate and basic components and laws; and the replacement of the Aristotelian conception of space – a differentiated set of innerworldly places – by that of Euclidean geometry – an essentially infinite and homogenous extension –from now on considered identical with the real space of the world" (Koyré, *From the Closed World to the Infinite Universe*, viii). Despite all the qualifications that this narrative deserves, in what follows I will attempt to discern some of the ethical and political effects that can be declined from this cosmological transition.

25. See for instance the following description of Newtonian mechanics by Nick Huggett: "final position plays no role at all: the straight path does not depend on distant places, and though an object might end up in a certain place, it certainly doesn't make sense to think of it as its natural 'goal'" (*Space from Zeno to Einstein*, 79–80). Huggett presents here a very useful rendition of the distinction between modern kinematics (which deals with the classical equivalent of natural motions) and dynamics (which deals with constrained motions, that is motions resulting from the action of forces).

26. Koyré, *From the Closed World to the Infinite Universe*, 201–2.

27. Casey defines the status of place in the modern imagination of space as "momentary subdivisions of a universal space quantitatively determined in its neutral homogeneity" (*The Fate of Place*, 134). I take from him the allusion to William Gilbert: "Place is nothing, does not exist, has no strength" (ibid., 135). In the scholium of the *Principia*, place becomes nothing more than a part of space, whereas positions add nothing other than a formal property of those places: "place is a part of space which a body takes up and is, according to the space, either absolute or relative. I say, a part of space; not the situation nor the external surface of the body. For the places of equal solids are always equal; but their surfaces, by reason of their dissimilar figures, are often unequal. Positions properly have no quantity; nor are they so much the places themselves as the properties of places" (*Scholium on Time, Place, Space and Motion*, III). Again, Huggett expresses

succinctly the effects of Newton's metaphysics of space on the notion of place: "every point of absolute space is exactly like every other, All points are identical, and absolute space is Euclidean: utterly flat and featureless. There is no way to distinguish experimentally one absolute place from any other" (*Space from Zeno to Einstein*, 161).

28. In his book on the origins of Greek cosmology, Couprie reconstructs David Furley's argument, according to which even the atomists believed in the limitation of the cosmos as a contained whole, akin to the image of a "walled city": "Both the Atomists, who believed in the infinite universe, and the Aristotelians, who did not, agreed that our world is itself a finite system, bounded by the sphere of the stars. The controversy was about what, if anything, lies beyond the starry sphere"; and elsewhere: "The controversy was not about the existence of a closed world, but about its status: is it all there is, or is there something else too?" (*The Greek Cosmologists*, 136, 2; cited in Couprie, *Heaven and Earth in Ancient Greek Cosmology*, 223).

29. Koyré, *From the Closed World*, 11. Jammer makes the case for identifying in the work of Cusa a "turning point in the history of astronomy" precisely in relation to this affirmation. The effects are not only metaphysical, but of a practical nature too: the fact that the ontological structure of the world is everywhere the same, that "the universe presents the same aspect from every point," is the necessary condition for the repeatability of experiments in modern science (*Concepts of Space*, 84).

30. In a universe that is by definition without limits and without center, how can we establish stable and solid reference points? Is it still possible, if all places are equal, to distinguish the different parts and directions of infinite space? If space is incapable of any action, how can we explain the movement of bodies that, in the absence of natural places, now seem restless and displaced, and have literally *nowhere* to go? And finally, why does the earth not fall, why don't the heavens collapse in this radically open, endless universe, where every grounding, every foundation seems now to be lost? On the solutions to the problem of reference, motion, and falling brought by the development of modern physics, see above, sections 5.3 and 5.4.

31. See Burtt, *The Metaphysical Foundations of Modern Physical Science*, 89–90: "The final why of events in the latter could be explained mainly in terms of their use to man; the final why of human activities in terms of the eternal quest for union with God. Now, with the superstructure from man up banished from the primary realm, which for Galileo, is identified with material atoms in their mathematical relations, the how of events being the sole object of exact study, there had appeared no place for final causality whatsoever. The real world is simply a succession of atomic motions in mathematical continuity."

32. In his commentary of the work of Edward Casey, Thomas Brockelman synthesizes that loss with remarkable effectiveness: "To be modern is to give up the 'sense of place' associated with the late medieval hierarchical world; in favor of a space and time conceived to be populated by infinite numbers of entirely exchangeable loci" ("Lost in Place? On the Virtues and Vices of Edward Casey's Anti-Modernism," 20). Panofsky expresses a similar idea when affirming that the "symbolic form" of perspective was "comprehensible only for a quite specific, indeed specifically modern, sense of space, or if you will, sense of the world" (*Perspective as Symbolic Form*, 34).

33. "O God, I could be bounded in a nutshell and count myself a king of infinite space, were it not that I have bad dreams," *Hamlet*, Act 2, Scene 2.

34. "Que l'homme contemple donc la nature entière dans sa haute et pleine majesté, qu'il éloigne sa vue des objets bas qui l'environnent. Qu'il regarde cette éclatante lumière mise comme une lampe éternelle pour éclairer l'univers, que la terre lui paraisse comme un point au prix du vaste tour que cet astre décrit et qu'il s'étonne de ce que ce vaste tour lui-même n'est qu'une pointe très délicate à l'égard de celui que ces astres, qui roulent dans le firmament, embrassent. Mais si notre vue s'arrête là que l'imagination passe outre, elle se lassera plutôt de concevoir que la nature de fournir. Tout ce monde visible n'est qu'un trait imperceptible dans l'ample sein de la nature. Nulle idée n'en approche, nous avons beau enfler nos conceptions au-delà des espaces imaginables, nous n'enfantons que des atomes au prix de la réalité des choses. *C'est une sphère infinie dont le centre est partout, la circonférence nulle part.* Enfin c'est le plus grand caractère sensible de la toute-puissance de Dieu que notre imagination se perde dans cette pensée. Que l'homme étant revenu à soi considère ce qu'il est au prix de ce qui est, qu'il se regarde comme égaré dans ce canton détourné de la nature. Et que, de ce petit cachot où il se trouve logé, j'entends l'univers, il apprenne à estimer la terre, les royaumes, les villes et soi-même, son juste prix. Qu'est-ce qu'un homme, dans l'infini?" (Blaise Pascal, 199; my emphasis for the rendition of the metaphor of the infinite sphere).

35. A. O. Lovejoy, *The Great Chain of Being*, 102. Lovejoy, however, goes on to contest the idea of the "demotion in the dignity of man within the Copernican revolution"; according to him it was only the assertion of the infinity of the world what dislocated that position, for "so long as the whole sensible universe remained thus limited and boxed-in, and so long as the planet occupied by man, whatever its spatial position, was still assigned a unique biological, moral, and religious status, the aesthetically and practically distinctive characteristics of the medieval cosmical scheme remained" (ibid. 103).

36. Burtt, *The Metaphysical Foundations of Modern Physical Science*, 10.

37. See *Proverbs* 25:28: "Like a city whose walls are broken through is a person who lacks self-control." In the *Discourse*, Descartes explains similarly the need to adopt a "provisional moral code" until he completes his investigation on knowledge, and compares such a code to a *place* where one can comfortably live while he is rebuilding his house: "before starting to rebuild your house, it is not enough simply to pull it down, to make provision for materials and architects . . . and to have carefully drawn up the plans; you must also provide yourself with some other place where you can live comfortably while building is in progress. Likewise, lest I should remain indecisive in my actions while reason obliged me to be so in my judgments, and in order to live as happily as I could during this time, I formed for myself a provisional moral code consisting of just three or four maxims" (*Discourse on the Method*, in *Selected Philosophical Writings*, 31). On the "shellessness" of the human condition after the breaking of the celestial domes, and the subsequent removal of the cosmological "safety structures," see the interesting reading by Peter Sloterdijk in *Bubbles: Spheres Volume I: Microspherology*, trans. Wieland Hoban (Los Angeles: Semiotext(e), 2011) (especially "The Allies; or: The Breathed Commune", 17ff), and *Neither Sun nor Death*, trans. Steve Corcoran (Cambridge: Semiotext(e), 2011).

38. "Archimedes used to demand just one firm and immovable point in order to shift the entire earth; so I too can hope for great things if I manage to find just one thing, however slight, that is certain and unshakeable" (René Descartes, *Meditations on First Philosophy: With Selections from the Objections and Replies* [Cambridge: Cambridge University Press, 1996], 16). As Richard Bernstein put it in his commentary of this passage from the opening of the second Meditation, at stake here is much more than an attempt at solving epistemological problems. This is rather a "quest for some fixed point; some stable rock upon which we can secure our lives against the vicissitudes that constantly threaten us. The specter that hovers in the background of this journey is not just radical epistemological skepticism but the dread of madness and chaos where nothing is fixed, where we can neither touch bottom nor support ourselves in the surface. With a chilling clarity Descartes leads us with an apparent and ineluctable necessity to a grand and seductive Either/Or. *Either* there is some support for our being, a fixed foundation for our knowledge, *Or* we cannot escape the forces of darkness that envelop us with madness, with intellectual and moral chaos" (Richard J. Bernstein, *Beyond Objectivism and Relativism: Science, Hermeneutics, and Praxis* [Philadelphia: University of Pennsylvania Press, 1983], 18). The relation between the development of science and the moral crisis of early modernity figures prominently too in a beautiful text by John Dewey, in which he describes how the practice of early modern science, by voiding the objective world of its

wealth of qualities, generated a "conflict and need for reconciliation between the scientific properties of the real and those which give moral authority" (John Dewey, *The Quest for Certainty*, in *Later Works, 1925–1953* vol. 4 [Carbondale: Southern Illinois University Press, 1988), 176). This conflict, which figures so prominently in Descartes and is the source for him both of optimism and anxiety, is as we will see also apparent in the crisis of the structures of theological and political authority that were inherited from the Middle Ages, and jeopardized, if not demolished, by the Scientific Revolution.

39. Lovejoy describes poignantly how human beings find themselves to be "alone in a dead infinity of matter that travels endlessly upon its barren rounds, without thought or understanding, with naught in it that is akin to man" (*The Great Chain of Being*, 72). Burtt also depicts the moral crisis that derives from the image of a world that is devoid of purpose, "hard, cold, colourless, silent, and dead"; the only thing that is in common "between man and this real world was his ability to discover it" (*The Metaphysical Foundations of Modern Physical Science*, 236, 79). Both passages echo Pascal's tribulations on the "eternal silence of infinite space" (*Pensées*, 201). According to a well-established narrative, this objectification of nature, its externalization and estrangement as a foreign realm of "dead stuff", is the starting point of the process through which human beings ceased to be mere cosmic spectators to become "lords and masters of nature" (for example in Koyré, *From the Closed World to the Infinite Universe*, viii). This famous synthesis of the Cartesian project should, however, be understood by considering what immediately follows his maxim: to become lords and masters of nature, apart from enjoying the "fruits" of the earth, would allow us to get rid of "innumerable diseases, both of the body and the mind," and would facilitate, "most importantly," the "maintenance of health," true foundation of every other good (*Discourse on the Method*, in *Selected Philosophical Writings*, 47). The fundamental role that Descartes attributed to medicine, as one of the most fecund benefits of practical philosophy should not be underestimated while analyzing this claim.

40. "For Copernicus, we are at the center of the world, not in virtue of our place in the hierarchy of being, or because of the privilege of geocentric position, but in terms of our ability to understand the world as a harmonious object of reflective thought" (McGuire, *Tradition and Innovation: Newton's Metaphysics of Nature*, xiv). This argument, employed among others by Pascal and Montaigne, finds a remarkable expression in Hume's essay of the "Dignity or Meanness of Human Nature". For Hume, the very essence of human thought is precisely the fact that it can reach and engulf from within even the most distant places, the most abstract principles, the most complex facts about the world and about himself: in man "we see a creature *whose thoughts*

are not limited by any narrow bounds, either of place or time; who carries his researches into the *most distant regions of this globe, and beyond this globe, to the planets and heavenly bodies*; looks backward to consider the first origin, at least, the history of human race; casts his eye forward to see the influence of his actions upon posterity, and the judgments which will be formed of his character a thousand years hence; a creature, who traces causes and effects to a great length and intricacy; extracts general principles from particular appearances; improves upon his discoveries; corrects his mistakes; and makes his very errors profitable" (David Hume, *Moral Philosophy* [Indianapolis: Hackett Publishing, 2006], 318, my emphasis).

41. Giovanni Pico Della Mirandola, *Oration on the Dignity of Man*, trans. A. Robert Gaponigri (Washington: Regnery Publishing, 1996), my emphasis.

42. "Men, good-natured as the sheep they herd, would hardly reach a higher worth than their beasts; they would not fill the empty place in creation by achieving their end, which is rational nature" (*Idea for a Universal History from a Cosmopolitan Point of View*, in Immanuel Kant, *On History*, trans. Lewis White Beck [Bobbs-Merril Co., 1963], thesis 4). Quite tellingly, Kant is dealing precisely with the fact of human antagonism, which he sees as a necessary condition for the achievement of progress: the emptiness of human nature, as I will try to prove in what follows, needs to be ethically and politically determined.

Chapter 10

Metaphysics of Equality

The open ontology of modern physics soon affirmed itself as a specifically political problem. The presuppositions of the infinite universe emptied nature of fixed ranks and orders, of qualitative emplacements and meaningful inequalities. The ontological chains which held parts fast in their virtuous relations to their wholes were irremediably broken, and in their stead there was nothing but the unmarked, endless extension of a space that had no centers, no directions, no permanent dispositions. But how can any meaningful distinctions be anchored in a world without differentiations? How can any principle of authority and moral value be grounded in a universe that has been flattened, which no longer accepts pre-established distinctions and appears instead to be marked by the fact of a fundamental ontological equality?

Such are the political consequences of the fall of cosmic hierarchies. Modern space carries no mark of emplacement, no rationale for the distinction and subordination of men. Now there is no longer any "proper" place for any given subject. Limits, hierarchies, and orders suddenly seem vulnerable and contingent. Every form of authority, every political disposition, stands now in need of a reason. Against this background, the task of politics seems to consist precisely in a kind of reconstruction, in the fabrication of orders for a world that no longer seems to have any. In a world that has lost its natural anchor, where the political effects of the logic of place no longer operate, the pieces of a broken whole must be brought back together. For that, politics needs to be grounded in a space that is not only open, but radically empty too.

10.1 Political Places: A Topology of the *Polis*

Politics has a special relation to place. Of course, in the foundation of cities a particular attention needs to be paid to the choice of a geographical site: there are natural facts that are determinant of the political fate of the city.[1] But cities and the land they stand on are bound together by more complex forms of political attachment. In the *Republic*, Socrates makes up a story about the rearing of citizens under the ground of the city, so that they will think of their fellow citizens as "brothers and born of the earth" and defend the land of the city, its *chora*, as if it were "a mother and nurturer."[2] In an inverted analogy, Heraclitus had already exhorted the citizens to "fight on behalf of the law" as they would do for their "city-wall."[3] This association of the laws and the ground in which they hold was not just metaphorical or arbitrary. Considered a traitor to Thebes, the body of Polyneices is left outside the walls of the city to be eaten by the dogs; for burying him and disobeying the law, Antigone is conducted to her death "down the long ramp leading to the plain outside the city."[4] There, outside the bounded place of the city, the kind of virtue that is at stake in the polis does not hold in the same way.

That delimitation, however, is not simply established by walls. For a city is not just a physical reunion of people living together, it is much more than "having a common place."[5] A city has to do with the *way* in which people live, which is ultimately what the laws of that city express.[6] What attaches someone to his city, hence, is a certain relation to the way in which that city is ordered; that order, in turn, corresponds with a specific arrangement of its elements, with the disposition of its parts in relation to the whole. That is why the study of politics proceeds by observing the kinds of constitutions that cities can have (that is, with the different dispositions that are possible, with various ways of arranging the parts in relation to the whole). And that is also why the ideal city, the best political arrangement imaginable, is literally an order that is "laid up in heaven" and can be found "nowhere on earth."[7] The perfectly ordered city is literally placeless. And yet, it is still disposed ordered according to a fundamental relation to place.

The reason is that here too, the logic of place is not simply locatory; it does not merely refer to ubiety. Rather, place is the site of a complex relation between capacity, position, and order that extends well beyond the realm of physics, and which resonates indeed with political implications. The reason, as Aristotle explains, is that our internal constitution, and our relations with ourselves and with others, can also be understood as kinds of motions, that we also proceed through natural and unnatural movements.[8] When we act virtuously, we find a pleasure that is likened to rest; when we do not, the parts of our soul are divided and violently torn, as if they were trying to break us apart.[9] So that our soul too also has parts that need to be arranged in the most virtuous possible way, and natural dispositions that differ in effectiveness, in dignity and value. The realm of ethics investigates precisely all the different dispositions of which we are capable, the complex relation between our limits and our capacities that makes us the kind of being that we are, and defines our relation to the world. Indeed, ἦθος means "accustomed place"; it is a name for the place that contains us.[10]

Of course, the realm of human affairs is different from physics. Stones move downward, and fire burns "here as in Persia," while human lives and actions admit of great variation and diversity in the shapes that they can assume.[11] But the lives of men, individually and taken at the collective level, are also disposed in different manners. They also know of different trajectories and arrangements, of potentialities that unfold or that are hindered and restricted, of relations that can be proper and improper, natural and unnatural, harmoniously balanced or violent and disordered. Like the cosmos and the soul, the polis is also a whole that can be disposed according to different principles.[12] Here too, the good ordering of the parts will result in a virtuous state, and an alteration that goes against its nature, in violence. Physics, ethics and politics seem to share hence the same principle of order: the harmony of the whole – whether that whole be the cosmos, the city or the soul – depends on the good arrangement of its parts, on a balance that can only be reached by disposing each of its elements in its proper and natural position, that is, in the place where each of them rightfully belongs.

Places, therefore, are political too. In every type of regime, under every constitution, the parts that compose a city are ordered in a specific way: they are assigned limits and positions, possibilities and capacities, different horizons of being.[13] Even in democratic cities – those that are most prone to disorder, for in them the natural order of things is often subverted, to the point that even horses in the streets "walk about as if they also had been granted liberty and freedom" – there is a clear allocation of positions, and a delimitation of the principle of ruling and being ruled in turn.[14] The *polis* always entails a distribution that determines what kind of life each of its components must lead in order to produce the happiest outcome for the city as a whole. Like the sun governs the cosmos and reason the human soul, such order generally requires that the superior element always be "authoritative" and rule over the inferior one, pursuing the good that is common to both.[15] Children must be mentored by adults, because they do not master the *logos* yet. Women must be governed by men, because they do so only partially. Slaves must be ruled by those who are free, because they are entirely deprived of it (at least those slaves who are said to be naturally so).[16] For each of these groups, a place corresponds in the city, well delimited and defined, which determines what they can and cannot do. What is natural for children is education, for women the private realm of the household and the family, for slaves the toils of crude reproductive labor; all of them must be kept away from the *agora* and the conduct of public affairs. In the city there are foreigners too: even if they are "there," they will always be marked by the fact that they come from somewhere else.

The order of the *polis* requires that each kind occupies itself with the activity that is proper to it, and none of the others. Citizens, Aristotle says, "must not lead the life of artisans or tradesmen," because those who work lack the time and the energy that are required for the pursuit of the common good.[17] Socrates had firmly established this principle when setting the class structure of the ideal city. Each of the elements of the *polis*, like the parts of a well-attuned soul, must excel in the realization of just one task, and devote to it the entirety of its time and all of its capacities.[18] When each part does what by its nature it is best at doing, what is befitting and proper to it, all of them join together in a harmonious and proportionate whole, like the sounds of a musical scale or the fixed proportions of the planets in the distribution of the sky.[19] Once and again, the same principle is hence reinstated: when each part is set in its proper place, within bounds that are properly defined and determined, the harmonious order of the city will make it thrive. When on the contrary that order is subverted, violence – the unnatural movement that takes things by force out of their natural places – brings about crisis and the degeneration of things.

10.2 To Follow Nature: Politics as the Order of Things

Keeping each thing in its place is precisely what Socrates calls justice. Like health, justice consists in ordering the elements according to their natural proportions and relations; injustice, like disease, comes from the subversion of that order, which does not fail to turn the city into "an enemy to itself."[20] From this perspective, justice will appear not only as a virtuous and noble end, but as a condition for the preservation of the city itself. The safety and endurance of the political order, the *salus rei publicae* that is the supreme law of all political communities, is directly connected with the internal balance of its elements, with the order and distribution that maintains it united and at peace with itself. Building on the Socratic analogy, Cicero affirms in *De re publica*: "What, in the case of singing, musicians call harmony is, in the state, concord (*concordia*); it constitutes the tightest and most effective bond of security; and such concord cannot exist at all without justice."[21] As the "tightest bond of security" for the republic, concord coincides with justice and sets the ultimate purpose of political laws. But precisely to achieve that purpose, those laws cannot be arbitrary inventions. Laws, like the political order that they establish, must be themselves "in harmony with nature," they must "inhere" in the natural order of things.[22] *Concordia* does not merely refer to a balance or proportion of the political elements between themselves, but also to the essential agreement of that balance with the natural order around them. Politics must be fashioned as a living image of the world, it must "follow nature" precisely in what is most orderly about it.[23] In that, the laws reveal their continuity with the natural totality – and conversely, what is natural acquires a specific ethical and political significance.

The order of human affairs – from the ethical to the domestic to the political – follows the principles of nature, the *instinctus* of nature as Isidore of Seville puts it, and must therefore be defined in accordance with it.[24] There is a principle of continuity, even of convertibility between nature and reason, between the immutable order that governs the world and the immanent facts of human political existence. Political laws must express the purposive order that is given to us by nature; our aspiration must be to achieve the most perfect correspondence with it.[25] Here again, it is the order of the whole what counts, what determines what is proper and best for each particular thing. And again, such order depends on a complex logic of relations and positions whereby each singularity is endowed with different capacities and possibilities. For the order of nature is far from being politically indistinct.

Indeed, politics must follow nature precisely in what is most unequal about it. The best government that a state can have, says

Plotinus, is not one that treats all citizens as equals but one that, like a painter who distributes different colors upon the canvas, gives to each part what is appropriate to it.[26] Augustine expresses this same principle with pristine clarity in a remarkable passage from the *City of God*: "The peace of all things is the tranquility of order. Order is the distribution which allots things equal and unequal, each to its own place."[27] The logic of place defines the political dimension of *scala naturae*. In the realm of human affairs too, the disposition of the chain of being requires hierarchical relations between the elements to achieve harmony and preserve its order. Therefore, each must accept the place that is properly assigned to it within the manifold diversity of creation. The order of nature imposes that everywhere the superior must govern the inferior; like God over the cosmos and fathers over their sons, the mission of rulers is to keep the political whole in order, to preserve its unity and purpose, to make each part strive for the general concord of the whole.[28] The medieval image of the "body politic" – where the "head" rules undisputedly over the lower parts, which are in turn hierarchically ordered according to their dignity, all being necessary in the precise place and function that has been assigned to them – reiterates the principle of government as an expression of the unequal natural order of things.[29] Determined by birth, the place of each is, precisely *qua* unequal, in natural agreement to the whole. But that agreement depends precisely on the maintenance of a strict logic of hierarchy between the parts, on the preservation of an order of positions that, through those differences, strives as one for the highest purpose of the whole.

Of course, history and politics often produce deviations from the natural course of things. Human beings can be dangerous or impious; they often do wrong and behave in unnatural manners; they can even become something monstruous, like a rabble claiming the right to distinguish between right and wrong.[30] But precisely as a form of corruption or degeneration, as a way of subversion against the order of nature, political excesses always remain in relation to that order itself. Like the movement that keeps an element out of its proper place, the political violence that brings an unnatural state of things is just an expression of the tension of mimesis and transience, a form of disorder that disappears when things are relocated right where they belong.[31] The purposive order of nature remains the fundamental measure of the political even in its tensions and deviations: for all things have a place to which they shall return.

10.3 Broken Chains: The Political Emptying of Nature

Putting an end to that correspondence, the rupture of the chain of being dislocated the political world too. Consider the famous *Discourse on voluntary servitude*, which Étienne de La Boétie opened by asking in bewilderment how it happens that

> so many men, so many villages, so many cities, so many nations, sometimes suffer under a single tyrant who has no other power than the power they give him; who is able to harm them only to the extent to which they have the willingness to bear with him; who could do them absolutely no injury unless they preferred to put up with him rather than contradict him.[32]

La Boétie's principle is revolutionary in that it presumes that it is human willingness, and not the conformity to any natural order of things, that provides the only basis and justification for the existence of political communities.[33] To be sure, the great theorists of natural law had already posited that political power and authority originate in the people, even that tyrants could be disobeyed and removed from power under very specific circumstances. La Boétie himself speaks in the *Discourse* of a "world governed by a nature which is reasonable," in which freedom is our original state (a statement very much in the spirit of Isidore's *una libertas omnium*, the idea that all men are born free which was eloquently defended by Suárez).[34] Despite these antecedents and elements of continuity, however, the *Discourse* is already describing a completely different world. For, if the ultimate foundation of all power and authority is nothing but the will of human beings to uphold them, there seems to be no external reference, no transcendent order to which men must conform, no justification for the concrete forms that the life of a political community should adopt. Every prince, as Machiavelli had anticipated to the great scandal of his contemporaries, is prince of a power that is not his own. Now, as La Boétie concludes, there is no reason why "anyone who has the face of a man" should not reject the fact of his subordination.[35]

With the collapse of hierarchies and differentiations, the logic of emplacement loses its grip on the political world. Nature no longer appears as something to be grown into, something to be fulfilled, an order that pre-exists the political and to which we should simply conform. Conversely, politics loses its referent and anchor, its rootedness in the natural order, and becomes instead eerily self-referential.[36] Gone are the organic correspondences, the virtuous hierarchies, the beautiful harmony of parts arranged in their proper places. Political orders appear now as historic and transient, independent of any hierarchies and purposes that would pre-exist their institution. To speak the truth about cities, hence, implies a very different kind of discourse from the speculations of natural theology.[37] As Hobbes will claim in the *Behemoth*, in a vein very close to La Boétie's, "political power hath no foundation but in the opinion and belief of the people."[38] Authority, and not truth, is now the source of the law.[39]

Nature, of course, has not disappeared from the picture. Men imitate the art of nature, Hobbes says in the opening line of the *Leviathan*, though this time not to become closer to it but to overcome it, to get out of nature and into the political condition.[40] In a quite complicated way, nature – human nature to be precise – is precisely what allows us to rescind the subordination to our original condition. The "laws of nature," a series of rational maxims that guide men in their agreement to lay down their unrestricted rights and erect a common sovereign power, are precisely what allows them to "come out" of the "ill condition in which man by mere nature is actually placed in."[41] Through the laws of nature, human beings become artificers of the political, which appears as a product of human reason rather than as an expression of any necessary and immutable natural order.

Grotius's mysterious statement in the *Prolegomena*, according to which "the mother of right – that is, of natural law – is human nature," acquires here a new and distinct meaning.[42] Nature has been emptied of all substantive and external content; now it just corresponds to a logic of form – the form of human reason – through which we politically determine ourselves. Nature does not disappear, but is somehow effaced, emptied of fixed orders and places, voided to the point of merely coinciding with the logical use of reason.[43] In the *Nicomachean Ethics*, Aristotle gave the following definition of natural justice: "that which is politically just . . . is natural if it has the same power everywhere."[44] Now the natural can be taken out of the equation. Under the foundations of modern politics, all we find is an empty space.

10.4 The Empty Space of Modern Politics

The metaphysics of natural places, and with it the entire logic of correspondence that had structured the political world too, did not survive the fall of the medieval cosmos. As the early modern

conception of the world asserted itself, the "natural" was progressively emptied of content. Nature was cosmologically drained
of qualitative emplacements, of permanent proportions and positions, of fixed trajectories and destinations. Every hierarchy of
being is dissolved in an infinite space that admits no local determinations, a space with no content and no beyond: it is a formless
and meaningless space, a space without exceptions and interruptions, without attributes or depth, the great equalizer of all things
on a single plane of existence.

The cosmological picture that remains – that of the great
equality of being in the empty space of the infinite universe – is
incompatible with the logic of place and the political principles
of harmony and subordination. Modern space extends abstractly,
absolutely indifferent to qualities; any region or point within it is
by principle equal to any other, equally immersed in an infinite
set of possible relations that are devoid of any meaningful, a priori character. No longer harbored in nature or in a metaphysical
beyond, the political world too appears empty of determinations.
If, as Hobbes pictures in the *Leviathan*, all human beings occupy
an equal position in nature, if nothing but sheer force can restrain
their right to dispute over the same things, it is because nothing
essential binds men to any political positions, because no place is
given as proper to them anymore.[45] All the previous distinctions
between them have now lost their ultimate grounding.

This is why the very origin of inequalities needs to be explained
and investigated. Once the world is voided from natural principles
of subordination, every order becomes susceptible of challenge,
and every political form stands in need of justification. To accept
a hierarchy as a pure given, as Rousseau says in the opening of his
Discourse, may be something proper for "slaves in the hearing of
their masters," but is unconceivable for beings who are free and
strive for the understanding of things.[46] Every instance of inequality, consequently, must be explained by history or positive right, by
a decision that must be reversible, by a contingent turn of events.

Metaphysically, every political place is now equal to every other,
like points in an infinite geometrical space: undistinguishable in
their essence, all of them are now reduced to mere positions, "possessing no independent content of their own" apart from the relations that exist between them at any given point in time.[47] Against
the background of a flat, neutral, and empty space, every political
distribution of being has now become inessential too. This means
that it is now a human task to fix the places for things. To determine

such places, we have to take our bearings, but since space has been empty of all bearings, we have no basis for that decision except the decision itself.

The creative explosion of political philosophy that took place in the seventeenth century originates precisely in this metaphysical problem. The rational cosmologies of early modern times deprived the political world of sources of legitimacy for pre-existing hierarchies and principles of order, emptying thereby the very foundation of political society.[48] Behind the assertion of the autonomy and self-referentiality of politics stands the loss of references for a political space that, with its detachment from the natural and the transcendent, has now lost its external principles of determination, a space that has become metaphysically groundless. The philosophy of the social contract, and the metaphysics of power upon which it is built, affirm thus politically what the imagination of an infinite, homogeneous, and ultimately empty space had already done in the rational metaphysics of early modern cosmology: the substitution of the logic of place by an unrestricted ontological equality, which now stands in need of political articulation.

What is empty and open in modern politics, hence, is something like a symbolic logic of association, a way of ordering political relations and modes of being. The empty space of modern politics refers to a set of logical relations which broke up, and then reorganized in a radically different manner, the system of associations and configurations that held fast values and distinctions, orders and ranks, bodies and positions, shaping and ushering thereby the great political revolutions of modernity. Such is the political import of the modern cosmological transition: the philosophy of infinite space carried within it nothing less than the promise of a political liberation which, however, did not cease to fall short almost from the moment of its formulation.

Notes

1. In the *Politics*, Aristotle emphasizes the importance of the choice of the site for the destiny of a city, as Plato does in the *Laws*. "Political work," as Luc Brisson puts it in his analysis of the latter, "is rooted in a physics of motion and change, and it is reflected in a limited set of geometrical dispositions" ("Polis as Kosmos in Plato's Laws", in Phillip Sidney Horky (ed.), *Cosmos in the Ancient World* [Cambridge: Cambridge University Press, 2019], 130). Between *topos* and *polis*, between the natural elements and the political disposition of those elements, there is a tension that will come to be determinant for the fate of each city. This

is very much the same spirit that animates Machiavelli's commentary in the *Discourses* on the importance of the natural location of new cities. For it is not enough to count on a resourceful and well-defensible city; to achieve political excellency, the founders will need to give it a *human form* too: "I maintain, then, that it is more prudent to place a city in a fertile situation, provided its fertility is kept in due bonds by laws. When Alexander the Great was proposing to build a city that should redound to his credit, Deinocrates, the architect, came to him and suggested that he should build it on Mount Athos, for, besides being a strong place, it could be so fashioned as to give the city a human form, which would be a remarkable thing, a rare thing, and worthy of his greatness" (Niccolò Machiavelli, *The Discourses*, ed. Bernard R. Crick [Harmondsworth: Penguin Books, 1970], I.I, 103).

2. "When the job had been completely finished, then the earth, which is their mother, sent them up. And now, as though the land (*chora*) they are in were a mother and a nurturer, they must plan for and defend it, if anyone attacks, and they must think of the other citizens as brothers and born of the earth" (Plato, *The Republic of Plato*, trans. Allan Bloom [New York: Basic Books, 2016], 414e, 94).

3. T. M. Robinson, *Heraclitus: Fragments: A Text and Translation with a Commentary by T. M. Robinson*, vol. 2 (Toronto: University of Toronto Press, 1987), fragment 44, 33.

4. Sophocles, *Antigone*, ed. Paul Woodruff (Indianapolis: Hackett Publishing, 2001), xxvi.

5. See Aristotle's formulation in *Politics*, 1280a32-b34: "But a state exists for the sake of a good life, and not for the sake of life only . . . [it] is not a mere society, having a common place, established for the prevention of mutual crime and for the sake of exchange [but rather] a community of families and aggregations of families in well-being, for the sake of a perfect and self-sufficing life" (*Aristotle's Politics: Writings from the Complete Works: Politics, Economics, Constitution of Athens*, ed. Jonathan Barnes and Melissa Lane [Princeton: Princeton University Press, 2017]). Indeed, the juridical realm of the polis extended well beyond the boundaries of the city, not only to include the agricultural lands of the countryside, but complex structures of political association of different villages living under common laws: "The geographical units of the polis of Athens were demes, villages associated under a common law . . . The Athenian citizen acquired his civic status by virtue of his membership in a deme, a geographical unit generally based on existing villages. The establishment by Cleisthenes of the deme as the constituent unit of the polis was in a critical sense the foundation of the democracy. It created a civic identity abstracted from differences of birth, an identity common to aristocracy and demos, symbolized by the adoption by Athenian citizens of a demotikon, a deme-name, as distinct from (though in practice never replacing, especially in the case

of the aristocracy) the patronymic" (Ellen Meiksins Wood, *Democracy Against Capitalism: Renewing Historical Materialism* [Cambridge: Cambridge University Press, 1995], 218).

6. "The polis, properly speaking, is not the city-state in its physical location; it is the organization of the people as it arises out of acting and speaking together, and its true space lies between people living together for this purpose, no matter where they happen to be" (Hannah Arendt, *The Human Condition* [Chicago: University of Chicago Press, 1958], 198).

7. *The Republic*, 502b, 295.

8. See *Nicomachean Ethics*, 1147a35-b1, 1144a24-26, *De Anima*, 433a29-b13.

9. *Nicomachean Ethics*, 1154b28, 1166b22-24: "the first part pulling in one direction while the second pulls in the opposite . . . as if these parts were trying to break the man apart." While discussing the ethical theory of Plato, Richard Parry notes the "difficulty of talking about parts of the soul." Sometimes, he says, "Socrates uses 'form' (*eidos*) and 'kind' (*genê*) (435b-c), other times a periphrasis such as "that in the soul that calculates" (439d-e). This warning should keep one from thinking of the soul as a committee of independent agents. Perhaps the least misleading way of thinking about the parts is as functions" (Richard Parry, "Ancient Ethical Theory," in *The Stanford Encyclopedia of Philosophy*). However, it is only from the perspective of the whole, of which each part is inseparable, that these kinds can appear as parts.

10. I take this etymological reading from Henry George Liddell and Robert Scott, *A Greek-English Lexicon* [Oxford: Clarendon Press, 1940]). The number and depth of spatial metaphors and references in the *Nicomachean Ethics* is breathtaking. Some of these are organic references, such as the comparison of ethical work with the *ground* that must be labored, cultivated so as to bear the right kind of fruit (1179b17-27). But others present an almost geometrical – and even, perspectival – reading of human relations. In each of its polyhedral faces, for instance, virtue constitutes a "mean" or an "intermediate state" between excess and deficiency. The mean is not only relative to us, but varies even for the same person according to the *specific position* that she occupies at each moment ("what is fitting, then, is relative to the position of a man and to the circumstances and to the object" 1122a24-26). Virtue is hence a matter of perspective: the good man acts by constantly "keeping an eye on the mean and working towards it"; he deliberates and calculates distances and proximities; he is like the archers "who have a mark to aim at" (1106b9, 1094a25). Of course, in the spur of the moment it is not hard to miss that moving mark, and one can easily lean too much in the "direction" of excess or in that of deficiency (1109b23-26). But we cannot state once and for all how much a man must "deviate" in order

to be censured for his actions: the "limits" and the "extent" of blame also depend on individual situations (1126a32-b5, 1109b17-23).

11. "What exists by nature is unchangeable and has the same power everywhere, like fire, which burns here as in Persia" (*Nicomachean Ethics*, 1134b26-8).

12. The investigation of the order of the city in analogy to the soul and the cosmos is in a sense the main object of *The Republic* and *The Laws*.

13. Already in Herodotus's *Histories*, the different political regimes are presented as a function of the relations between the parts that compose the polis (see *Herodotus*, trans. A. D. Godley [Cambridge: Harvard University Press, 1920], book 3, ch. 80ff). Whichever is the "authoritative" element in a *polis* – be it the multitude, the wealthy, the best men, or a single individual – determines the character of the political community and the kind of city that each polis is (*Politics*, 1278b8ff, 1281a11ff). What order is best will be conditioned in each case by the specific character and the practical needs of a particular city, although there are forms of order that are best for the whole as such: those forms, which are more complex and balanced, result from a combination of authoritative elements, where the care of each of those parts is "inseparable from the care of the whole" (*Politics*, 1288a35ff, 1337a29-30).

14. *Politics*, 1283b42–1284a1. For an interpretation of the "democratic disorder" of positions, see C. L. R. James, *Every Cook Can Govern* (Oakland: PM Press, 2010,) 142.

15. *The Republic*, 442c.

16. See *Politics*, 1280a32ff, 1254b13. On the relation between *logos* and political capacities see Jacques Rancière, *Disagreement: Politics and Philosophy* (University of Minnesota Press, 1999), 22–6.

17. "The citizens must not lead the life of artisans or tradesmen, for such a life is ignoble and inimical to excellence. Neither must they be farmers, since leisure is necessary both for the development of excellence and the performance of political duties" (*Politics*, 1328b39–1329a1). Aristotle's remarks echo Plato's statement in the *Laws*, where he claims that the rulers need to conduct "ordered ways of life," which "leave them no pressing work to do, no genuinely appropriate occupation" (*Laws*, 806d7–807a5, cited in Brisson, "Polis as Kosmos in Plato's Laws," 136). Of course, those who work are essential for the polis: they provide it with all the resources that the city needs in order to survive and thrive. But precisely as such, they are to be excluded from political participation; what is proper to them is not politics but labor. This is the "division between those who rule and those who labour, between those who work with their minds and those who work with their bodies, between those who rule and are fed and those who produce food and are ruled," which Ellen Meiksins Wood, illustrates through a passage by the Chinese

philosopher Mencius: "Why then should you think . . . that someone who is carrying on the government of a kingdom has time also to till the soil? The truth is that some kinds of business are proper to the great and others to the small. Even supposing each man could unite in himself all the various kinds of skill required in every craft, if he had to make for himself everything that he used, this would merely lead to everyone being completely prostrate with fatigue. True indeed is the saying "Some work with their minds, others with their bodies. Those who work with their minds rule, while those who work with their bodies are ruled. Those who are ruled produce food; those who rule are fed" (*Democracy Against Capitalism: Renewing Historical Materialism*, 189–95).

18. Again, the distinction between producers, auxiliaries, and rulers, and the allocation of individual beings to each of the three categories, is to be justified through a story – one that makes each of the classes correspond to the three kinds of souls that populate the city (*The Republic*, 415a-d). As Socrates puts it, the fact that "the shoemaker by nature rightly practices shoemaking and does nothing else, and the carpenter practices carpentry, and so on for the rest" turns out to be "a kind of image of justice" (*The Republic*, 443c).

19. *The Republic*, 443d–444a.

20. The comparison between justice and health (or rather, between injustice and disease) happens at a crucial point of the *Republic* where Socrates is finally ready to define justice as the pursuit of the "proper business" of each of the elements of the whole. There, he portrays injustice as "a power such that, wherever it comes into being, be it in a city, a clan, an army, or whatever else, it first of all makes that thing unable to accomplish anything together with itself due to the faction and difference, and then it makes that thing an enemy both to itself and to everything opposite and to the just" (*The Republic*, 351b-a). In the *Laws*, the Athenian Stranger also sets the avoidance of "civil strife" and "internal war" as the first task for "him who brings the state into harmony" by "ordering its life" (*Laws* 628ab, in *Plato in Twelve Volumes* [Cambridge: Harvard University Press, 1967], vol. 11).

21. Cicero, *De re publica*, II.69, in *The Republic and The Laws*, ed. Jonathan Powell, trans. Niall Rudd (Oxford: Oxford University Press, 2009), 58. Scipio's previous sentence expresses the political logic of place with succinct clarity: "Just as with string instruments or pipes or in singers' voices a certain harmony of different sounds must be maintained (and trained ears cannot bear the effect if that harmony is thrown out or becomes discordant), and as that harmony, though arising from the management of very different notes, produces a pleasing and agreeable sound, so a state, by adjusting the proportions between the highest, lowest, and intermediate classes, as if they were musical notes, achieves harmony" (ibid.).

22. "Law in the proper sense is right reason *in harmony with nature.* It is spread through the whole human community, unchanging and eternal, calling people to their duty by its commands and deterring them from wrong-doing by its prohibitions" (Cicero, *De re publica,* 3.33, 69, my emphasis). In *De Legibus,* the law is defined as "the highest reason, inherent in nature, which enjoins what ought to be done and forbids the opposite" (1.18-9, 104). Later in that same passage, Cicero defines again the law as "a force of nature, the intelligence and reason of a wise man, and the criterion of justice and injustice" (ibid.).

23. The expression comes from the moral letters of Seneca: "For this reason, Lucilius, let us keep to the way which Nature has mapped out for us, and let us not swerve therefrom. If we follow Nature, all is easy and unobstructed; but if we combat Nature, our life differs not a whit from that of men who row against the current. Farewell." (Lucius Annaeus Seneca, *Moral Letters to Lucilius: Epistulae Morales Ad Lucilium,* trans. Richard Mott Gummere [Studium Publishing, 2018], letter 122, 19). According to the *Digest* of Roman law, there are a number of things that "nature teaches all animals, including human beings," a formula being used by Ulpian in the third century precisely to define natural law (see Ken Pennington, "Lex Naturalis and Jus Naturale," *The Jurist: Studies in Church Law and Ministry* 68, no. 2 (2008): 569–91).

24. Isidore's definition in the "Treatise of Laws" was then recuperated in the *Decretum Gratiani,* a compilation of canon law from the twelfth century that would be extremely influential in the development of modern European law (in the *Divina Commedia,* Dante includes Gratian among the circle of Doctors of the Church that surround Thomas Aquinas).

25. According to Aquinas, the principles of nature are "naturally known" by human beings: they are "impressed on [us] by nature," as "general rules and measures of all things relating to human conduct, whereof the natural reason is the rule and measure, although it is not the measure of things that are from nature" (*Summa Theologiae,* question 91, article 3, "Whether there is a human law," reply to objection 2). Since we have no "proper knowledge of each single truth," however, civil law and the law of nations, which are derived from the *ius naturale,* often find great difficulties in translating and adapting its precepts; sometimes, they even restrain or even enter in open contradiction with the mandates of nature, as shown for instance by the great theological debates on slavery, the rights of the heathen or the regimes of property.

26. This is the complete passage from *Enneads* III.2.11: "No, but the rational forming principle makes all these things as their sovereign, and wishes them to be as they are, and makes the things which are called bad according to reason, because it does not wish that all

should be good, just like a craftsman who does not make everything eyes in his picture; in the same way the formative principle did not make everything gods but some gods, some spirits (a nature of the second rank), then men and animals after them in order, not out of grudging meanness but by a reason containing all the rich variety of the intelligible world. But we are like people who know nothing about the art of painting and criticise the painter because the colours are not beautiful everywhere, though he has really distributed the appropriate colours to every place; *and cities are not composed of citizens with equal rights, even those which have good laws and constitutions*; or we are like someone who censures a play because all the characters in it are not heroes but there is a servant and a yokel who speaks in a vulgar way; but the play is not a good one if one expels the inferior characters, because they too help to complete it" (*Enneads, Volume III*, 1967, 79–80, cited in Lovejoy, *The Great Chain of Being*, 64–5, my emphasis). In *Enneads* III.3.3, Plotinus states the principle of inequality as pertaining to the very essence of the scale of nature: "Is this then so, because the creator measured them out with the deliberate intention that all things ought not to be equal? Not at all; but it was according to nature for things to come about so" (ibid., 119).

27. Augustine, *The City of God* (New York: Modern Library, 1993), XIX.13, 690. This chapter of the *City of God*, which bears a remarkable title, begins with a synthesis of the organic logic through which nature imposes in all things the order of position and place: "The peace of the body then consists in the duly proportioned arrangement of its parts . . . Peace between man and man is the well-ordered concord. Domestic peace is the well-ordered concord between those of the family who rule and those who obey. Civil peace is a similar concord among the citizens" ("Of the universal peace which the law of nature preserves through all disturbances, and by which every one reaches his desert in a way regulated by the just Judge" [ibid.]).

28. This principle had found perhaps its clearest exposition in Cicero: "Do we not perceive that whatever is best has been granted domination by nature herself, to the great advantage of the weak? Why else does God rule over man, mind over body, reason over desire, anger, and the other wicked elements in the same soul?" (*De re publica*, 3.36, 71).

29. On the political extension of the Pauline metaphor of Jesus Christ as the "head of the Church" and of the faithful as his body (*Ephesians* 1:22–23), see Stephen H. Rigby, "The Body Politic in the Social and Political Thought of Christine de Pizan. Reciprocity, Hierarchy and Political Authority": "this metaphor was then developed by early Christian writers such as Ambrose and Isidore of Seville, by public documents and theological works of the Carolingian period, and by eleventh- and

twelfth-century writers such as Honorius Augustodunensis and Hugh of St Victor. It continued to be used in the later middle ages, even after it had also started to be applied to particular political communities such as kingdoms or cities ... In using the human body as a model of how society should be organized, medieval philosophers such as John of Salisbury and Giles of Rome were adopting the traditional Platonic and Stoic conception of nature as a model of how a divinely-ordained and rational order is constituted and as a pattern for how human virtue should be exercised." Quoting Pierre Manent, Bernard Flynn sustains that in the expression "body politic," the "body" did not work simply as a metaphor: "How better to define the pre-modern order? If one were to look for one synthetic trait that would characterize pre-modernity, it would be defined as an order founded on filiation. Everyone's place was in principle determined by her or his birth; both one's name and one's estate were determined through inheritance. In this society there were only families, poor or rich, common or noble, and each was governed by the "head of the family" ... Western pre-modern society had no public space in the ancient sense; rather, what was considered to be public was the family, which meant that the logic of filiation and paternity, that the same representation of human ties and bonds, circulated throughout the whole society" (Bernard Flynn, *The Philosophy of Claude Lefort: Interpreting the Political* [Evanston: Northwestern University Press, 2006], xxiii–xxiv). See also the description of the political chain of feudal power in Perry Anderson: "The liege lord in his turn would often be the vassal of a feudal superior, and the chain of such dependent tenures linked to military service would extend upwards to the highest peak of the system – in most cases, a monarch – of whom all land could in the ultimate instance be in principle the eminent domain. Typical intermediary links of such a feudal hierarchy in the early mediaeval epoch, between simple lordship and suzerain monarchy, were the castellany, barony, county or principality. The consequence of such a system was that political sovereignty was never focused in a single centre" (Perry Anderson, *Passages from Antiquity to Feudalism* [London: Verso, 1978], 148).

30. A common point to the critique of democracies was precisely the charge that they produced states of chaos and disorder that were conducive to tyranny or, even worse, to anarchy, to the absence of any principle or order. The "mobs" install a government of excesses and disproportion, which makes violence to the natural order of things and does not fail to produce civil discord and the degeneration of public virtue. See for instance the discourse by Megabyzus reproduced in Herodotus's *Histories*: "the tyrant, in all his doings, at least knows what is he about, but a mob is altogether devoid of knowledge; for how should there be any knowledge in a rabble, untaught, and with no natural sense of what is right and fit? It rushes wildly

into state affairs with all the fury of a stream swollen in the winter, and confuses everything" (*Histories* 3,1 cited in Jorge Tamames, *For the People: Left Populism in Spain and the US* [London: Lawrence and Wishart, 2020], 9).

31. As Christian theologians had explained, it is the norm that creates the transgression; being defined by the norm, transgression only reinforces the norm: "And where there is no law there is no transgression" (*Romans* 4:15).

32. Étienne de La Boétie, *De La Servitude Volontaire*, in *The Politics of Obedience* (Montreal: Black Rose Books, 2007), 112.

33. On the problem of the will as a decisive marker of political modernity, see Yirmiyahu Yovel, *Kant and the Philosophy of History* (Princeton: Princeton University Press, 1980).

34. In the *Digest* of Roman law figure already some antecedent expressions of the doctrines of popular sovereignty and the right of disobedience to unjust laws and political authorities, which was expressed, among others, by Marsilius of Padua, Thomas Aquinas, and Francisco Suárez. Likewise, the *Digest* included an affirmation that "all persons are born free," a fact expressed by Isidore of Seville under the formula of the "one liberty of all" that was to be included in the *Decretum Gratiani* (see Paul Vincent Spade, "Medieval Political Philosophy," Stanford Encyclopedia of Philosophy, note 24). Suárez would consequently affirm, in a gesture prefigurative of social contract theories, that "man is by his nature free and subject to no one, save only to the Creator" (Suárez, *De Legibus ac Deo Legislatore*, in *Opera Omnia*, vol. 5 [Paris: Bibliopolam Editorem, 1856], 176; cited in Ivone Moreira, "Suárez in Eighteenth Century British political thought. Burke's political thought and Suárez's inheritance", *CAURIENSIA. Revista anual de Ciencias Eclesiásticas* 13, 480). La Boétie's statement of a "world governed by a nature which is reasonable" deserves to be quoted in full, for even as he defends the existence of a natural order of reason, that order implies that even beasts can undo the fact of their subordination and be *placed* in the pulpit of the defense of freedom: "Therefore it is fruitless to argue whether or not liberty is natural, since none can be held in slavery without being wronged, and in a world governed by a nature, which is reasonable, there is nothing so contrary as an injustice. Since freedom is our natural state, we are not only in possession of it but have the urge to defend it. Now, if perchance some cast a doubt on this conclusion and are so corrupted that they are not able to recognize their rights and inborn tendencies, I shall have to do them the honor that is properly theirs and *place, so to speak, brute beasts in the pulpit to throw light on their nature and condition*. The very beasts, God help me! if men are not too deaf, cry out to them, Long live Liberty!" (*De la Servitude Volontaire*, 120–1, my emphasis).

35. "Can that be called a happy life? Can it be called living? Is there anything more intolerable than that situation, I won't say for a man of mettle nor even for a man of high birth, but simply for a man of common sense or, to go even further, *for anyone having the face of a man*? What condition is more wretched than to live thus, with nothing to call one's own, receiving from someone else one's sustenance, one's power to act, one's body, one's very life?" (*De la Servitude Volontaire*, 142, my emphasis).

36. Blandine Kriegel, *The State and the Rule of Law* (Princeton: Princeton University Press, 1995), 57.

37. "With [Machiavelli], we are told, a new political discourse is inaugurated, not a reflection on the essence of a good regime or the art of government, but a discourse that aims at politics as such, circumscribing its domain and detaching politics from metaphysics and theology" (Farhang Erfani, "Fixing Marx with Machiavelli: Claude Lefort's Democratic Turn," *Journal of the British Society for Phenomenology* 39, no. 2 (2008), 202). See also Carlo Galli's detailed analysis of how politics for Machiavelli already "takes place in a space that is neither ordered nor qualified by natural characteristics" (Carlo Galli, *Political Spaces and Global War* [Minneapolis: University of Minnesota Press, 2010], 21).

38. Thomas Hobbes, *Behemoth; or, The Long Parliament* (New York: Barnes and Noble, 1969), 16. While distancing himself from Hobbes's theory of the irreversibility and absoluteness of the transfer of powers to the sovereign, Spinoza expresses the same logic in a famous passage from his letters: "the sovereign power in a State has right over a subject only in proportion to the excess of its power over that of a subject" (*Letters*, V, cited in Étienne Balibar, *Spinoza and Politics* [New York: Verso, 1998], 104).

39. For an analysis of the Hobbesian (and then Schmittian) claim that "Autoritas, non veritas, facit legem," see Laila Yousef Sandoval, "Carl Schmitt y la Evolución del "Ius publicum europaeum": interpretación y crítica desde las nuevas epistemologías de las relaciones internacionales", PhD diss., Madrid, Universidad Complutense de Madrid, 2018, 162.

40. "NATURE (the Art whereby God hath made and governes the World) is by the *Art* of man, as in many other things, so in this also imitated, that it can make an Artificial Animal," Thomas Hobbes, *Leviathan*, ed. Richard Tuck (Cambridge: Cambridge University Press, 1996), 9.

41. "And thus much for the ill condition in which *man by mere nature is actually placed in*, though with a possibility to come out of it, partly because of our passions, partly because of our reason," 13 (*Leviathan*, XIII, 90, my emphasis).

42. *Prolegomena*, §16, cited in Jon Miller, "Hugo Grotius," in *The Stanford Encyclopedia of Philosophy* (2005). See also: "The law of nature

is a dictate of right reason, which points out that an act, according as it is or is not in conformity with rational nature, has in it a quality of moral baseness or moral necessity; and that, in consequence, such an act is either forbidden or enjoined" (ibid. I.1.10.1).

43. For an elaboration of the Straussian argument on the "effacement of nature by history," see Flynn, *The Philosophy of Claude Lefort*, xv. Later in the book, Flynn suggestively describes the early modern political dilemma as the experience of the "dissolution of the classical, as well as the Christian, onto-theological markers of certainty" and the encounter of "a certain void in the very place where the ancient discourses rested upon a divine or a natural order" (ibid., 12–14).

44. *Nicomachean Ethics*, 1134b19-20.

45. See *Leviathan*, chapters XIII–XXI.

46. "Still less can one inquire if there would not be some essential link between the two inequalities; for that would be asking, in other terms, whether those who command are necessarily worth more than those who obey ... a question perhaps good for Slaves to discuss in the hearing of their Masters, but not suitable for reasonable and free Men who seek the truth" (Jean-Jacques Rousseau, *Discourse on the Origins of Inequality (Second Discourse); Polemics; and Political Economy* [Hanover: University Press of New England, 1992], 18).

47. The sentence is from Cassirer's description of modern space, which has fascinating political undertones: "The ultimate basis for the homogeneity of geometric space is that all its elements, the "points" which are joined in it, are mere determinations of position, possessing no independent content of their own outside of this relation, this position that they occupy in relation to each other. Their reality is exhausted in their reciprocal relation: it is a purely functional and not a substantial reality. Because fundamentally these points are devoid of all content, because they have become mere expressions of ideal relations, they can rise no question of a diversity of content. Their homogeneity signifies nothing other than this similarity of structure, grounded in their common logical function, their common ideal purpose and meaning" (Ernst Cassirer, *Philosophie der Symbolischen Formen, Vol. 2: Das mythische Denken*, cited in Panofsky, *Perspective as Symbolic Form*, 30, 77). Indeed, it is interesting to compare this account with Carlo Galli's description of the connection between spatiality and political equality in the *Leviathan*: "The radical assumption Hobbes makes, through his embrace of materialistic atomism, is that natural space is "empty" and not open to any "beyond" relative to itself – and this, of course, implies that space has no quality. Because every stereometric, organic, and qualitative structure of space is alien to Hobbes, so too does he refuse every natural hierarchy among men, deny that Justice exists in nature as an Order of Being, or accept the notion that it is possible to "*unicuique*

suu, tribuere" ("to give each his due")" (Carlo Galli, *Political Spaces and Global War*, 27). See also James's definition in the *Principles of Psychology*: "Each point, so far as it is placed, is then only by virtue of what it is not, namely, by virtue of another point" (William James, *The Principles of Psychology* [New York: Holt, 1907], 154).

48. In his compelling study of the relation between democracy and relativism, Carlo Invernizzi Accetti identifies in the denaturalization of the political the origin of an epistemological problem that has haunted the democratic *ethos* until our very days. In pre-modern societies, in fact, "a hierarchical order of authority was assumed to be implicit in the natural order of things, and this prevented the question concerning the foundations for its legitimacy from being raised in a politically meaningful manner"; political modernity can be understood as the substitution of that order for "a conception of freedom that is ultimately 'empty,' in the sense that it does not contain any necessary reference to a substantive conception of truth or justice" (Carlo Invernizzi Accetti, *Relativism and Religion: Why Democratic Societies Do Not Need Moral Absolutes* [New York: Columbia University Press, 2015], 10ff).

Chapter 11

Political Universals

The radical opening of the world, and the ontological gap that it installed at the heart of modern political society, became the source of a tension of which our politics still bears the marks. The fundamental dynamic of political modernity, in fact, can be read as the interplay of forces striving to keep open and close back the emptiness that now lies beneath political institutions. On one pole of that tension is the presentation of freedom and equality as the absence of metaphysical determinations, that is, as a *political experience of the void* which seeks to actualize itself by negating all given forms of social subordination. On the other pole stands an *abstract political logic*, which saturates that void by projecting upon it the positive, rational vectors of a universalist political geometry. The empty space of modern politics becomes thus the site of a political struggle: it harbors quite naturally a general promise of emancipation, but also the immediate sublation of that promise through an implacable physics of power. This inner ambivalence, this dialectical tension between the opening and the closure of the political void, is from this perspective the very object of the political philosophy of universalism.

11.1 Closure of the Void: Space in the State of Nature

In the seventeenth century, speculations about the nature of space often included a logical experiment consisting in nothing less than the destruction of the world.[1] The general form of that experiment consisted in imagining what would remain of the world if God decided to annihilate everything that existed in it; as we have seen,

Gassendi used this very formulation as a means to assert the physical existence of the void. Similarly, Hobbes writes in *De Corpore* that "In the teaching of natural philosophy, I cannot begin better (as I have already shewn) than from *privation*; that is, from feigning the world to be annihilated."[2] The hypothetical annihilation of what appears as given becomes therefore a logical and philosophical tool to investigate the fundamental structure of the world. But this method was not restricted to metaphysics and natural philosophy; the study of politics too became the object of such radical gestures of suspension of what exists. To "begin from privation," that is, from feigning the disappearance of the concrete materiality of the world as it is known, is arguably the logical structure of the classical genre of political utopias, which knew an impressive revival among Renaissance and early modern political philosophers. Like in the logical experiments of a world emptied of its contents, the political nowheres of More's Amaurot, of the City of the Sun of Campanella, of Bacon's New Atlantis, offer insight and foresight on the fundamental principles of politics precisely because they allow for the suspension and removal of all aspects of the political as it is historically given. Those are the conditions under which an investigation of the foundations of society (but also the ironical detachment from it, or the horizon of an ideal political community) become available to the critical spirit: once the contents of the political world have been removed, and we find before ourselves a sort of blank political space.[3]

The non-places of utopias are not very far from another rhetorical device that would be even more determining for the philosophical fate of modern politics. In the scenes of the state of nature, we become witnesses of a similar gesture: it is precisely the emptying of the political world, the "feigned" removal of its concrete and historical contents, that allows us to deduce its fundamental structure, and hence to discern the necessary principles of political society. Here too, the voiding of the political world is what allows us to legislate about its content. To that empty space we give then the name of "nature": only there, in a space that is apparently devoid of given determinations, can the scene acquire its full constitutional force.

In its archetypal form, the philosophical scene of the state of nature does not appear to have spatio-temporal coordinates. The scene allegedly happens in a time that is pre-political, prior to association, as an origin or a beginning that is not in history but purely logical (and indeed, at stake is precisely a logical investigation, in the sense that its end-result is a political logic). Strictly speaking, it is also a scene that happens nowhere, in no identifiable concrete place. Precisely at a time when cartography aimed at rendering the world with renewed geometrical precision, the state of nature has no particular location, no specific thereness, for it describes not a place but a condition, the kind of life that men would have, in every possible time and place, if they lived without common institutions. Happening nowhere, its effects hold thus everywhere; its placelessness begets a sort of universal political rationality.

This is the spatial paradox of the state of nature. The state of nature is a place of indetermination, and yet it is the very point from which the logical vectors of the modern state (including the principles of sovereignty, citizenship and representation) are politically determined. In the absence of a law, we assist to the setting of the law for all political places: what is predicated upon the state of nature should obtain in principle everywhere, in every political locus. Like in infinite space, every political point is now equal to any other. Every point, that is, except the one corresponding to the scene itself, which works as a site of founding and projection, something like the Archimedean point that Descartes required to ground the entire edifice of knowledge.[4] The state of nature is the leaning point of the political logic of universalism, the non-place that determines the distribution of political places for times and places to come.

From that leaning point, the emptiness of the world is politically determined almost with the same gesture that had opened it. Voided of teleological and substantive content, nature is now even more rigidly structured by form – by the predication of abstract principles endowed with universal value.[5] The same ontological operation that empties the world of all essential differentiations, affirming thereby the negative equality of human beings, immediately closes that opening upon itself, legislating upon it with binding and irrevocable principles. The emptiness of space is not politically void: it represents, on the contrary, the affirmation of an unprecedented force of law, the capacity to determine again, through the methodical mechanisms of abstract rationality, the universal form and structure of the political world.

11.2 The Logic of Projection: Space and Universality

Anticipating some of the criticisms that his account of the origin of the state could encounter, Hobbes says that the "greatest objection" that could be raised against his reasoning is one of "practice."[6] For people may react asking precisely "where and when" this original contract was established, and seeing that the scene described has no concrete time and place, they might as well conclude that there was never such condition, that the agreement never took place, and hence that they are not bound in any way to its obedience.

Confronted with this mighty objection, Hobbes argues two different things, which may appear at first difficult to reconcile. Even though the state of nature was probably never a general condition all over the world, he says first, it is possible to get glimpses of it wherever states do not yet exist (as in the "many places of America" where the "savage people" live without a common power), or where they exist no longer, because they have collapsed under the strain of civil war.[7] This seems to be Hobbes's answer to the empirical question of the "where and when": although we cannot see the state of nature as such, we do see traces of its origins and its effects. Whenever there is a dissonance in the temporality of politics, wherever the political condition is undeveloped, delayed or interrupted, the state of nature emerges as a possibility ready to be actualized, at once a reminder of our political origin and a threatening specter about what may lie ahead.

The second answer that Hobbes gives is even more intriguing. For now he despises a merely "practical" approach to the understanding of politics, as if asking for visible, material instantiations of the logic of the state was a naïve and completely insufficient approach. The entire political history of mankind may for that matter be but a trifling succession of ignorance and mistakes; in a sense, that is irrelevant to the issue at stake. It so happens, Hobbes argues, that the "skill of making and maintaining Commonwealths" does not consist of practice only, but of certain rules, "as doth arithmetic and geometry," which can be methodically found out with the help of reason even if they have not been so in the past.[8] In other words, his account of the logic of the state holds not despite, but precisely due to its logical and abstract character. The detachment from the concrete, from the details of history and geography, does not detract from its validity; on the contrary, it only adds to it, for it now makes it universal.

Thus, Hobbes's second answer leaves the empirical realm of proof and observation and turns politics into an object of abstraction. Politics has a rational logic, endowed with principles and rules, which holds for human affairs generally, independently of any concrete place or moment in time. The objection of practice is thus nullified, and the question of the "when and where" becomes all but insignificant: like it happens in arithmetic and geometry, what is found through the correct use of the method of investigation must be taken to hold everywhere and at every particular time.

The state of nature appears thus as a scene of universal predication. Provided the logic is applied well, what is obtained from that scene will now be taken to hold equally in all times and places; what "derives" from the state of nature, to use the formula that Kant will employ in his essay on perpetual peace, must be taken as the original basis for every political constitution.[9] Since a rational matrix informs politics according to the same principles in every concrete political locality, the political principles that are thus produced can be projected universally, from the "nowhere" of nature to every "there" in the political world. From the state of nature, those fundamental principles of reason can now be projected upon the entire world, as a sort of universal political legislation.[10]

A second form of spatiality is hence presupposed by the universality of political reason. The state of nature requires in fact something like a smooth surface of projection, a domain of uninterrupted regularity that will receive and sustain its mandates without exceptions and inconsistencies. In that universal space, whatever obtains politically in a given place must now also obtain, in principle, everywhere else.[11] The political space is thus presumed as a space of rational sameness and continuity, a space of continuous coherence that, like the principles of reason, admits of no fractures or disruptions. This is the latent spatiality that is implied by the state of nature: a form of homogenous emptiness, equally affected in all of its points by the same principles and rules, which at once presupposes and guarantees the universality of political principles.[12] Reduced to a medium of abstract coherence, space gives ground to the universal projections of contractualism. But for that, every form of spatial difference must be first silenced and repressed. The ontological neutrality of space unifies the world and, in the same gesture, makes its content disappear.

11.3 Colonial Geometries

In the *Metaphysics of Morals*, Kant boldly affirms that political communities are a necessary consequence of our existence on the Earth. Being a sphere, our planet "unites all the places on its surface", so that men cannot "disperse infinitely" and are forced to coexist with one another.[13] The single plane of the Earth makes it so that men cannot avoid living side by side, for no land is remote enough to be out of reach for human beings. From this fact derives the essential postulate of public right: "when you cannot avoid living side by side with all others, you ought to leave the state of nature and proceed with them into a rightful condition, that is, a condition of distributive justice."[14] The physical space of the world, hence, makes it so that no local specificity can ultimately override the universal norms of reason. But exactly as the unity of the globe forces us to enter into a political condition, we must conclude from it that there is no outside either for political norms, no political places that would not fall under their domain. If that was not the case, if an exception was to be declared, there would ultimately be no way to circumscribe its effects. The entirety of political space would become vulnerable, and potentially at least, no place would go unaffected. Both in its positive and negative forms, hence, the Kantian argument unifies the world in a single political space under the guidance of reason. That space is marked by a strict form of continuity, being governed everywhere by the same principles and rules. Any potential for disruption is ultimately effaced in the uninterrupted regularity of space. The unity of the globe is politically formalized in a notion of political spatiality for which there is no exception.

The logic of such space, however, is marked a fundamental political ambivalence. On the one hand, the univocity of political space is what sustains the modern cosmopolitan horizon – upon which depends the possibility of a universal community of equals, a shared experience of the world according to a single set of principles and norms, and the idea of political temporality as progress in relation to that horizon. These three vectors of political universalism, which converge in the modern idea of emancipation, find in space a common necessary condition.[15] Space gives the factum of interconnection, space gathers and unifies, it synthesizes what is particular, and thus grants the very possibility of a common cosmopolitan experience.

But on the other hand, such space is far from being politically indifferent. To begin with, there is what we may call an empirical problem: the very unity of the globe, which allows for the commonality of political experience, is also what presents space as the object of a struggle, as an incessant fight for separation, for territory and control. Logically, such a premise can be synthesized in a simple statement: an infinite space cannot be conquered, but a globe can. This is the fundamental paradox carried by the political universality of space: an entire geometry of power is predicated upon its premises, projecting the specter of European rationality over the entire surface of the globe.

Europe poses itself as the center of a world without centers, as the legislating agent in which the world becomes aware of its own coherence, of its own existence *as one*.[16] Everything else dissipates under a single political horizon; all parallels, "in whatever direction they lie," now have a common vanishing point.[17] All the places of the Earth, and the peoples who inhabit them, become objects of legislation; the planet itself appears as vast stretch of *terra nullus*, a smooth, blank surface that the colonizer crosses to find the "to-be-colonized simply 'there.'"[18] The seas, as Grotius passionately argued in his *Mare Liberum*, are now declared to be free, and hence open to all; the lands are presumed empty, available and ready for possession. Devoid of qualities, ruptures or folds, space just lies there, isotropic and indifferent, as the passive surface of a universal projection. For that, any particularity or specificity must be made insignificant, dissolved into a space that can be measured and cartographed from afar: borders are traced and retraced upon an abstract coordinate system; straight lines, parallels and meridians, are drawn from scratch over a pristine, geometrized plane.[19] All political places disappear in the colonial imagination of a unified and indistinct space.

There is something in the colony, however, which resists its own disappearance and makes such closure impossible. To the contemporaries of Hobbes, the colonies appear as a form of asynchrony, a form of presence of the past in the present (in a peculiar temporal paradox, the New World refers to an original innocence, or a primitive stage of development, long lost to the European imagination, and thus becomes in a sense also much older than it). But the colony is also the place of an irreducible spatial exteriority, a form of alterity that cannot be simply subsumed under the smooth homogeneity of universal space. The colony, in fact, remains a sort of constitutive exterior, where the order of public law is affirmed precisely through its suspension, so that European states confront one another beyond the realm of the law: even in the eyes of the legislator, the political homogenization of space can never be final and complete.[20] But the colony also defies such homogenization from within: inside its territory, a strict logic of place must be reinstated by the colonizer granting unequal rights to unequal subjects, and hence forms of political subjection that are incompatible with the presumed universality of the modern principles of liberty and equality.[21] The place of the colonized must be strictly delimited again, and the open space of universality, walled to prevent their incursions. The colony remains a segmented political space, a place of exception that resists its absorption into the smooth, unified space of political universalism.

The colony hence becomes a marker of a fundamental contradiction inscribed at the heart of the modern political project. In the colony, the multiple attempts to unify the rational domain of the political – a space liberated from any external determination, where freedom and equality were to be structured, *via* the mechanisms of the social contract, by the universal principles of reason – become inseparable from their own negation. Such is the contradiction between the metaphysical opening of the world and the physics of power that animates modern politics. The colonial geometry of universalism shows that the "empty ontology" of modern space was never in fact politically void.

11.4 Political Mechanicism: The Physics of Power

The empty space of abstract universalism is not only negated externally by the geometry of colonialism: it is also internally broken by its own logic. To get a grip on the world, to govern the empty space of modern politics, the political geometry of abstract universalism relies in fact on a physics of power which neutralizes its own cosmopolitan ambitions, and annuls the attempt at projecting a structure of purposiveness upon an empty political background.

Indeed, the early modern philosophy of the state shares a metaphysics and an epistemology with the new science: both require a world empty of transcendence, without inherent values or meanings; a world of measurable and commensurable quantities, of rational proportions and relations. The European state is thus composed of individual bodies like an object is composed of particles and atoms; political relations depend on the interaction of forces and masses, which proceed with mechanical regularity; power consists in the capacity to move and to force others to move, to the point that words such as "freedom" or "liberty" are abused if applied to anything other than motions and their impediments.[22] The body politic is said to be in that respect indistinguishable from other physical bodies; like every other natural mechanism, including the great machine that is the world itself, the state too is presented as a self-moving engine.[23] Political sovereignty, the "artificial soul" of that machine, is nothing but the spring of its motion; as such, it is the essential *given* of a general political mechanics, but also, as we shall see, the source of its internal contradiction.

Above all, sovereignty maps onto of a physics of extension. There is a foundational relation between sovereignty and spatiality, which makes of the exclusive dominion over a territory a *sine qua non* condition of statehood.[24] Behind this clause of exclusive territoriality is the principle according to which two bodies (we might add, two sovereign bodies) cannot occupy the same region of space at the same time.[25] The territory is hence conceived according to a rigid, two-dimensional system of relations inside/outside: the Westphalian system of international law is essentially a Cartesian framework in which the body politic is spatially determined, defined by geometrical lines against the background of an assumedly neutral and indifferent space.

Within that framework, the boundaries of sovereignty define the ream of applicability of law and the reach and capacity of each state. Boundaries are in that respect both linear and absolute: crossing them implies to become subject to another's dominion.[26] The inside of sovereignty is thus clearly distinct from its outside, where states relate to one another as ontological equals co-existing on a common horizontal plane, which is governed by norms and laws of an abstract and rational character. There is no longer a transcendent order to adapt to; there are no principles or qualities that could dictate an order of positions, a hierarchy or an asymmetry between states. The monist aspirations of universal empires, of the *Respublica Christiana* and the existential wars of religion, must give way to a complex physics of actions and reactions, in which every relation is premised upon both the commensurability and the independence of its members.[27]

The international society of states is hence driven by a sort of political mechanics, a dynamic equilibrium whereby "every weight in the political mass [finds] somewhere a counter-weight."[28] In the Westphalian political space, power is no longer an object but a mechanical relation: power is a logic of engagement, a permanent dynamic of material confrontations and exchanges between individual bodies, which takes place against the background of a neutral space governed by objective laws. However, this political logic is also the source of an internal contradiction. For the same political mechanics that sustain the Westphalian system of public law seem to be at play within European states too. States are not only engaged with from the outside: they are also the object of internal pressures, of an interplay of political forces that challenge the givenness of sovereignty and call into question its absolute character and vocation. The closure of the political void encounters here a second form of resistance: the same physics of power that consecrates the absolute sovereignty of the state threatens at the same time to bring it down.

Notes

1. The origins of this gesture can be traced back to the Middle Ages, when scholastic theologians would employ them as a means to investigate not only metaphysical questions, but also matters pertaining to natural philosophy. But forms of this experiment were already present in classical physics and philosophy. See for instance this passage from Sextus Empiricus: "And even if, in imagination, we abolish all things, the place wherein all things were will not be abolished, but remains possessing its three dimensions – length, depth, breadth, – but without solidity; for this is an attribute peculiar to body" (Sextus Empiricus, *Against Physicists*, trans. R. G. Bury [Cambridge: Harvard University Press, 1936], II.12, 217). For the relevance of this experiment in Gassendi, see section 6.1 above.

2. Hobbes, *De Corpore*, in *The English Works of Thomas Hobbes of Malmesbury* (London: J. Bohn, 1839], part 2, ch. VII, 91, cited in Grant, *Much Ado About Nothing*, 208). Arguably, the kind of metaphysical gesture implied by this experiment is not very different from Descartes's radical suspension of the world in the first *Meditation*, where he decides to "demolish everything completely and start again right from the foundations" to establish an indubitable basis for the sciences that would be "stable and likely to last", and hence asserts that "the sky, the air, the earth, colours, shapes, sounds and all external things are merely the delusions of dreams devised to ensnare his judgement (Descartes, *Meditations on First Philosophy*, 12, 15).

3. It is certainly striking that one of the most salient features that the three cities have in common is the socialization of labor. Precisely at the dawn of modern capitalism, the philosophical genre of political utopias identifies in the process of production the main source of contradiction between the promise of emancipation carried by political modernity and the subsistence of something like a political logic of place that keeps assigning unequal positions and fragmented horizons to human beings.

4. *Meditations*, 16.

5. That form is the form of reason, which corresponds to the methodical development of the logic of deduction. Through this equation, nature becomes something like an empty placeholder, fitting quite perfectly within the worldview of infinite space, for the sum of

legislative, rational, and universal processes concerning the order and government of things. The origin of this identification of nature and reason can be traced back once again to the developments of natural law, and finds a clear formulation for example in Grotius: "The law of nature is a dictate of right reason, which points out that an act, according as it is or is not in conformity with rational nature, has in it a quality of moral baseness or moral necessity; and that, in consequence, such an act is either forbidden or enjoined" (*Prolegomena* I.1, cited in Jon Miller, "Hugo Grotius," in *The Stanford Encyclopedia of Philosophy*, 2005).

6. *Leviathan*, XX, 135.
7. *Leviathan*, XIII and XX, 77, 135. Of course, the interplay between historicity and abstraction is extremely fertile and complex in Hobbes's text, and the subliminal role that the "New World" played for the early modern political imagination has deservedly been the object of much critical attention. On this point see for instance Sergio Landucci, *I filosofi e i selvaggi* [Turin: Einaudi, 2014]; and Sylvia Wynter, "Unsettling the Coloniality of Being/Power/Truth/Freedom: Towards the Human, After Man, Its Overrepresentation – An Argument," *CR: The New Centennial Review* 3, no. 3 (2003): 257–337). However, even if we bracket or qualify the logical dimension of the state of nature, and emphasize instead all the elements of particularity involved in its political construction, it is still quite interesting that the norms derived from it should apply universally. Doesn't this imply a conception of the homogeneization of the political that allows to abstract, even from the distant reality of the "savages," a set of political norms that are presented as a logic of statehood endowed with universal value?
8. "But one may ask them again, when or where has there been a kingdom long free from sedition and civil war? In those nations whose Commonwealths have been long-lived, and not been destroyed but by foreign war, the subjects never did dispute of the sovereign power. But howsoever, an argument from the practice of men that have not sifted to the bottom, and with exact reason weighed the causes and nature of Commonwealths, and suffer daily those miseries that proceed from the ignorance thereof, is invalid. For though in all places of the world men should lay the foundation of their houses on the sand, it could not thence be inferred that so it ought to be. *The skill of making and maintaining Commonwealths consisteth in certain rules, as doth arithmetic and geometry*; not, as tennis play, on practice only: which rules neither poor men have the leisure, nor men that have had the leisure have hitherto had the curiosity or the method, to find out" (*Leviathan*, XX, 135, my emphasis).
9. "[A *republican constitution*] is the only constitution which can be derived from the idea of an original contract, upon which all rightful legislation of a people must be founded. Thus as far as right is

concerned, republicanism is in itself the original basis of every kind of civil constitution, and it only remains to ask whether it is the only constitution which can lead to a perpetual peace" (Immanuel Kant, *Perpetual Peace. A Philosophical Sketch*, in Immanuel Kant and Reiss, *Kant: Political Writings*, ed. Hans Siegbert [Cambridge: Cambridge University Press, 1991], 99–100).

10. Certainly, Western philosophers in early modern times did certainly not invent the political quest for universals, which is at least as old as philosophical reflection. What they did develop and refine to a previously unseen degree, however, was the logical and rhetorical machinery which could lead to the production and projection of those universals themselves, the "enunciative position" that, although being always necessarily particular, has the capacity or the power to be universalized or generalized in its effects (see Doreen B. Massey, *For Space*, 64). It is my claim that if that machinery can now function with such a degree of power and capacity, it is because one condition particularly facilitated its projection: the uninterrupted regularity of space.

11. Universality is in a particular relation with space; universals are, after all, ideas that "obtain everywhere and for which a particular somewhere, a given place, is presumably irrelevant" (Casey, *The Fate of Place*, xii). Precisely in that respect, modern space can be understood as a sort of necessary condition for the projective logic of contractualism. Carlo Galli is not far from this claim when he says that the "Modern spatial logic . . . is Hobbesian – or, if you will, Cartesian – in character. It is governed by available, amorphous natural space (devoid of "places," concrete bonds and meaning) and by the Subject's need to define rationally the smooth, artificial space of politics for himself. This spatial logic is a dimension of thought that, in its pure form, was never realized in history (although the French Revolution came close), but it nonetheless contains, *in nuce*, the political logic of modernity" (Galli, *Political Spaces and Global War*, 36).

12. Massey, *For Space*, 111.

13. See the following two passages from the *Metaphysics of Morals*: "This right, to present oneself for society, belongs to all human beings by virtue of the right of *possession in common of the earth's surface on which, as a sphere, they cannot disperse infinitely but must finally put up with being near one another*; but originally no one had more right than another to be on a place of the earth" (8:358, 329, my emphasis); and "this kind of possession (*possessio*) – which is to be distinguished from residence (*sedes*), a chosen and therefore an acquired *lasting* possession – is a possession in common because *the spherical surface of the earth unites all the places on its surface*; for if its surface were an unbounded plane, people could be so dispersed on it that they would not come into any community with one another, and

community would not then be a necessary result of their existence on earth (6:263, 414–15, my emphasis). (Both citations are from the edition by Mary J. Gregor in *Practical Philosophy* [Cambridge: Cambridge University Press, 1996].) On the normative importance of the sphericity of the earth for Kant's political elaborations, see Angela Taraborrelli, "Cosmopolitanism and Space in Kant's Political Thought," 2019. It is interesting to note that a similar political role is arguably attributed by Hobbes to language in the beginning of the *Leviathan*, where he describes it as "a profitable invention for continuing the memory of time past, and the conjunction of mankind, dispersed into so many and distant regions of the earth" (*Leviathan*, IV, 16). The argument is then rerouted in an opposite direction: the divine curse fell on Babel dispersed human beings once gain into distant regions and a general lack of understanding which, as he will go on to demonstrate, had dire political consequences.

14. "From the private right in the state of nature there proceeds the postulate of public right: when you cannot avoid living side by side with all others, you ought to leave the state of nature and proceed with them into a rightful condition, that is, a condition of distributive justice" (*Metaphysics of Morals*, 6:308, 451–2).

15. Mirroring the argument from the *Metaphysics of Morals*, space plays a decisive role too in Kant's formulation of the principle of universal hospitality which serves as basis for the creation of a peaceful international order of states. Indeed, the freedom of movement and commerce – which is the very condition of the common interest that might unite different peoples of the world – is spatially determined, i.e. it is based on the fact of our shared experience of space and the Earth. See for instance "Perpetual Peace: A Philosophical Sketch," in *Political Writings*, edited and translated by H. S. Reiss (Cambridge: Cambridge University Press, 1991), 93–130. It might be a worthy philosophical task to explore the role that modern space and the new cosmology played in the imaginaries of alternative constructions of modern political universalism, such as the work of Moses Mendelssohn: "Thus, the religion of the Jews, which is so much decried as an exclusive and unsocial system, is, in reality, a universal religion; and, like the sun in the heavens, sheds its light and its warmth upon all, without distinction" (*Jerusalem or On Religious Power and Judaism*, edited and translated by Allan Arkush [Waltham: Brandeis University Press, 2011], 13).

16. This is one condition that was not available for the universalist aspirations of the *Respublica Christiana*. For the unification of the world does not reflect a transcendent principle or horizon, which would bring back together what was broken and kept apart. Now there are no different orders, no celestial cities, no metaphysical doubling of the space of the world. With the scientific revolution, *the world*

itself has been now unified: the earth in a single spherical surface, the political realm in a single political space under the unquestionable mandates of reason. See Laila Yousef Sandoval: "la consideración del planeta como globo, como esfera, ha logrado su mayor nivel de autoconciencia" (*Carl Schmitt y la Evolución del "Ius publicum europaeum"*, 134). Yousef presents a brilliant rendition of Schmitt's account of the emergence of a "universal conception" of the planet in the seventeenth and eighteenth centuries. According to Schmitt, the "ius publicum europaeum" expresses both the juridical and spatial articulation of this modern notion of the universal (ibid., 141ff).

17. "All parallels, in whatever direction they lie, now have a common vanishing point" (Panofsky, *Perspective as Symbolic Form*, 28).

18. "Similarly, the 'unbounded' quality of openness has been the basis of the ideology of much colonialism (and in turn capitalism), such as in and through the doctrine of *terra nullus* (vacant land), on the basis of which whole continents were declared open for occupation and exploitation" (Jai Sen, "On Open Space: Explorations Towards a Vocabulary of a More Open Politics," *Antipode* 42, no. 4 (2010): 994–1018). The second quote is from Massey, who explains European colonization as a political operation based on the "imagination of space as a continuous, smooth surface that the coloniser, as the only active agent, crosses to find the to-be-colonized simply 'there'"(*For Space*, 63). Carlo Galli discerns in Montaigne's essay "Of Cannibals" an essential moment of the "spatial dequalification and moral undifferentiation" of the world, by which America is not "placed in qualitative opposition with Europe, but rather on the same plane as it", in the same line of Francisco de Vitoria's theorization of "the moral and material unity of the world through the American Indians" (*Political Spaces and Global Wars*, 18, 20). Casey retraces an association between colonization and the theology of space in the late Middle Ages: "It seems hardly coincidental that the great age of Discovery in the fifteenth and sixteenth centuries – an age that set out expressly to explore a terra incognita of interconnected places within the larger space of the earth itself as well as the still larger space of the heavens – immediately followed upon the speculations of theologians and philosophers in the thirteenth and fourteenth centuries. From an entirely imagined and divine status that was fully gained by 1400 AD, such spaces became actual in the form of an earth and a sky that lay ready for discovery and possession not only by thought and faith but also by arms and men" (Casey, *The Fate of Place*, 115).

19. On the colonial "repression of the spatial" and its relationship with the establishment of "foundational universals" by the colonizer powers, see Massey, *For Space*, 70ff. Following that repression, the Earth can appear *politically* as the domain of an "indifferent sameness-of-place" (Casey, *The Fate of Place*, xiii); it is a "perfectly unified

world, a world where bodies and the gaps between them were only differentiations or modifications of a continuum of a higher order" (Panofsky, *Perspective as Symbolic Form*, 41).

20. For Schmitt, the space of the globe was divided into three spaces marked by their different juridical logics: Europe, where the Westphalian system of public right was the norm of political relations; the open seas, as an intermediary space which was open to all and where such system of laws did not operate; and the colonies, where European states can confront each other without restrictions from the law. The colony, from this perspective, is for Schmitt akin to the state of nature in that it is a zone of exception, a space that is open and bounded where the norms are suspended in favor of a logic of sovereign force (see Yousef Sandoval, *Carl Schmitt y la Evolución del "Ius publicum europaeum"*, 134–7, and Carl Schmitt, *Land and Sea: A World-Historical Meditation* [Candor: Telos Press Publishing, 2015]).

21. The second aspect of the spatial irreducibility of the colony refers to its internal segmentation, an order of political positions and relations that is naturalized and based on an essential hierarchy again. See for instance Frantz Fanon's description of the colonial logic that determines the "place of the native" in *Wretched of the Earth*: "It is not enough for the settler to delimit physically, that is to say with the help of the army and the police force, the place of the native. As if to show the totalitarian character of colonial exploitation the settler paints the native as a sort of quintessence of evil"; "The first thing which the native learns is to stay in his place, and not to go beyond certain limits"; "The native is always on the alert, for since he can only make out with difficulty the many symbols of the colonial world, he is never sure whether or not he has crossed the frontier" (Frantz Fanon, *The Wretched of the Earth* [New York: Grove Press, 1968], 41, 52, 53).

22. This is in fact Hobbes's description of liberty as the absence of external impediments to move in the *Leviathan*: "for whatsoever is so tied or *environed* as it cannot move but within a certain space, which space is determined by the opposition of some external body, we say it hath not liberty to go further" (*Leviathan*, XXI, 136). On Dewey's critique of social atomism as a metaphysical presupposition of the social contract, see Richard J. Bernstein, *The Pragmatic Turn* (Cambridge: Polity, 2010), 73: "The essence of the Social Contract theory is not the idea of the formulation of a contract; it is the idea that men are mere individuals, without any social relations until they form a contract".

23. See the famous "mecanomorphic" description of the state as an "artificial man" in the introduction to the *Leviathan* (Introduction, 3–5; and Burtt, *The Metaphysical Foundations of Modern Physical Science*, 236, 297). See also Schmitt's interpretation of Hobbesian

political mechanicism as a decisive moment in the general technifi-
cation and neutralization of the political: "El resultado es que esta
máquina, como la técnica toda, se independiza de todos los objeti-
vos y convicciones políticas y adquiere frente a los valores y frente
a la verdad, la neutralidad propia de un instrumento técnico. Así se
cumple a lo largo del siglo XVII un proceso de neutralización que,
con absoluta lógica interna, culmina en la tecnificacion general" (*El
Leviathan en la teoría del estado de Thomas Hobbe*s, 54, cited in
Yousef Sandoval, 70).

24. On Weber's definition of modern statehood as the "monopoly of
legitimate physical violence within a particular territory," see Max
Weber, *The Vocation Lectures* (Indianapolis: Hackett Pub, 2004), 33.

25. "After all, it is not difficult to transpose from physics to politics one
of the most ancient rules which states that it is impossible for two
bodies to occupy the same space at the same time" (Johannes Fabian,
Time and the Other: How Anthropology Makes Its Object [New
York: Columbia University Press, 1983], 29, cited in Massey, *For
Space*, 73).

26. "For whosoever entereth into another's dominion is subject to all the
laws thereof" (*Leviathan*, XXI, 145). See also the following rendition
of the principle of territorial sovereignty by J. F. Osborne: "neighboring
states with clearly demarcated boundaries, within which state sovereignty is held to be uniformly and evenly distributed across space. In
crossing boundaries, sovereignty then transfers entirely to the neighboring state. Westphalia inaugurated what has been the basic paradigm
for understanding statehood and territory over the next three and a
half centuries (James F. Osborne, "Sovereignty and Territoriality in the
City-State: A Case Study from the Amuq Valley, Turkey," *Journal of
Anthropological Archaeology* 32, no. 4 (2013), 776).

27. "The modernist conception of nation-states or cultural isolates resonates with the billiard-ball view of the world proposed by physical
mechanics. First the entities exist in their full identities, and then they
come into interaction. There is a distinct inside and outside" (Massey,
For Space, 72). As Christopher Bickerton expresses it, the "international society of the modern nation state was premised upon the
independence of its members" (Christopher J. Bickerton, *European
Integration: From Nation States to Member States* [Oxford: University Press, 2012], 13; right before this assertion, however, Bickerton,
quotes Hegel's passage from the *Philosophy of Right* according to
which, "without relations with other States, the State can no more be
an actual individual than an individual can be an actual person without a relationship with other persons" [ibid]. That tension between
independence and interdependence is, as we will soon see, one of the
main internal problems of the Westphalian physics of power).

28. Friedrich von Gentz, *Von dem politischen Zustande von Europa vor
und nach der französischen Revolution*, cited in Perry Anderson, *The*

New Old World (London: Verso Books, 2011), 491. Perry Anderson reconstructs the genealogy of the conception of Westphalian Europe as a balanced and virtuous system of power. Hence the division of the continent into different political states of an equal status and footing is for Gibbon "productive of the most beneficial consequences to the liberty of mankind"; for Montesquieu, progress in Europe derives from the fact that "strong nations are opposed to strong: those who border each other have nearly the same courage" (ibid., 477–8). Ultimately, this idea – which portrays the logic of general progress as the result of the mechanical confrontation of particular interests on a general plane of equivalency – is not very different from Adam Smith's famous metaphor of the invisible hand in his *Theory of Moral Sentiments*, curiously expressed in terms of a proportional distribution of the property of the surface of the earth: "The rich . . . are led by an invisible hand to make nearly the same distribution of the necessaries of life, which would have been made, had the earth been divided into equal portions among all its inhabitants, and thus without intending it, without knowing it, advance the interest of the society, and afford means to the multiplication of the species (Adam Smith, *The Theory of Moral Sentiments* [Indianapolis: Liberty Classic, 1976], 304). The logic is also close to Kant's beautiful image of the unsocial sociability of the human kind: "But once enclosed within a precinct like that of a civil union, the same inclinations have the most beneficial effects. In the same way, trees in a forest, by seeking to deprive each other of air and sunlight, compel each other to find these by upward growth, so that they grow beautiful and straight – whereas those which put out branches at will, in freedom and in isolation from others, grow stunted, bent and twisted. All the culture and art which adorn mankind and the finest social order man creates are fruits of his unsociability. For it is compelled by its own nature to discipline itself, and thus, by enforced art, to develop completely the germs which nature implanted" (Kant, *Idea for a Universal History with a Cosmopolitan Purpose*, in *Political Writings*, 46). Much has been written about the historical and ideological correlations between the emergence of the Westphalian system of public law and the early developments of European capitalism. From a metaphysical perspective, it is perhaps relevant to note how both share in this same logic of political mechanics, where the confrontation of individual bodies against the background of a neutral space is now identified as the source of motion, conflict, progress and strength.

Chapter 12

The Autonomy of Politics

To rule upon a political void, the logic of modern sovereignty is constituted as absolute. The rupture of the chain of being, and the destruction of all figures of natural and theological transcendence that gave an order and a foundation to the political, cannot efface the place that those figures occupied: the transcendent figure is destroyed, but the place subsists as the fundamental emptiness of a power that can no longer be embodied.[1] In the immanent, mechanistic world of modern politics, that place is hence occupied by the state, which replaces logically the absolutes that have been lost: in the universal abstraction of the state, the political body is unified, subsumed under a single form; the projective geometry of modern power, and the mechanics of political relations, rely entirely upon it.[2] But as in the case of space, the absoluteness of the state is also fatally pressured, both from outside and from within, bringing back the specter of an irreducible openness that ultimately cannot be foreclosed.

12.1 Space and Political Theology

In their descriptions of the universe, the authors of the new science often made use of political metaphors. Copernicus, for instance, likened the sun to the ruler of the world, since it resides at its center; Thomas Digges portrayed the infinite universe as the "gloriouse court of ye great god"; in a vivid and emphatic image, Otto Von Guericke described the ineffable power of nothingness as being "more noble than the blood of monarchs" and superior to "the jurisdiction of all kings".[3] A common trope of the early modern scientific imagination, picked up by Newton in the *General Scholium*, describes the space of the world as the realm of God's rule: God governs over the infinite extension of the universe as an absolute king does over his domains.[4] These political metaphors translate more than evocative images of vastness and power. Like in the Shakespearean plays where great princes bear the name of their own kingdoms, space and God are thus presented as participating in the same nature.

In the work of More or Newton, space derives its absolute character precisely from its relation to the divine maker and ruler of the world. It is precisely *as* the extension of God that space acquires a number of essential metaphysical qualities, including its self-sufficiency, completeness, independence and omnipresence, which are essential to its status as an absolute framework. Only as an attribute of God can space become the region of regions, the *ultima ratio* of mechanics, that which is in itself and not relative to anything else. In the physics of absolute space are thus preserved the traits of an absolute entity, the all-powerful God, otherwise destined to depart a world which no longer required its presence. That is what the political metaphors of the divinity of space ultimately express: a secularized theology of the absolute, a derivative form of absoluteness, which lays the metaphysical ground of material mechanics and, indeed, of the entire physical world.

The analogy, in fact, works both ways. We know only too well that early modern thinkers borrowed the language of the theologians to conceive of political sovereignty, to the point that the state itself could be likened to a "mortal God" that is owed reverence by its subjects.[5] But in that, political philosophers were simply following the path that had been strenuously opened by the spatial imagination of modern science. Absolute space and political sovereignty are not simply contemporary concepts, but are also bound by a deep logical affinity, almost by a form of equivalence. Like space, political sovereignty also relies on a process of unification, on the logical subsumption of all forms of authority under the *puissance souveraine* of the state.[6] The space of politics is now empty too, cleared of the complex relations of hierarchy, order and position that had been inherited from the logic of place. Like matter in the empty space of the universe, political bodies appear now as ontological equals on a single, universal plane of existence; on that plane the absolute state becomes the ultimate system of reference, at once foundation and background for all political relations. Space and sovereignty are two secularized forms of the divine absolute, two expressions of the same transcendent notion of power, two traces of the disappeared divinity that they must now replace, as logical absolutes in the world, to secure the metaphysical foundation of modern politics and physics.

Precisely as such, however, space and sovereignty were also affected by similar tensions and contradictions. When Leibniz denounced the inconsistency of the Newtonian conception of space, for instance, one of his strongest arguments was related to the fact that an absolute entity cannot be divided into parts, for then space would be "not only immense in the whole, but also immutable and eternal in every part. There will be an infinite number of Eternal things besides God."[7] The problem of the division of absolute space brings us to two unsustainable positions that are in fact charged with political undertones. On the one hand, we risk having the *absolute restrained*: each point, insofar as it must be absolute in itself, represents a limit to every other part and hence to the absolute as a whole. On the other, we seem to have *different absolutes* coexisting at the same time, as if multiple sovereigns tried to rule at once over the same realm. In both cases, the political reality of the absolute is compromised, to the point of becoming the origin of its own negation.

12.2 Absolute and Relative: An Ontology of Limits

The Westphalian sovereign depends on the political logic of absoluteness. The sovereign appears originally as the sole bearer of authority, a form of *potentia absoluta* that governs politics unrestrictedly and from above. This is why the sovereign has no parts: its power must be undivided, it must have no conditions or fragmentations. The polity, in fact, needs the sovereign to acquire its own unity and independence. By contrast, the sovereign is not in need of anything else: while everything must be subject to the sovereign, the sovereign itself cannot be subject to anything at all – not even to its own acts.[8]

Precisely as absolute, however, the logic of sovereignty is constitutively tensioned within the Westphalian physics of power. Political sovereignty is in fact spatially restrained in its very essence: sovereignty is bound in space, it is defined by a territorial limit, by an inside/outside distinction that is foundational of modern sovereignty as such. Beyond the spatial limits of sovereignty another sovereign entity begins, both standing beside one another on an equal plane of political existence. Multiple sovereignties thus coexist, each endowed with an absolute power that ceases to be entirely on the other side of the line. Political power both absolute and contained within strict bounds: its form of absoluteness, hence, seems to be essentially defined by a limit.[9] In the absence of any superior power, of any common authority above the sovereign states, the Westphalian system is thus marked not only by a political tension – the constant threat of conflict between multiple sovereignties tied up in agonistic relations with one another – but also by a metaphysical one. For being limited, each of those sovereign entities lays claim to a form of power that in itself depends on the negation of limits. There is a tension, in the Westphalian system, between the absolute and the universal: political sovereignty, as a result, is both fragmented and unified.

This constitutive tension, which Schmitt synthesized in the cosmological image of a pluriverse of sovereign states, explains why cosmopolitanism will permanently appear as the fulfillment of a logical necessity.[10] From a metaphysical perspective, the notion of a universal contract represents a sort of redemption of the original logic of political sovereignty, ending the state of nature from a universal standpoint, and achieving hence the formal unification of the entirety of political space.[11] For in the absence of such unification, to put it in terms that are close to the Leibnizian critique of absolute space, the Westphalian system appears as little more than an order of coexistence of sovereigns, where each state is placed in a series of external relations with other states; seen from an international perspective, the logic of political space seems to correspond with "the order of political bodies among themselves."[12] Such a pluralist ontology, embedded in notions of immanence and limitation, is obviously at odds with the political premises of modern sovereignty. There is a tension, in the understanding of Europe as a spatial balance of powers, between absolutism and relationality, between the logic and the mechanics of political sovereignty. The dialectics of integration and fragmentation, which still define the present of European politics, perhaps have here a metaphysical origin.

This tension, however, does not only manifest itself from the outside. The political absolute is pressured internally too by a similar attempt to contain its originally unrestricted power. The development of European liberalism, in this respect, can be read from the perspective of an ontology of limits, understood as so many restrictions and bounds that the state cannot trespass, or conversely, as situations in which the power of the state itself can be legitimately countered and neutralized.[13] To restrain such absolute power, however, liberalism relies on the same political mechanics that had grounded such power in the first place. Government will thus result from an internal balance of separated and independent powers, like physical forces that counter one another; instead of being subsumed under a single form, power is now fragmented and mediated, distributed among several political bodies that can occupy different positions and be bounded by different relations. Here too, the political absolute is confronted with an internal contradiction: it is now threatened by the same logic that made it rise.

12.3 Modern Spheres: Space as a Political Transcendental

This partition of power clashed against one of the main premises of the rise of the absolute state: the creation of a unified political space under the sovereign's exclusive control. Behind the attempts to secure an autonomous domain of the political, in fact, lies the need of the state to acquire a distinct and separate existence, to assert its superiority over any intermediary bodies and jurisdictions, to guarantee the dominion of the universal over the particular, the concrete, the fragmented. The absolute state appeared then as a transcendent political apparatus, severed from its roots, separated from the immanent forms of sociability that it governed from above. Liberalism emerges precisely as a reactive movement to this alienation of the absolute sovereign: to protect the rights and liberties of individuals, to restrain the ability of the sovereign to interfere with social needs, interests and relations, the political power of the state had to be divided, and its political space, contoured again.

With Locke and Ferguson, the liberal response to the absolute emancipation of the state begins to acquire its positive form. A restriction of the state's coercive powers is then taken not only as a defensive fortification against the intrusions and excesses of the sovereign, but even as a contribution to the flourishing and development of society. This same principle, which identifies in the realm of sociability – and not in politics – the true soul of the life of nations, limits the scope and capacities of the state to the mere preservation of the pre-political conditions of social exchanges and relations. The power of the state, hence, is not only quantitatively limited, but qualitatively too. The duty of the sovereign, as Smith would put it in *The Wealth of Nations*, "is that of erecting and maintaining those public institutions and those public works . . . [that are] advantageous to a great society."[14] The role of the state, which is nothing more than a political trustee of the citizens, and hence becomes dependent on them, is to preserve and provide the necessary conditions for their manifold associations to thrive. Here, the political operates under the premise of its separation from the social logic of production and exchange, presented as two different domains that need to assert their relative autonomy, if not to be protected from one another. At stake in this constitutive scission is much more than the determination of legal limits to the prerogatives of modern states. At stake is a process of political enclosure parallel to the one that had been taking place in the English countryside: the restriction of the political capacity of the state, which is now to be contained within a separate and imaginary sphere, leaving outside a significant volume of meaningful social life, and hence, significant expressions of power too.[15] This is the anti-modern gesture of European liberalism: an abstract vault covers the political space again, so as to separate it from "what it is not."

The relation of society and the state is thus transformed into a transcendental problem. Critical philosophy and political liberalism coincide in the elaboration of an ontology of limits, an investigation of the conditions that must be the case for a state of affairs to be possible and carried to its end. Under liberalism, the task of public law and the philosophy of the state becomes precisely the demarcation and containment of political space as separated from the exclusive domains of civil and economic life. Here, the severance of the state from social life no longer appears as a threat to be quelled, but rather as a transcendental necessity, a condition that must be met for the realization of the modern promises of freedom and political equality. In fact, it is precisely *qua* limited and separated, at a distance from the social life of the nation, that the political sphere can appear as being untouched by any form of particularism or fragmentation, as an open space where all differences between individuals can be suspended and neutralized, where political freedom can be realized despite the segmentation of social life. From the standpoint of liberalism, politics realizes its universal vocation only within the bounds of a transcendental sphere.

12.4 Critique of the Political Void

With one and the same gesture, the French revolutionaries completed the political emancipation of the state and forever changed its nature.[16] Freed from any form of particularism or fragmentary jurisdiction, the universal state can now appear as a pristine political space, a pure realm of general interest, the unobstructed locus of a political life in which people participate as free and equal citizens. The revolution, as Marx would claim in his writings on the Paris Commune, had "cleared the soil of France"; it dissolved the fixed significance of markers of hierarchy and distinction; it proclaimed a logic of citizenship that is indifferent to birth, rank, religion, and property, to any particular identity, to every exception and peculiarity.[17] The transparent sphere of modern politics appears then as a smooth political space, an open and universal realm of free access and equal participation.

But as the German idealists would make clear enough, every transcendental constitution betrays a process of social institution.[18] The universal sphere of the political, as Marx would point in his essay on the *Jewish Question*, can in fact only exist as an *abstraction*, as a "celestial community" to which people belong as imaginary members, at a distance from their rootedness in the social practices of production, property, and labor.[19] In declaring the formal equality of individuals, Marx explains, the political revolutions of modernity do not emancipate men from social relations of oppression and inequality: they simply abolish the direct political character that those relations had displayed under the *ancien regime*, but leave unaffected the source of their social power. Men (for the universal, here too, only applies to them) are thus forced to live two lives, one as members of a political community of equals, another as social beings whose existence bears the marks of deeply unequal relations, conditions, and situations. There is a dissociation between the political status of individuals, which determines their identity as citizens, and their position within social and economic space, a scission between

> life in the political community, in which he considers himself a communal being, and life in civil society, in which he acts as a private individual, regards other men as a means, degrades himself into a means, and becomes the plaything of alien powers. The relation of the political state to civil society is just as spiritual as the relations of heaven to earth.[20]

Here the transcendental separation of politics and society becomes both a metaphysical and a political problem. For the same gesture that proclaims the political equality and capacity of the citizens separates, at the same time, those capacities from the social conditions and circumstances in which they must be exerted. Political power is at once diffused throughout the entire political body and estranged from its sources in the processes of social reproduction. Far from superseding the frictions of the particular, hence, the political sphere is set in a constitutive tension against its outside. An irresolvable friction links together the aspiration to universality, which makes politics appear as an empty realm of abstract equality and freedom, and its constitutive exteriority, a social logic marked by the fragmentation and inequality of social being within the nascent capitalist society.

This abstraction of the universal from the segmentation of social being becomes the basis of an unstable political program. The theories of popular sovereignty, in fact, are premised upon a contradictory principle, the political equality of social non-equals, which at once elevates the political above the socio-economic order and confines its effects into a limited order of existence.[21] That limitation, however, is not a sign of mere partiality or incompleteness. On the contrary, it is the very *premise* of universality as such, it is the condition of possibility of political emancipation under the logic of capitalist societies. Indeed, the fiction of an open and empty social space, by which beings who are unequal accept or are forced to treat each other as equals, is not exclusive of the political sphere: it is also the ideological presupposition of the market itself, of the capitalist exchange, of waged labor. The functioning of capital also requires that every differential trait of being be abolished, dissolved in a plane of convertibility, reduced to abstract units of labor, value, and time.[22] Ultimately, capital depends on an empty space too.

The two imaginary, decentered spheres of the political and the economic express the same metaphysical logic, crystalized in the image of an empty space of equal belonging and participation, which at once declares the universal emancipation of the citizen and produces the conditions for its subordination. This is the last form under which the political absolute will appear: as the purpose to abolish that separation of the spheres, to make the space of the social and the political coincide, and finally redeem the political promise of that image.

Notes

1. The rupture of the chain of being generated an immense ontological and political displacement. The seminal work of Ernst Kantorowicz has often been taken as a reference point for the evaluation of such political upheaval, which ultimately resulted in the culmination and

dissolution of medieval politics. In the *ancien régime*, says Claude Lefort, by drawing on Kantorowicz's work, the king had two "bodies": the physical and the sacred, the empirical and the symbolic. A part that embodied the whole, the king was a person who incarnated at the same time the very identity and the unity of society, a single empirical body raised to the status of a representative for the entire "body politic." This doubling, however, was only possible within a complex economy of transcendence: the king was the mediator between the visible and the invisible, between the immanent and the transcendent, between the sensible existence of the political community and the supernatural source of meaning that, descending from elsewhere, invested him with sacred power and authority. That political body was according to Lefort destroyed by the modern democratic revolutions: "C'est la 'révolution démocratique' se produisant par l'intermédiaire des deux révolutions américaine et française du 18e siècle qui 'détruit le corps du roi'. Si, pour la représentation politique classique, le Corps du roi assurait l'unité organique et mystique du royaume, 'quand tombe la tête du corps politique, du même coup, la corporéité du social se dissout. Alors se produit ce que j'oserai nommer une désincorporation des individus.' Cette dernière n'est pas synonyme d'une désintégration, voire d'une annihilation, du monde social. Elle décrit plutôt l'émergence d'une société envers laquelle, dans l'ordre heuristique ou gnoséologique, il devient impossible d'user du schème unitaire pour expliquer la relation entre l'État et la société : l'unicité du principe gouvernemental n'est plus la raison de l'unité nationale. Il n'est plus possible de concentrer toutes les fonctions politiques en un seul point, en une seule personne, qui aurait un pouvoir absolu sur toutes les affaires de l'État" (Gaëlle Demelemestre, "Le concept lefortien du pouvoir comme lieu vide," *Raisons politiques* 46, no. 2 (2012): 175–93; see also Claude Lefort, *L'Invention démocratique: les limites de la domination totalitaire* [Paris: Fayard, 1994], 172).

2. Carlo Invernizzi Accetti reconstructs succinctly the Arendtian formulation of the problem of foundation in modern politics: before modernity, "a hierarchical order of authority was assumed to be implicit in the natural order of things, and this prevented the question concerning the foundations for its legitimacy from being raised in a politically meaningful manner . . . At the beginning of modernity, Arendt contends, this assumption began to be called into question. Indeed, for her, the theory of the divine rights of monarchs already constituted a response to this problem, which consisted in making explicit something that had previously been assumed to be implicit: that the foundation for the legitimacy of the political order ultimately lay in the sanction received by the transcendent will of God. A conceptual absolute was therefore posited as the foundation

for early modern theories of absolute monarchy" (Carlo Invernizzi Accetti, *Relativism and Religion*, 10).

3. Cited in Koyré, *From the Closed World to the Infinite Universe*, 33, 38, and Grant, *Much Ado About Nothing*, 216. See for instance this passage from Copernicus: "Then in the middle of all stands the sun. For who, in our most beautiful temple, could set this light in another or better place, than that from which it can at once illuminate the whole? Not to speak of the fact that not unfittingly do some call it the light of the world, others the soul, still others the governor. Tremigistus calls it the visible God; Sophocles' Electra, the All-seer. And in fact does the sun, seated on his royal throne, guide his family of planets as they circle round him" (cited in Burtt, *The Metaphysical Foundations of Modern Physical Science*, 45).

4. "The supreme God is a Being eternal, infinite, absolutely perfect; but a being, however perfect, without dominion, cannot be said to be Lord God; for we say, my God, your God, the God of Israel, the God of Gods, and Lord of Lords; but we do not say, my Eternal, your Eternal, the Eternal of Israel, the Eternal of Gods; we do not say, my Infinite, or my Perfect: These are titles which have no respect to servants. The word God usually signifies Lord; but every lord is not a God. It is the dominion of a spiritual being which constitutes a God; a true, supreme, or imaginary dominion makes a true, supreme, or imaginary God" (Newton, *General Scholium*, 389).

5. "This is the generation of that great LEVIATHAN, or rather (to speak more reverently) of that *Mortal God* to which we owe, under the *Immortal God*, our peace and defence" (*Leviathan*, XVII, 109). The reference is to the famous passage in Schmitt's *Political Theology*: "All significant concepts of the modem theory of the state are secularized theological concepts not only because of their historical development – in which they were transferred from theology to the theory of the state, whereby, for example, the omnipotent God became the omnipotent lawgiver – but also because of their systematic structure, the recognition of which is necessary for a sociological consideration of these concepts. The exception in jurisprudence is analogous to the miracle in theology. Only by being aware of this analogy can we appreciate the manner in which the philosophical ideas of the state developed in the last centuries" (Carl Schmitt, *Political Theology: Four Chapters on the Concept of Sovereignty* [Cambridge: MIT Press, 1985], 36).

6. The expression is from Bodin's definition of sovereignty in *The Six Books of the Republic* I, 1 (cited in J. W. Allen, *A History of Political Thought in the 16th Century* [Routledge, 2013], 407). As Perry Anderson eloquently describes, medieval politics was based on a complex structure of multiple, fragmented authorities: "The consequence of such a system was that political sovereignty was never focused in a single centre. The functions of the state were disintegrated in a vertical

allocation downwards, at each level of which political and economic relations were, on the other hand, integrated. This parcellization of sovereignty was constitutive of the whole feudal mode of production" (Perry Anderson, *Passages from Antiquity to Feudalism*, 148; see also Ellen Meiksins Wood's description of the medieval "clash" of economic and political powers, resulting from the fact that the medieval logic of political domination was essentially of an extra-economic nature, and did not depend on controlling the autonomous processes of production; *Democracy against Capitalism*, 272ff). In a quite poetic manner, Casey describes the physico-political underpinnings of the metaphysics of unification at the dawn of the modern age as an attempt at the articulation of the universe as a "totalized whole" that is the "single aim of Roman conquest, Christian conversion, early modern physics, and Kantian epistemology" (Casey, *The Fate of Place*, 78).

7. *The Leibniz–Clarke Correspondence*, "Mr. Leibniz Fourth Paper", 37. As Leibniz goes on to say, "Space being uniform, there can be neither any external nor internal reason, by which to distinguish its parts, and to make any choice among them. For, any external reason to discern between them, can only be grounded upon some internal one. Otherwise we should discern what is indiscernible, or choose without discerning . . . A God, who should act by such a will, would be a God only in name" (ibid., 39).

8. "Maiestie or Soveraigntie is the most high, absolute, and perpetuall power over the citisens and subiects in a Commonweale . . . that is to say, The greatest power to command" (Bodin, *Six Books of the Republic*, cited in Ricardo Sanín-Restrepo, *Decolonizing Democracy: Power in a Solid State* [Rowman and Littlefield, 2016], 150. See also *Leviathan*, XVI). The idea that such "greatest power" must not be bound even by its own acts originates in natural law; as Rousseau would claim in his *Social Contract*, the likes of Grotius and Bodin had robbed the people of their inalienable rights and invested the monarchs with them (see Miller, "Hugo Grotius"). Meiksins Wood quotes an eloquent passage, written in the sixteenth century by Sir Thomas Smith, about the unrestricted character of representation from the perspective of the parliamentarist tradition: the sovereign, wrote Smith alluding to the English Parliament, "hath the power of the whole realme both the head and the bodie. For everie Englishman is entended to bee there present, either in person or by procuration and attornies, of what preheminence, state dignitie, or qualitie soever he be, from the Prince (be he King or Queene) to the lowest person of England. And the consent of the Parliament is taken to be everie man's consent" (cited in Meiksins Wood, *Democracy Against Capitalism*, 205).

9. Pascal famously derided this notion of justice that would be determined by a river or be honored on one side only of the same mountain:

"On la verrait plantée par tous les États du monde et dans tous les temps, au lieu qu'on ne voit rien de juste ou d'injuste qui ne change de qualité en changeant de climat, trois degrés d'élévation du pôle renversent toute la jurisprudence. Un méridien décide de la vérité, en peu d'années de possession les lois fondamentales changent. Le droit a ses époques, l'entrée de Saturne au Lion nous marque l'origine d'un tel crime. Plaisante justice qu'une rivière borne! Vérité au-deçà des Pyrénées, erreur au-delà" (Pascal, "L'économie du monde", *Pensées*, 60).

10. "A world state that embraces the entire globe and all of humanity cannot exist. The political world is a pluriverse, not a universe" (Carl Schmitt, *The Concept of the Political* [New Brunswick: Rutgers University Press, 1976]). Schmitt relies on the Hobbesian understanding of inter-state relations as a sort of state of nature, where the absence of any common superior authority makes it impossible to suppress the possibility of conflict between different Commonwealths: "To speak impartially, both things are very true: that *man to man is a kind of God*; and that *man to man is an arrant wolf*. The first is true, if we compare citizens amongst themselves; and the second, if we compare cities" (Thomas Hobbes, *Man and Citizen: Thomas Hobbes's De Homine*, ed. Bernard Gert [Gloucester: P. Smith, 1978], 89, cited in Yousef Sandoval, *Carl Schmitt y la Evolución del "Ius publicum europaeum"*, 73). The conclusion of a universal contract, for Schmitt, would neutralize such possibility of conflict and hence, politics itself. But that is exactly the picture that Kant draws in his essay on *Perpetual Peace:* a gradual advancement of the principles of republican federalism that would be conducive to a universal state and the eradication of conflicts. From the perspective that I have defended, it is curious that Kant culminates his essay by stating that the international "state of public right," which would bring about the perpetual peace of cosmopolitanism "is not just an *empty idea*" (*Towards Perpetual Peace*, in *Political Writings*, 130). On the contrary: as Kant's articles make clear, the powerful projection of an empty universal space is indeed rigidly structured by defined political principles and conditions. From a philosophical perspective, the connection between abstract universalism and modern forms of enlightened imperialism are striking indeed; see for instance this passage from a letter that Jefferson addressed to Monroe in 1801: "however our present interests may restrain us within our limits, it is impossible not to look forward to distant times, when our multiplication will expand it beyond those limits, and cover the whole northern, if not the southern continent, with people speaking the same language, governed in similar forms, and by similar laws" (in Perry Anderson, *American Foreign Policy and its Thinkers*, New Left Review no. 83 (2013): 6–7).

11. On the original connection between cosmopolitanism and early modern social contract theory, and the role of the philosophy of natural

right in the foundation of international law, see Pauline Kleingeld and Eric Brown: "some natural law theorists assume that nature implanted in humans, in addition to the tendency to self-preservation, *also* a fellow-feeling, a form of sociability that unites all humans at a fundamental level into a kind of world community . . . Grotius, Pufendorf, and others did draw out these implications and thereby laid the foundation for international law . . . envisioned as a "great society of states" that is bound by a "law of nations" holding between all states ("Cosmopolitanism," in *The Stanford Encyclopedia of Philosophy*, 2019).

12. *The Leibniz–Clarke Correspondence*, "Mr Leibniz Third Paper", 26.

13. Of course, the chronology of the decay of absolute states follows a complex and irregular trajectory. For a good description of it, see Perry Anderson's *Lineages of the Absolutist State*, 10: "Spanish absolutism suffered its first great defeat in the late sixteenth century in the Netherlands; English absolutism was cut down in the mid-seventeenth century; French absolutism lasted until the end of the eighteenth century; Prussian absolutism was only overthrown in the twentieth century"). From the early theorizations of the right to disobey or rebel, however, the long, conflictual history of liberalism and democracy can be read precisely in terms of an ontology of limits that, as I will try to prove in the next two sections, is compatible with a materialist account of the fall of the absolute state (see for instance this passage from Ellen Meiksins Wood, who identifies the "origin of modern constitutional principles, ideas of limited government, the separation of powers, and so on" in the ascent of the modern propertied classes that become "lords themselves asserting their independent powers against the claims of monarchy"; *Democracy against Capitalism*, 204).

14. Adam Smith, *An Inquiry into the Nature and Causes of the Wealth of Nations*, ed. Edwin Cannan (New York: Bantam Classic, 2003), 874.

15. "Civil society represents a separate sphere of human relations and activity, differentiated from the state but neither public nor private or perhaps both at once, embodying not only a whole range of social interactions apart from the private sphere of the household and the public sphere of the state, but more specifically a network of distinctively economic relations, the sphere of the market place, the arena of production, reproduction and exchange, [a precondition of which] was the modern idea of the state as an abstract entity with its own corporate identity" (Ellen Meiksins Wood, *Democracy against Capitalism*, 239). On the genealogy of the concept of the "public sphere," see Craig Calhoun, "Civil Society and the Public Sphere: History of the Concept," in *International Encyclopedia of the Social and Behavioral Sciences*, ed. James D. Wright [Oxford: Elsevier, 2001], 701–6.

16. José Luis Villacañas describes the effect of the modern doctrine of popular sovereignty as "a revolution in the Copernican manner":

"de la misma forma que el curso de los planetas no se puede estudiar ni ordenar sin atender al movimiento del propio observador, el Estado ya no es la estructura heredada, independiente de los súbditos, que determina de forma soberana su lugar en el cosmos social, sino que, antes bien, resulta de la voluntad de los dominados hasta ahora, de las fuerzas del propio cosmos social que lo construyen racionalmente. A nadie puede pasar desapercibida esta convergencia entre la revolución de la ciencia moderna y la ratio políticamente revolucionaria" (*La Nación y la Guerra: Confederación y Hegemonía como Formas de Concebir Europa* [Murcia: DM Librero-Editor, 1999], 27, cited in Yousef Sandoval, *Carl Schmitt y la Evolución del "Ius publicum europaeum,"* 98). Indeed, the doctrine of popular sovereignty displaces the ontological center of politics *outside* the realm of the state: the people, the only source of legitimacy from which political decisions emanate, is never already *there*, and so it must confer legitimacy to the state through the process of political representation. Hobbes had already claimed that the people, which is now at once the efficient and final cause of politics, is only unified in the act of its political constitution. In other words, the people only exists through its political representation, when it transfers its legitimacy to the state, when it is no longer or not fully *there*. All future attempts at making the people whole again, at restoring its unity and political centrality, would face in one way or another this same metaphysical problem.

17. "The gigantic broom of the French Revolution of the eighteenth century swept away all these relics of bygone times, thus clearing simultaneously the social soil of its last hindrances to the superstructure of the modern State edifice raised under the First Empire" (Karl Marx, *The Civil War in France*, in *Karl Marx and Frederick Engels: Selected Works in One Volume* [New York: International Publishers, 1968], 289).

18. Robert Brandom, *Tales of the Mighty Dead: Historical Essays in the Metaphysics of Intentionality* (Cambridge: Harvard University Press, 2002), 216. It is interesting in this respect to notice the political undertones of Casey's description of the transcendental deduction of space: "The only thing that can de deduced from a transcendental argument – of a Kantian sort – is the presupposition of *empty space* ... as such – as categorial ... – it fails to capture what is specific to place, namely the capacity to hold and situate things, to give them a local habitation" (*The Fate of Place*, 20).

19. Karl Marx, *On the Jewish Question*, in *Marx: Early Political Writings* (Cambridge University Press, 1994), 36. In is interesting to compare Marx's critique of political abstraction with De Maistre's denunciation of the universal political categories that inspired the French revolutionaries: "La constitution de 1795, tout comme ses ainées, est faite pour l'*homme*. Or, il n'y a point d'*homme* dans le monde. J'ai vu,

dans ma vie, des Français, des Italiens, des Russes, etc.; je sais même, grâces à Montesquieu, *qu'on peut être Persan*: mais quand à l'homme, je déclare ne l'avoir rencontré de ma vie; s'il existe, c'est bien à mon insu" (Joseph Marie Maistre, *Considérations Sur La France*, ed. Pierre Manent [Brussels: Editions Complexe, 1988], 87).

20. "Where the political state has attained its true development, man – not only in thought, in consciousness, but in reality, in life – leads a twofold life, a heavenly and an earthly life: (Marx, *On the Jewish Question*, ibid.). The universal rights of the citizen, the early Marx famously concluded, are the private rights of the isolated bourgeois said in the voice of abstraction.

21. Meiksins Wood, *Democracy against Capitalism*, 223.

22. The "clearing" of the social space by capital is indeed the object of Marx's famous metaphor in the *Communist Manifesto*: "All fixed, fast-frozen relations, with their train of ancient and venerable prejudices and opinions, are swept away, all new-formed ones become antiquated before they can ossify. All that is solid melts into air; all that is holy is profaned; and man is forced to face his real conditions of life, and his relations with his kind" (Karl Marx and Friedrich Engels, *The Communist Manifesto* [London: Pluto Press, 2008], 38). In that clearing, the "freedom" of individuals as workers acquires hence the double meaning of being juridically emancipated from any subjection and boundary that would prevent them to sell their labor-power, but also of being deprived of the property of the means of production that determines the position that they occupy in the "empty" social space of capitalist relations: "this worker must be free in the double sense that as a free individual he can dispose of his labour-power as his own commodity, and that, on the other hand, he has no other commodity for sale, i.e. he is rid of them, he is free of all the objects needed for the realization of his labour-power" (Karl Marx, *Capital: A Critique of Political Economy*, vol. 1, ed. Ben. Fowkes [New York: Vintage Books, 1977], 272–3; capital thus required the removal of all obstacles to the free movement of workers, and the "abolition of all laws that prevent workers from moving from one sphere of production to another and from one local seat of production to any other" [ibid., vol. 3], 298).

Democracy and the Critique of Space

"A space is something that has been made room for."[1]
"Le temps ne crée pas de radicalité, ce sont les radicalités qui s'inventent un temps."[2]

The Forgetfulness of Space

A sort of temporal obsession haunts the dominant conceptions of emancipation that we have inherited from the twentieth century. It might be enough, in tracking the origin of such obsession, to consider the tactical debate at the dawn of the workers' movement from which emerged the categorical distinction on the left between reform and revolution. What originally distinguished revolutionaries and reformists was not an idea of the end *per se* – an archetype of social emancipation through the overthrow of capitalism and the bourgeois state – but a disagreement on the means that should be employed to reach that goal. A certain function of time distinguishes the two: reform and revolution express two opposing statements about the temporal structure of political change. Both diverge fundamentally in their categorization of what counts as a political means, or conversely, of the temporality of the political production of ends. But both share an adherence to a temporal frame that understands social transformation as the unfolding of a linear historical sequence, leading through different routes and rhythms from social causes to political effects. Ultimately, the efficacy of each of those routes is a matter of historical judgment, a sort of measurement of their performance, taken from the standpoint of the end. The idea of socialism, the movement that brings about the abolition of the actual state of things, is thus drawn as an essentially temporal horizon. The central political problem is how to get there.

It is a classic instinct of the critique of Marxism to underline the instrumental rationality that is at work in this kind of projection. Politics is thus reduced to a sort of technological problem, to the mechanical calculation of means and ends, and most often, to the anticipation of futures that never were. Against this instrumental form of activity, for instance, Arendt affirms that what is emancipatory about politics is precisely its not being conditioned by causal antecedents or determinate outcomes. For her, politics begins precisely when we break with instrumentality itself, when we start something new, unanticipated, unpredictable, which could be neither expected from what happened before, nor calculated by the laws of cause and effect.[3] A free action always appears as its own end, an end in itself that is subordinated to nothing outside of it, which does not require an authorization from the standpoint of what will be accomplished, from the anticipation of any future state of things. The emancipatory character of politics, then, does not lie in the end, but in the capacity to begin.[4]

Like miracles, however, beginnings seem to occur out of nowhere.[5] Freedom suspends momentarily the attachments and determinations of social existence; in their stead, one can spontaneously breathe in an emptiness, in a sort of liberated void. But actions, and the temporality that they bear or embody, cannot persist in the void. Actions need to encounter bodies, ideas, relations; they need to affect and be affected by them; they need, in sum, to take place among the things that they set to transform. This is possibly why, in the case of Arendt, this temporality that survives, the radical autonomy of action and freedom as radical beginnings, cannot be understood without something like a spatial correlate. Freedom exists only for and before others; it appears in the space of what is common to them, in the "public space" that is forged precisely through their actions, their recognition, the significant exchange with others.[6] Arendt famously explained that this public realm of action has been threatened in modernity by the "rise of the social," and the consequent invasion of the public sphere by the instrumental relations of work, interests and desires (a process, according to her, at once mirrored and accelerated by Marxism). Still, one could say that her model of an open, unobstructed space of appearance, where unequal human beings can recognize and treat each other as equals, is something like the spatial reverse of the temporality of action; not exactly a condition of possibility, but the fertile ground where freedom and action can get a grip on the world, persist, and thrive.

Taken together, these two images of thought (temporality without an end and the ideal of the public sphere) complete the Arendtian critique of Marxism and arguably mark the coordinates for a non-instrumental paradigm of the political. However, one might doubt the efficacy of this solution. One could even argue that instead of providing the necessary spatial supplement to the temporal autonomy of politics, the notion of the public sphere expresses on the contrary a certain forgetfulness of space – or to be more precise, of the spatial limits and horizons of social existence, of what we might call a political topology of being.

Political Nowheres

Against all forms of political abstraction, the materialist critique would not cease to emphasize the embeddedness of political existence in situations that are marked, defined and delimited by the processes of social reproduction.[7] A basic premise of Marxism is that the social life of subjects is overdetermined by their position in the productive structure – that there is no such thing as a universal realm for subjects to deal with each other as equals, and that in fact such a fiction is the ideological presupposition of the market and the capitalist exchange. Moreover, the critique of ideology denounces the very logic of separation that holds the image of different "spheres" in society, and the general distinction of the private and the public, as a way of guaranteeing the dissociation of political identities and socio-economic life, so that political equality can well coincide with class inequality and social exploitation.

From the perspective of materialism, hence, the celebration of the autonomy of politics inevitably results in a mystification. The social space is never empty: it is always fragmented and segmented, broken into different planes and unequal horizons of possibility. Against the imagination of an open and autonomous public sphere, which naturalizes and makes invisible the fact of social fragmentation, the materialist critique would hence claim that political subjects cannot be thought of as disembodied agents roaming through an abstract logical *nowhere*, but that on the contrary, they are always already immersed in a context of social relations that saturate their lives with practical significance. The political void is thus contrasted with a social landscape where the relations of production carve out and define the boundaries of social positions, trajectories and capacities, setting the limits and the conditions under which those capacities can be distributed and effectively exercised.

However, for the purpose of critique – nothing less than to liberate the modern promise of political freedom and equality from its capitalist corset – it was not enough to emphasize how the presumably "empty" space of abstract universalism was always already saturated with politically significant, distributive relations of order and qualification. Nor was it possible to move beyond the idea of an "empty space" of free participation and equal belonging by simply replacing it with another, more productive image. For that idea was not just a figment of the imagination, nor a mere ideological construction. It was rather the political expression of a metaphysical construct, the modern logic of universalism, which sustained at the same time a new cosmological imagination, the theoretical edifice of modern physics, and a conception of freedom and equality that was essential to the political construction of modern Europe.

This is why, ultimately, the idea of social emancipation appeared not in opposition to that universal logic, but rather as a critique of its incompletion, of the fact that the political universal had been mutilated and restrained, colonized by the economic logic of capitalism, the particular interests of class, and the power-geometry of private property and social domination. The idea of emancipation appeared then as a form of fulfillment of universalism, a "second clearing" of social space, soon to be disencumbered and liberated.

This is perhaps one of the reasons behind the contemporary crisis of emancipatory politics: the undoing of that universal logic, a process which happened over a century ago in the discipline of physics, has only defectively been mirrored in our political imaginaries.[8] The scission that once animated the political logic of universalism – opposing the spatial emptiness of a political sphere and the temporal fetishism of the replacement of capital – now only subsists as a ghostly reflection. The ultimate horizon of the politics of emancipation is blurred as a result; we still hold on to it as an imaginary destination, but in truth, we no longer know where to go.

The Spatial Contradictions of Modern Universalism

From the moment of its formulation, the political logic of universalism was confronted with at least two major spatial contradictions. The first contradiction, which is external to the nature of the state, is due to the fact that political sovereignty is spatially contained.

Multiple political universals coexist side by side with one another, each being restrained within the limits of clearly defined borders. The result of this contradiction is a permanent possibility of conflict; this is why Hobbes affirmed that states live in a state of nature between themselves. The international political space appears consequently as unstable and dangerously irrational; it is the task of international law to rationalize that space, to make it homogenous and commensurable to norms, to reduce its contingency and arbitrariness, to make the international life of states compatible with the universal vocation expressed by each of its elements.

The political geography of the globe, however, would only become more complex, instead of less. The striated space of the colonies, the freedom of the seas and the constant remaking of the borders of continents and states, the competing claims of modern empires, the uneven development of capitalism and its perennial functioning through conflict and contradiction – one after the other, all the attempts at stabilizing a coherent political world-space were to be frustrated and overturned. Schmitt saw precisely in this resistance to homogenization and pacification a distinctive trait of international politics: for him, the self-awareness of the world-space as one, the spatial principle of a *nomos of the Earth*, does not and cannot preclude conflict, but is on the contrary based on it as a presupposition.[9] To combat this assumption is exactly the purpose of a cosmopolitan political project: underneath its various formulations – from Kant's horizon of perpetual peace to the romanticizing mythologies of multilateralism, integration, and the very contemporary aspirations for a "constitution of the Earth" – lies the explicit *desideratum* of a pacification of the globe through its unification, that is the configuration of a universal political space brought to coincidence with the spatial totality of the planet.[10] From this perspective, behind every conflict and war lies a denial of that aspiration, a failure of the ideal that sees in the rational unification of the Earth a sort of unrealized modern destiny, which still calls upon us for its completion.

The second contradiction of universalism also has to do with the containment of the universal within precise boundaries that it is not supposed to transcend, but this time as an internal form of limitation. The fiction of an open, empty political space acquires hence the shape of a sphere – the most perfect of forms, but also one that is limited, separated, unable to extend its domain to the entirety of social being. To abolish that separation of the social and the political, to make the principles of modernity truly universal in their reach, thus becomes the ultimate task of emancipation: in Marxist terms, this requires at once the transformation of the pro-letariat into a universal subject, which would end the segmentation of social being into different classes and positions, and the abolition of the bourgeois state, which would end its role as a political instru-ment for the preservation of capitalist relations and hence for the oppression of one class by another. In the communist society, the sphere of politics would thus be dissolved into a social space that is finally reunified with itself, a truly open and universal space that, in turn, would reorder the space of the world too. For the revolution will extend through the surface of the Earth, effectively abolishing the existence of nation states, and producing instead new forms for the free cooperation and federation of peoples. The interna-tionalist spirit of the communist struggle (in itself a pure instance of the logic of universalism) prefigures this socialist version of cos-mopolitanism: the politics of emancipation only make sense from the perspective of the whole, of a unified Earth and the liberation of all. Ultimately, the "second clearing" of the socialist revolution also depends on a cosmological dimension.

After the cosmopolitan and socialist attempts, the so-called age of globalization would finally bring to completion the dream of a universal synthesis – positing the failure of both as a premise, even as a condition of possibility for the neoliberal unification of the globe. Of course the internationalization of capital, its tendency to overcome all national barriers and conform a unified world mar-ket, is according to Marx a logical development, which is "given in the concept of capital itself."[11] Lenin had likewise described how the total subsumption of the Earth by capital was the ultimate goal of the imperialist struggle, precisely the prospect that the interna-tional alliance of the proletariat was summoned to disrupt. But the historical achievement of such purpose, the ultimate "totalization" of capital as a spatial and logical form, has only happened under very particular conditions.[12] In fact, the celebration of the *unum*, the final synthesis of planetary space in the concept of globaliza-tion, does not quite aim at overcoming the spatial contradictions of universalism; on the contrary, it only seems to reinforce them, and even to rely on them.

Indeed, the open and unified space of globalization depends both on the political fragmentation of authorities and jurisdic-tions, which it multiplies and concentrates in different entities and dimensions that overlap but are never synthesized, and on the rein-forced containment, even on the subjection of political spheres, which were weakened as a result both within nation states and on the transnational plane. What ultimately unifies the world is not politics, but the sheer logic of capital: the abstract universal, finally realized in the pristine image of the Earth as one, lacks any form of substantive political expression.[13] The universal, hence, is never politically given: only this absence of a political instance of unification made the neoliberal completion of the modern project apparently possible.

Even more striking than its historical imposition, however, is the speed at which this ideal of unification faced the threat of collapse. Within a few decades from its affirmation, the globalized Earth confronted an acceleration of internal crises (2001, 2008, 2020), only to find itself threatened externally too: in the ecological emergency the neoliberal project reaches a limit, an existential menace to which, precisely because it lacks a political form, it finds itself unable respond. Perhaps this instability expresses a third spatial contradiction of modern universalism: at the exact point of its unification, this open universal space is violently turned into its opposite, into a closed, fragile totality, the very subsistence of which appears to be at risk. Today, it would seem that the globalized world has become a cosmos again, except in the worst possible political version: not as a virtuous order of places but rather as a violent experience of finitude. Of the modern political cosmology not much seems to be left, except the feeling of weakness, exposure, and vulnerability – this time, however, without any real promise of emancipation. This sudden contraction, this turning-inside that now imposes itself like a destiny, is hence the starting point for any effort of reorientation, and the contemporary premise for a political critique of space.

A Space with No Outside

If every age is defined by a form of spatial imagination, the age of globalization must be marked above all by the impossibility to conceive of an outside.[14] The entire Earth appears subsumed under the image of a world market; all of its points are fully integrated within a single, ideal space for the circulation of capital. There is, simply put, no conceivable exteriority to that uninterrupted space: there is no longer a boundary, and certainly no other space that could be opposed to this one. In the pure givenness of global space – a space of flows and synchronic mobility, where every point is accessible and interconnected at once; a space of instantaneity and simultaneous presence, what Virilio calls a "speed-space" – the logic of universalism seems to find its mythological completion.[15]

Such totality, however, is never concretely given, never instantiated or embodied as one; it remains a synthetic abstraction, only unified by the impossibility of an alternative, by the absence of otherness and interruptions. Global space has no apparent political expression; there is no institution, not even a set of institutions, which can claim the entirety of such space as its own. A temptation appears hence to conceive of a transformation in the nature of political power: what corresponds to the porous, all-encompassing totality of capital would not be a unified, coherent, and centralized entity, in the manner of an international *Leviathan*, but a series of transnational networks and layers of power. Power is thus constituted as a non-place, a system of relays and non-linear political relations, which are diffused throughout an essentially open space. Political sovereignty is thus detached from its inherited spatial contradictions: it no longer has a center, a border, an exteriority.[16] Like in the infinite sphere of Cusanus, now power seems to be everywhere and nowhere at all.

But space has no outside in another sense too. The space of globalization is a space without an outside insofar as capital has no further space to absorb, no virgin land to subsume, no exteriority where it could further project itself. In a global space, capital has literally nowhere else to go; every frontier and division is now found within itself; all that is available to leap over its contradictions is the internal mobility of its elements. Like the cosmos described in the *Timaeus* – an animal that finds nourishment in its own waste – now capital can only feed upon itself: virtualizing, colonizing, overexploiting.[17] In becoming universal, capital does not find an open field for its expansion; it rather reaches a limit and folds back upon itself. Space becomes then the opposite of a universal promise: a closure, a limit, no longer a source of optimism, but of insecurity and paralysis.[18] In a world that becomes one, we seem to have no vision of the whole, except for the possibility of a catastrophe.

On What is Empty

Precisely because there is nothing outside of it, because it subsumes the totality of places within itself, global space becomes paradoxically less visible, instead of more. As a totality, space is in fact somehow impossible to apprehend: there is no "other place" from which it could be seen, no perspective from the outside, no point from which it could be perceived as one. Global space is thus not only naturalized, but also dissimulated, never fully in sight. All we are able to discern are concrete or particular instantiations, manifestations of the totality in fragments, a multiplicity of planes, positions and trajectories against a background that can only be imagined, but never becomes concrete.[19] This retraction, however, only solidifies the political univocity of global space. In a space without exteriority, every idea of an alternative becomes in fact inaccessible – there is simply nowhere else to go. Global space is consequently naturalized as a destiny, stabilized, objectified. Keeping the appearance of openness, space captures and suffocates.[20] Becoming invisible, space negates the possibility of change.

In the absence of a political beyond, all forms of alternative and resistance find themselves confined within a closed world: they become internal forces that proceed from the inside of that same space, aiming at a re-composition of what is already there. There is no new world to be found, no possibility of an island, no "other camp" to desert to. In a beautiful short text, Benjamin described an afterlife that looked exactly like this same life here except for a small, almost imperceptible detail. Likewise, political programs are somehow secularized, and now aim not at the replacement or uprooting of society, but rather at a change of its direction, perhaps just an acceleration, pushing its logic right to the edge.[21] The ancient atomists claimed that no movement would be possible if there existed no void in the world, for motion requires an empty space for things to move into. Similarly, in the absence of an outside, the void that makes political movement possible must now be found within – not as a beyond to which we can aspire, but as the absence of an ultimate grounding, as the contingency of social formations, and hence as the very possibility of change. The emptiness that sustains democratic politics, thus, attests to the impossible closure of society upon itself, the fact that political universals cannot be embodied or reified, that they are politically produced, always the object and the result of a struggle.[22] What is empty is no longer an ideal political space, but the fact that, for that struggle, no final outcome can ever be given.

Contingency and indetermination, however, are a thin base for a political project. The mere "default of a god," to use the famous Heideggerian phrase, does not bring by itself any sense of political liberation.[23] Lacking both reference and direction, struggling to connect a democratic politics and the critique of international political

economy, the movement of resistance to the neoliberal form of globalization has often found itself at a strategic loss. It is telling that
for years the slogan of the movement, "another world is possible,"
aimed at affirming that an alternative could exist, even if it was
impossible to specify exactly which one, not to mention to theorize
its implementation. At the hour of the ecological breakdown, after
successive crisis of capitalist globalization, the question has become
all the more pressing. How to think democracy and emancipation
from the perspective of this spatial crisis? How to conceive of political change under the conditions imposed by global space?

The Striated Polis

It is not surprising that, in parallel with the thousand elegies on
the openness of global space, the last few decades have witnessed
a renewed attention to the situatedness of social life. A multiplicity
of spatially inspired concepts (environments, habitats, dispositifs,
bubbles, spheres, fields) have evoked figures of enclosure, of limitation and containment; a new "physics of power" has aimed at
reconstructing the social production of spaces and times. "One of
the primary objects of discipline," says Foucault in *Discipline and
Punish*, "is to fix; it is an anti-nomadic technique."[24] But to fix does
not necessarily mean to arrest movement: it suffices to channel it
through specific trajectories, to give it a pace and a logic, to make
it correspond to a certain order of space. Power concentrates or
separates, isolates and juxtaposes; it gives positions and rhythms to
things. Thus, the same space can be open and porous for the mobility of some elements and closed and impenetrable for others; what
is apparently at the margins of space can be at the same time the
center of a different periphery. This is perhaps the basic premise of
the "spatial turn" in the critical tradition: space is never a given,
it is never a thing. Space is always a regime that is politically governed, and politically disrupted too.

In *A Thousand Plateaus* – itself a quite interesting spatial notion
– Deleuze and Guattari describe the idea of a "striated space,"
a space of fixity that is saturated with positions, references and
values, a space that can be mapped and counted, measured and
quantified.[25] Confronted to the striated is the idea of a "smooth
space" without limits or landmarks, a purely qualitative space of
different layers and intensities, a space where orientation coincides
with discovery. Interestingly, the account is loaded with political
undertones. All becoming and change happen in smooth space,

which is said to be the basis of resistance and revolution; progress, however, can only crystallize in the striated. In these notions
resonate Nietzsche's "early artist metaphysics" of the Apollinian
and the Dionysian: the God of individuation "congeals the form"
and the shape of things, only to find that shape disrupted by a force
that "annihilates the ordinary bounds and limits of existence."[26]
The emergence of form always exceeds that which is formed: the
limits are pushed from within, they are retraced by what they can
no longer contain. Indeed, it is interesting that smooth and striated
space do not simply oppose one another in the *Nomadology*: on
the contrary, they are said to be the object of a reciprocal necessity.
The smooth is always being translated, petrified into the striated;
the striated melts and expands into the smooth.

Something fundamental happens in the relation expressed by
that movement. Things do not happen in an empty space that
would be already there; rather, the happening of things remakes
the space in which they are – as a transformation or a disruption of
space, of a particular regime of space of which those things are at
once an instance and a modification. At the junction of the striated
and the smooth, of that which holds still and that which disrupts,
something happens that forces us to raise the question again: what
does it mean to be placed, to be positioned, to be contained by
space? Is it possible to think of emancipation from limitation and
together with it, to think the autonomy of that which is always
already in place, always already limited? The challenge, in other
words, is to think of the limit as the very place where autonomy
is constantly at stake, this time not in association with a political
void, but as a transformation of space.

Democracy at the Limit

In his lectures on Nietzsche, Heidegger presents a reading of the
will to power as a work of delimitation of chaos, as the imposition
of limits, regularity, and form upon a universe entirely made of
force and becoming. Interestingly, Heidegger calls this operation
of delimitation a "praxis": the will to power consists of setting
limits, of "a fixing and thus a limiting" of life.[27] But here too, such
fixing cannot find any permanence or stability. Limits are set and
then overcome, transgressed by practices that establish new, further horizons, which are themselves overcome in the positing of a
further limit and fixation (from a spatial perspective, that motion is
remarkably close to Marx's description of the logic of capital in the

Grundrisse, where he speaks of the "tendency of capital to relate to every limit on its self-realization" as to a barrier that must be overcome: capital constantly fixes and exceeds what is fixed, it moves through contradictions that are "constantly overcome but just as constantly posited").[28] At the limit, at the point where ending and beginning coincide, the living being is exposed each time "to what has not been fixed, what becomes and can become, the possible."[29] A composite of openness and determination, of containment and dislocation, the limit is at once a place of closure and opening, the place where the opening discloses itself, where it is made room for, so that it can appear as a possibility of action.[30]

Limits, hence, are not simple instances of the negative; they are more than mere reifications or external constraints. Of course, limits hold environments and situate things. But a limit also moves with the thing that it limits; it is something like its margin of possibility, a horizon that can be pressured, pushed in different directions by different forces, torn until the point of contradiction, broken and then recomposed. From a materialist perspective, this means that the limit is a place of containment, but also the locus of an ongoing struggle; it means that limits fix and order modes of being, but also that they express movement, tension, and growth. Perhaps this is what Gramsci's notion of the "war of position" ultimately implies: orders are fissured only at the limits, in those points of rupture and concentration where causes and effects become manifest and political interventions acquire a visibility, a potentiality, a temporality of their own.[31] Limits aggregate and accumulate power, they generate political distributions of space. But even when those regimes are assaulted, when they collapse or are politically abolished, limits do not disappear: they just sediment in different ways.

This is the idea with which I would like to conclude this book: an idea of autonomy as a work on the limit, a dislocation in the order of things whose direction is always as yet undecided. Against those who imagine a linear replacement of such order, or its suspension in an ideal nowhere, the idea of the limit affirms instead a sort of political topology – a study of the transformation of spaces, of the plasticity of political forms.[32] From this perspective, the political universal appears as something that is always concretely given, always materially spaced. Its limits are nothing but the effect of a process, of an encounter of forces, of a disruption that was once returned into space. Politics never occurs in a clearing; there is always something that is already in place, a tension of limits that curbs the movement of things. But each limit gestures as well at a different motion, and the possibility of limiting being in different ways.

Notes

1. Martin Heidegger, "Building, Dwelling, Thinking," in *Poetry, Language* (New York: Harper & Row, 1971), 154.

2. Jacques Rancière, *Moments politiques: interventions 1977–2009* (Paris: Fabrique, 2009), 154.

3. For Arendt, political actions express the ontological condition of "natality," the human capacity to begin, to make *archai*, at once principles *and* beginnings, which interrupt any subordination to mechanisms and determinations: "to take initiative, to begin, . . . to set something in motion. Because they are *initium*, newcomers and beginners by virtue of birth, men take initiative, are prompted into action" (Hannah Arendt, *The Human Condition* [Chicago: University of Chicago Press, 1958], 177. See also the commentary by Miguel Vatter, "Natality and Biopolitics in Hannah Arendt," *Revista de Ciencia Política* 24, no. 2, (2006): 137–59). Reiner Schürmann explains that the category of natality, which is for Arendt the "central category of political thought" (*The Human Condition*, 9), must be understood in the wake of Heidegger's exploration of the historicity of Dasein, as an attempt to displace its emphasis on mortality, the tension of Dasein as a being-towards-death, by opposing to the expectation of death a genetic experience of memory: in remembering our own birth, our own origin and "beginning," we are able to act as beginners ourselves, to suspend our determinations, our existential orientation towards death as a future, and affirm instead the singular, prolific freedom of our existence in the world. To begin, hence, is to give birth to an autonomous action that bears its own temporality within itself (Reiner Schürmann, *Des Hégémonies Brisées* [Toulouse: T.E.R., 1996], 67, n.3).

4. In a political revolution, for instance, coincide "the idea of freedom" and the notion of a "new beginning" (Hannah Arendt, *On Revolution* [New York: Penguin Books, 2006], 29, 212). For Arendt, "the problem of the beginning [is the problem] of an unconnected, new event breaking into the continuous sequence of historical time" (*On Revolution*, 204–5). This is the temporality that survives the critique of instrumentalism: not as a quantum of chronology, but as an essential fact marking both the freedom and limitation of our ontological condition. It is the temporality of an interruption, an exceptional event that generates its own conditions of possibility. It is, one could claim, a conception of autonomy as temporality *without an end*, an idea which has taken a wealth of forms in recent political thought, including its radical emancipatory variants, as an alternative to the instrumental conception of the political in terms of logical mediations between means and ends. See for instance Giorgio Agamben, *Means Without End: Notes on Politics* (Minneapolis: University of Minnesota Press, 2000).

5. In *On Revolution*, Arendt thematizes explicitly the relation between the beginning and the nowhere, interpreting it *as if* it carried an abolishment of the spatio-temporal order of the social: "Not only

is it not bound into a reliable chain of cause and effect, a chain in which each effect immediately turns into the cause for future developments, the beginning has, as it were, nothing whatsoever to hold on to; it is as though it came out of nowhere in either time or space. For a moment, the moment of beginning, it is as though the beginner had abolished the sequence of temporality itself, or as though the actors were thrown out of the temporal order and its continuity" (*On Revolution*, 206). The theological undertones are relevant here: in *The Human Condition*, Arendt says herself: "Action is, in fact, the one miracle-working faculty of man . . . The miracle that saves the world, the realm that saves human affairs from its normal, 'natural' ruin is ultimately the fact of natality, in which the faculty of action is ontologically rooted" (*The Human Condition*, 246–7).

6. This is the conception of public space as a "space of appearance," "where I appear to others as others appear to me, where men exist not merely like other living or inanimate things, but to make their appearance explicitly" (*The Human Condition*, 198ff). "Unlike the spaces which are the work of our hands," Arendt says of such space, "it does not survive the actuality of the movement which brought it into being, but disappears not only with the dispersal of men – as in the case of great catastrophes when the body politic of a people is destroyed – but with the disappearance or arrest of the activities themselves. Wherever people gather together, it is potentially there, but only potentially, not necessarily and not forever" (ibid.).

7. "Hence we see that whether a use-value is to be regarded as raw material, as instrument of labour or as product is determined entirely by its specific function in the labour process, by the position it occupies there: as its position changes, so do its determining characteristics" (Karl Marx, *Capital: A Critique of Political Economy* [New York: Penguin Books in association with New Left Review, 1990], vol. 1, part 3, ch. 7, 289).

8. To retrace the origin of such implosion in the physics of the twentieth century, and to investigate the association between the demise of Newtonian space and the crisis of the modern logic of universalism, would be a necessary complement to the effort sustained in this book. Perhaps the four logical principles that I have used to reconstruct the modern logic of universalism – infinity, emptiness, abstraction and absoluteness – could be used again as vectors for the investigation of its crisis, and for the reconstruction of its multiple scientific and political effects. On this point, and on the "subconscious" survival of the Euclidean-Newtonian worldview within our everyday lives, see Karel Čapek, *The War with the Newts*, translated by Ewald Osers (New York: Catbird Press, 2004).

9. Carl Schmitt, *The Nomos of the Earth in the International Law of the Jus Publicum Europaeum* (New York: Telos Press, 2003).

10. Luigi Ferrajoli, "The Case for a Planetary Constitution", *Il Manifesto*, March 21, 2020.

11. Marx, *Grundrisse* (New York: Penguin Books, 1973), 408. By its nature, capital "drives beyond every spatial barrier"; it aims at conquering "the whole earth for its market," and at the same time "it strives to annihilate this space with time, i.e. to reduce to a minimum the time spent in motion from one place to another" (ibid. 539; see also David Harvey's analysis of how the failure to "achieve spatial integration disturbs the universality of the value form" in *The Limits to Capital* [New York: Verso, 2006], 375ff. On the conception of "space-time compression" through technological progress, see David Harvey, *The Condition of Postmodernity: An Enquiry into the Origins of Cultural Change* [Oxford: Blackwell, 1989]). In the *Communist Manifesto*, that same drive was described in terms of a "cosmopolitan character" of capitalist production and consumption: "The need for a constantly expanding market chases the bourgeoisie over the whole surface of the globe. It must nestle everywhere, settle everywhere, establish connections everywhere" (*Communist Manifesto*, 38).

12. "[Capital] has totalized itself both intensively and extensively. It's global in reach, and it penetrates to the heart and soul of social life and nature" (Ellen Meiksins Wood, "Back to Marx," *Monthly Review* 49, no. 2 (1997): 5).

13. "Finance capital, since it is so abstract, seems distant from the lives of most people; but that very abstraction is what gives it the general power of an a priori, with increasingly universal reach" (Michael Hardt and Antonio Negri, *Commonwealth* [Cambridge: Harvard University Press, 2009], 7).

14. "Las grandes transformaciones históricas suelen ir acompañadas, en verdad, de una mutación de la imagen del espacio. En ella radica la verdadera médula de la amplia transformación política, económica y cultural que entonces se lleva a cabo" (Carl Schmitt, *Tierra y Mar: Una Reflexión Sobre La Historia Universal* [Madrid: Trotta, 2007], 49).

15. See Jai Sen, "On Open Space: Explorations Towards a Vocabulary of a More Open Politics," *Antipode* 42, no. 4 (2010): 994–1018; and Paul Virilio, *Speed and Politics: An Essay on Dromology* (New York: Columbia University Press, 1986).

16. See for instance Hardt and Negri's characterization of empire as a non-explicit form of power, an *ou-topia* where power has no longer a place but is "both everywhere and nowhere" (Michael Hardt and Antonio Negri, *Empire* [Cambridge: Harvard University Press, 2000], 190, 232; Bashir Abu-Manneh describes the notion of empire as "spatially limitless, temporally eternal, socially all-encompassing, politically centerless, and universally peaceful," see "The Illusions of Empire", *Monthly Review*, June 1, 2004).

17. See David Harvey, *A Companion to Marx's Capital, Volume 2* (London: Verso Books, 2013), 376). The reference to the *Timaeus* can be found at 33bd.

18. This is perhaps close to what Fredric Jameson describes as "the strange new feeling of an absence of inside and outside," which expresses the fact that "the security of the Newtonian era [has been] withdrawn" (Fredric Jameson, *Postmodernism, or the Cultural Logic of Late Capitalism* [Durham: Duke University Press, 1991], 116–17; cited in Doreen Massey, *For Space*, 79). Heidegger explained in *Being and Time* the relation that the "nowhere," the being out of place, entertains with the crisis of anxiety: "Thus neither does *Angst* 'see' a definite 'there' and 'over here' from which what is threatening approaches. The fact that what is threatening is *nowhere* characterizes what *Angst* is about. *Angst* 'does not know' what it is about which it is anxious. But 'nowhere' does not mean nothing: rather, region in general lies therein, and disclosedness of the world in general for essentially spatial being-in. Therefore, what is threatening cannot approach from a definite direction within nearness, it is already 'there' – and yet nowhere. It is so near that it is oppressive and stifles one's breath – and yet it is nowhere. In what *Angst* is about, the 'it is nothing and nowhere' becomes manifest. The recalcitrance of the innerwordly nothing and nowhere means phenomenally that *what* Angst *is about is the world as such*" (Martin Heidegger, *Being and Time: A Translation of Sein Und Zeit* [Albany: State University of New York Press, 1996], section 40, 174–5). It would perhaps be interesting to develop a political analysis of the notion of democratic anxiety as related to the idea of a global nowhere.

19. Ellen Meiksins Wood describes the political effects of this dissolution: "disaggregating society into fragments, with no overarching power structure, no totalizing unity, no systemic coercions – in other words, no capitalist system, with its expansionary drive and its capacity to penetrate every aspect of social life" (*Democracy against Capitalism*, 245).

20. See for instance Ernesto Laclau, *New Reflections on the Revolution of our Time*, 72–82. For Laclau, space represents and representation spatializes: both fixate meaning, stabilize and arrest the life of becoming, they capture and suffocate what is essentially fluid, changing, multiple and self-differing – and turn it thus into something stable, coherent and lifeless. In representing, space orders, it forecloses openness and contingency, and thus destroys the temporal "dislocation" which is at the heart of the political (ibid.; also cited in Massey, *For Space*, 20ff).

21. This was precisely the puzzle signaled in the mysterious accelerationist passage of the *Anti-Oedipus*: "But which is the revolutionary path? Is there one? – To withdraw from the world market, as Samir Amin advises Third World countries to do, in a curious revival of

the fascist 'economic solution'? Or might it be to go in the opposite direction? To go still further, that is, in the movement of the market, of decoding and deterritorialization? For perhaps the flows are not yet deterritorialized enough, not decoded enough . . . Not to withdraw from the process, but to go further, to *accelerate the process*, as Nietzsche put it: in this matter, the truth is we haven't seen anything yet" (Gilles Deleuze and Felix Guattari, *Anti-Oedipus: Capitalism and Schizophrenia* [New York: Viking Press, 1977], 239).

22. Of course, the association of democracy and emptiness refers to the political philosophy of Claude Lefort. For Lefort, the destruction of political figures of transcendence cannot efface the *place* that such figures occupied: the transcendent body is destroyed, but it symbolically subsists as the fundamental *emptiness* of a power that can no longer be embodied – that leaves the place of the symbolic One forever vacant. The "empty places" of democratic power, multiplied by the fracture and fragmentation of that unity, attest thereby to society's impossible, to its impossible political self-identity. Chantal Mouffe reinterprets Lefortian democracy in terms of a specific political agonism: "The public space, in Lefort's account, is the social space where, in the absence of a foundation, the meaning and unity of the social is negotiated – at once constituted and put at risk. What is recognized in public space is the legitimacy of debate about what is legitimate and what is illegitimate" (see Claude Lefort, *L'Invention démocratique: les limites de la domination totalitaire* [Paris: Fayard, 1994], 172ff; and Chantal Mouffe et al., *Deconstruction and Pragmatism* [Taylor and Francis, 2003], 149). Interestingly, one of Lefort's last texts deals precisely with the political perils of the idea of the unification of the globe in a "world space" (Claude Lefort, *La Complication: retour sur le communisme* [Paris: Fayard, 1999]; see also Bernard Flynn, *The Philosophy of Claude Lefort: Interpreting the Political*, 267ff).

23. "The era is defined by the god's failure to arrive, by the 'default of god' . . . The default of god means that no god any longer gathers men and things unto himself, visibly and unequivocally, and by such gathering disposes of the world's history and man's sojourn in it" (Martin Heidegger, *Poetry, Language, Thought* [New York: 1971], 91).

24. Michel Foucault, *Discipline and Punish: The Birth of the Prison* [New York: Vintage Books, 1995], 218. For Foucault, discipline is the "counterpart" of law; it appears to undermine or transgress the law, but in fact it does nothing but to develop it: discipline gives the law its actual and effective content, it practically encloses and demarcates what the abstract universality of the law affirms at the very same time. The matrix of social power works hence beneath and above the order of law, but always *together with it*: it alternatively embodies, punctuates and suspends the law, it encompasses and substantiates formal legalism through the structuring delimitation of social capacities, possibilities and positions.

25. Gilles Deleuze and Felix Guattari, *Nomadology: The War Machine* (New York, Semiotext(e), 1986), 20ff (published originally as ch. 12 of *A Thousand Plateaus: Capitalism and Schizophrenia* [Minneapolis: University of Minnesota Press, 1987]). See also Edward Casey, *The Fate of Place*, 301ff.

26. See the following references from *The Birth of Tragedy* (New York: Vintage Books, 1967): Apollo, who "forms states" (p. 124) and is the "God of individuation and of just boundaries" (p. 72), "knows but one law – the individual, i.e. the *delimiting of the boundaries of the individual*, measure in the Hellenic sense" (p. 46). The "rapture of the Dionysian," on the other hand, brings forth the "annihilation of the ordinary bounds and limits of existence" (p. 59). Standing in a similar reciprocal relation, Nietzsche affirms that despite the "Apollinian tendency to *congeal the form* to Egyptian rigidity and coldness, lest the effort to prescribe to the individual wave its *path and realm* might annul the motion of the whole lake, the *high tide of the Dionysian* destroyed from time to time all those little circles in which the one-sidedly Apollinian "will" had sought to *confine* the Hellenic spirit" (p. 72; my emphasis for all of the above).

27. "Das Schemabedurfnis ist bereits Ausblick auf Festmachendes und damit Eingrenzendes." I am using Andrew Mitchell's translation of the original text in "Praxis and Gelassenheit" (Francois Raffoul and David Pettigrew (eds.), *Heidegger and Practical Philosophy* [Albany: State University of New York Press, 2002], 331). The translation of the passage by Joan Stambaugh, David Farrell Krell, and Frank A. Capuzzi reads "The need for a schema already looks for what stabilizes and thus limits" (Martin Heidegger, "The Will to Power as Knowledge," *Nietzsche* [San Francisco: Harper and Row, 1979], vol. 3, 85ff).

28. Marx, "The Circulation Process of Capital," *Grundrisse* (London: Penguin, 1993), notebook IV, section 2, 422, 410. Capital sweeps away all "fixed, fast-frozen relations"; everything that ossifies will melt into air (*The Communist Manifesto*, 38).

29. Heidegger, *Nietzsche*, vol. 3, 87.

30. "A space is something that has been made room for, something that is cleared and free, namely within a boundary, Greek *peras*. A boundary is not that at which something stops but, as the Greek recognized, the boundary is that from which something *begins its presencing*. That is why the concept is that of *horismos*, that is the horizon, the boundary. Space is in essence that for which room has been made, that which is let into its bounds" (Martin Heidegger, "Building, Dwelling, Thinking", in *Poetry, Language, Thought*, 154).

31. "La struttura massiccia delle democrazie moderne, sia come organizzazioni statali che come complesso di associazioni nella vita civile costituiscono per l'arte politica come le 'trincee' e le fortificazioni permanenti del

fronte nella guerra di posizione: essi rendono solo 'parziale' l'elemento del movimento che prima era 'tutta' la guerra" (Antonio Gramsci, "Note sul Machiavelli", in *Quaderni del carcere* [Rome: 1979], 102–3). The challenge, from this perspective, is to think of revolution neither as an end nor as a beginning, but as a "partial movement" that makes other, subsequent motions possible: the thought and praxis of emancipation, as shown by historical experience, becomes even more fundamental *after* the revolution than before. It would perhaps be interesting to develop a study of the theories of hegemony and revolution (but also, for instance, of the Poulantzian notion of the state as a "field of forces") from this spatial perspective.

32. "To form itself, the public has to break existing political forms. This is hard to do because these forms are themselves the regular means of instituting change" (John Dewey, *The Public and Its Problems* [New York: Henry Holt, 1927], 31). This association of democracy and the disruption of forms already appeared in book VIII of the *Republic*, where Socrates famously affirms that in democratic cities all sorts of human beings come to be, because democracy contains all species of regimes within it: there are many incipient shapes moving, waiting to emerge and erupt within this single, unstable and over-encompassing political form (whether for Socrates this is a good thing is a matter of discussion: democracy is the *best* place for a philosopher to look for a regime, but it is also the most prone to rapid corruption and decay. Ultimately, this is the paradox of democracy: the city that provides more room for creativity, innovation and self-correction is also the first one to fall into the vicious circles of transformation and decay). The topological dimension of democracy, however, does not merely refer to the *in which* of political transformations, but to the spatial character of those transformations themselves. See for instance this characteristic passage by Jacques Rancière: "On dit qu'il n'y a plus d'horizon d'attente. Mais il faut inverser l'idée d'un grand horizon historique dont les promesses auraient permis la nouveauté politique et artistique. L'histoire ne fait rien et ne promet rien. Ce sont les actions politiques et les opérations artistiques qui créent une historicité propre, et éventuellement alors des horizons d'attente. Le temps ne crée pas de radicalité, ce sont les radicalités qui s'inventent un temps. J'essaye de penser les choses non pas en termes de nouveauté radicale, de commencement ou de fin, mais plutôt en termes de topographies, de systèmes de distribution des possibles qui mettent en jeu des temporalités différentes. Un présent de l'art ou de la politique se constitue à partir de couches hétérogènes qui ne sont pas forcément contemporaines, qui constituent une réinvention perpétuelle du passé" (*Moments Politiques*, 154).

Bibliography and Works Cited

Abu-Manneh, Bashir. "The Illusions of Empire." *Monthly Review*, June 2004.

Accetti, Carlo Invernizzi. *Relativism and Religion: Why Democratic Societies Do Not Need Moral Absolutes*. New York: Columbia University Press, 2015.

Agamben, Giorgio. *Means Without End: Notes on Politics*. Minneapolis: University of Minnesota Press, 2000.

Allen, J. W. *A History of Political Thought in the 16th Century*. Abingdon: Routledge, 2013.

Anderson, Perry. *Passages from Antiquity to Feudalism*. London: Verso Books, 1978.

Anderson, Perry. *The New Old World*. New York: Verso Books, 2011.

Anderson, Perry. "American Foreign Policy and its Thinkers." *New Left Review*, no. 83 (2013): 6–7.

Anderson, Perry. *Lineages of the Absolutist State*. London: Verso Books, 2013.

Andolfo, M. *Testimonianze e Frammenti Degli Atomisti Antichi*. Milan: Bompiani, 2001.

Aquinas, Thomas. *Summa Contra Gentiles*. Notre Dame: University of Notre Dame Press, 1975.

Aquinas, Thomas. *Summa Theologiae*. https://www.newadvent.org/summa/2091.htm#article3.

Arendt, Hannah. *The Human Condition*. Chicago: University of Chicago Press, 1958.

Arendt, Hannah. *On Revolution*. New York: Penguin Books, 2006.

Aristotle. *Metaphysics, Volume I*. Cambridge: Harvard University Press, 1933.

Aristotle. *On the Heavens*. Cambridge: Harvard University Press, 1939.

Aristotle. *Physics*. Cambridge: Harvard University Press, 1957.

Aristotle. *The Nicomachean Ethics*. Dordrecht: Springer Netherlands, 1980.

Aristotle. *Complete Works of Aristotle, Volume 1: The Revised Oxford Translation*. Princeton: Princeton University Press, 2014.

Aristotle. *Aristotle's Politics. Writings from the Complete Works: Politics, Economics, Constitution of Athens*. Princeton: Princeton University Press, 2017.

Arnobius. *The Case against the Pagans*. Westminster: Newman Press, 1949.

Augustine. *Augustine: The City of God*. Edinburgh: T&T Clark, 1871.

Augustine. *The City of God*. New York: Modern Library, 1993.

Augustine. *On Christian Teaching*. Oxford: Oxford University Press, 1999.

Augustine. *On the Trinity*. Cambridge: Cambridge University Press, 2002.

Augustine. *Confessions*. Indianapolis: Hackett Pub. Co, 2006.

Augustine. *The Confessions of Saint Augustine* (Latin Text). Accessed August 8, 2020. http://www.stoa.org/hippo/noframe_entry.html.

Bacon, Francis. *The New Organon*. New York: Cambridge University Press, 2000.

Bacon, Francis. *The Philosophical Works of Francis Bacon*. Abingdon: Routledge, 2011.

Bakker, Frederik, Delphine Bellis, and Carla Rita Palmerino, eds. *Space, Imagination and the Cosmos from Antiquity to the Early Modern Period*. Cham: Springer International Publishing, 2018.

Balibar, Étienne. *Spinoza and Politics*. London: Verso Books, 1998.

Barnes, Jonathan. *The Presocratic Philosophers*. London: Routledge, 1982.

Benveniste, Emile. *Indo-European Language and Society*. Miami: University of Miami Press, 1973.

Berger, John. *The Look of Things: Essays*. New York: Viking Press, 1974.

Bergson, Henri. *Creative Evolution*. Translated by Mitchell Abidor. New York: New York Review of Books, 2019.

Bernstein, Richard J. *Beyond Objectivism and Relativism: Science, Hermeneutics, and Praxis*. Philadelphia: University of Pennsylvania Press, 1983.

Bernstein, Richard J. *The Pragmatic Turn*. Cambridge: Polity, 2010.

Berstein, Serge. *La Démocratie libérale*. Paris: Presses Universitaires de France, 1998.

Bertt, G. S. *The Philosophy Of Gassendi*. London: Macmillan, 1908.

Bickerton, Christopher J. *European Integration: From Nation States to Member States*. Oxford: Oxford University Press, 2012.

Biener, Zvi. "De Gravitatione Reconsidered: The Changing Significance of Experimental Evidence for Newton's Metaphysics of Space." *Journal of the History of Philosophy* 55, no. 4 (2017): 583–608.

Boethius. *Theological Tractates. The Consolation of Philosophy*. Cambridge: Harvard University Press, 1918.

Boethius. *On the Holy Trinity*. Translated by Erik C. Kenyon, 2004. Accessed January 8, 2021. http://pvspade.com/Logic/docs/Boethius-DeTrin.pdf.

Bonometti, Donata. "L'Anno Nuovo del Decamerone." Accessed September 20, 2020. https://www.pienidigiorni.com/single-post/2020/09/20/l-anno-del-nuovo-decamerone.

Borges, Jorge Luis. *Labyrinths: Selected Stories and Other Writings*. New York: New Directions Publishing, 1964.

Boyde, Patrick. *Dante Philomythes and Philosopher: Man in the Cosmos*. Cambridge: Cambridge University Press, 1983.

Brackenridge, J. Bruce. *The Key to Newton's Dynamics: The Kepler Problem and the Principia*. Berkeley: University of California Press, 1995.

Brandom, Robert. *Articulating Reasons: An Introduction to Inferentialism*. Cambridge: Harvard University Press, 2000.

Brandom, Robert. *Tales of the Mighty Dead: Historical Essays in the Metaphysics of Intentionality*. Cambridge: Harvard University Press, 2002.

Breaugh, Martin, Christopher Holman, Rachel Magnusson, Paul Mazzocchi, and Devin Penner. *Thinking Radical Democracy: The Return to Politics in Post-War France*. Toronto: University of Toronto Press, 2015.

Bréhier, Emile. *Chrysippe*. Paris: Félix Alcan, Editeur, 1910.

Brisson, Luc. "Polis as Kosmos in Plato's Laws." *Cosmos in the Ancient World*. Cambridge: Cambridge University Press, 2019, 122–41.

Brockelman, Thomas. "Lost in Place? On the Virtues and Vices of Edward Casey's Anti-Modernism." *Humanitas* 16 (2003): 36.

Brown, Oscar James. *Natural Rectitude and Divine Law in Aquinas: An Approach to an Integral Interpretation of the Thomistic Doctrine of Law*. Toronto: Pontifical Institute of Mediaeval Studies, 1981.

Bruno, Giordano. *Giordano Bruno: Cause, Principle and Unity: And Essays on Magic*. Cambridge: Cambridge University Press, 1998.

Bruno, Giordano. *De l'Infinito, Universo e Mondi* [1584]. Accessed January 8, 2021. https://iniziazioneantica.altervista.org/1500-1600/bruno/DeInfinitoUniverso.pdf.

Burtt, Edwin A. *The Metaphysical Foundations of Modern Physical Science: A Historical and Critical Essay*. New York: Humanities Press, 1932.

Bustinduy, Pablo. "Two or Three Battles: Organicity and Temporality in Cartesian Ethics." *Ramon Llull Journal of Applied Ethics* 4 (2013): 9–29.

Calhoun, Craig. "Civil Society and the Public Sphere: History of the Concept." International Encyclopedia of the Social and Behavioral Sciences, 2nd ed. Oxford: Elsevier, 2001, 701–6.

Čapek, Karel. *The War with the Newts*. Translated by Ewald Osers. New York: Catbird Press, 2004.

Čapek, Milič, ed. *The Concepts of Space and Time*. Dordrecht: Springer Netherlands, 1976.

Casey, Edward S. *Getting Back Into Place: Toward a Renewed Understanding of the Place-World*. Bloomington: Indiana University Press, 1993.

Casey, Edward S. *The Fate of Place. A Philosophical History*. Berkeley: University of California Press, 1998.

Cavarero, Adriana. *Horrorism: Naming Contemporary Violence*. New York: Columbia University Press, 2009.

Cicero. *The Republic and The Laws*. Oxford: Oxford University Press, 2009.

Clarke, Samuel. *The Leibniz–Clarke Correspondence, Together with Extracts from Newton's Principia and Opticks*. New York: Philosophical Library, 1956.

Cornford, F. M. "The Invention of Space." *The Concepts of Space and Time: Their Structure and Their Development*, edited by Milič Čapek. Dordrecht: Springer Netherlands, 1976, 3–16.

Couprie, Dirk. *Heaven and Earth in Ancient Greek Cosmology: From Thales to Heraclides Ponticus*. New York: Springer, 2011.

Couprie, Dirk, and Radim Kočandrle. *Apeiron: Anaximander on Generation and Destruction*. New York: Springer International Publishing, 2017.

Coxon, A. H. *The Fragments of Parmenides: A Critical Text With Introduction and Translation, the Ancient Testimonia and a Commentary*. Las Vegas: Parmenides Publishing, 2009.

Deleuze, Gilles, and Félix Guattari. *Anti-Oedipus: Capitalism and Schizophrenia*. New York: Viking Press, 1977.

Deleuze, Gilles, and Félix Guattari. *Nomadology: The War Machine*. New York: Semiotext(e), 1986.

Deleuze, Gilles, and Félix Guattari. *A Thousand Plateaus: Capitalism and Schizophrenia*. Minneapolis: University of Minnesota Press, 1987.

Demelemestre, Gaëlle. "Le Concept Lefortien du Pouvoir comme Lieu Vide." *Raisons Politiques* 46, no. 2 (2012): 175–93.

D'Eramo, Marco. "Populism and the New Oligarchy." *New Left Review* 83 (2013): 5–28.

Descartes, René. *Selected Philosophical Writings*. Cambridge: Cambridge University Press, 1988.

Descartes, René. *Meditations on First Philosophy: With Selections from the Objections and Replies*. Cambridge: Cambridge University Press, 1996.

Dewey, John. *The Public and Its Problems*. New York: Henry Holt, 1927.

Dewey, John. *The Later Works of John Dewey, 1925–1953*, vol. 4. Carbondale: Southern Illinois University Press, 1988.

Dijksterhuis, Eduard Jan. *The Mechanization of the World Picture: Pythagoras to Newton*. Princeton: Princeton University Press, 1986.

Dodd, James. *Crisis and Reflection: An Essay on Husserl's Crisis of the European Sciences*. Dordrecht: Springer Netherlands, 2005.

Duhem, Pierre Maurice Marie. "The Empyrean as the Place of The Universe." *The Concepts of Space and Time: Their Structure and Their Development*. Dordrecht: Springer Netherlands, 1976, 43–5.

Duhem, Pierre Maurice Marie. *Medieval Cosmology: Theories of Infinity, Place, Time, Void, and the Plurality of Worlds*. Chicago: University of Chicago Press, 1990.

Duhem, Pierre Maurice Marie. *Le Système du monde: Histoire des Doctrines Cosmologiques de Platon à Copernic*. Paris: A. Hermann, 1913.

Edwards, Mark. *Aristotle and Early Christian Thought*. Abingdon: Routledge, 2019.

Einstein, Albert. "Foreword." In Max Jammer, *Concepts of Space. The Histories of Space in Physics*. New York: Dover, 1993.

Elden, Stuart. *The Birth of Territory*. Chicago: Chicago University Press, 2013.

Eliade, Mircea. *Cosmos and History: The Myth of the Eternal Return*. New York: Harper and Brothers, 1954.

Erfani, Farhang. "Fixing Marx with Machiavelli: Claude Lefort's Democratic Turn." *Journal of the British Society for Phenomenology* 39, no. 2 (2008): 200–14.

Ertman, Thomas. *Birth of the Leviathan: Building States and Regimes in Medieval and Early Modern Europe*. Cambridge: Cambridge University Press, 1997.

Fabian, Johannes. *Time and the Other: How Anthropology Makes Its Object*. New York: Columbia University Press, 1983.

Fanon, Frantz. *The Wretched of the Earth*. New York: Grove Press, 1968.

Ferrajoli, Luigi. "The Case for a Planetary Constitution." *Il Manifesto*, March 21, 2020. https://global.ilmanifesto.it/the-case-for-a-planetary-constitution/.

Flynn, Bernard. *The Philosophy of Claude Lefort: Interpreting the Political*. Evanston: Northwestern University Press, 2006.

Foucault, Michel. *Power/Knowledge: Selected Interviews and Other Writings, 1972–1977*. Brighton: Harvester Press, 1980.

Foucault, Michel. *La Pensée du dehors*. Paris: Fata Morgana, 1986.

Foucault, Michel. "Of Other Spaces." *Diacritics* 16, no. 1 (1986): 22–7.

Foucault, Michel. *Discipline and Punish: The Birth of the Prison*. New York: Vintage Books, 1995.

Fukuyama, Francis. *The End of History and the Last Man*. New York: Free Press, 2006.

Furley, David. *The Greek Cosmologists. The Formation of the Atomic Theory and Its Earliest Critics*. Cambridge: Cambridge University Press, 1987.

Galilei, Galileo. *Opere*. Florence: Edizione Nazionale, 1966.

Galilei, Galileo. *Galileo on the World Systems: A New Abridged Translation and Guide*. Berkeley: University of California Press, 1997.

Galli, Carlo. *Political Spaces and Global War*. Minneapolis: University of Minnesota Press, 2010.

Gerson, Lloyd, ed. *The Cambridge Companion to Plotinus*. Cambridge: Cambridge University Press, 1996.

Graham, Daniel W. *Explaining the Cosmos: The Ionian Tradition of Scientific Philosophy*. Princeton: Princeton University Press, 2009.

Gramsci, Antonio. *Quaderni del Carcere*. Rome: Editori Riuniti, 1971.

Granada, Miguel A. "Kepler and Bruno on the Infinity of the Universe and of Solar Systems." *Journal for the History of Astronomy* 39, no. 4 (2008): 469–95.

Grant, Edward. "Medieval and Seventeenth-Century Conceptions of an Infinite Void Space beyond the Cosmos." *Isis* 60, no. 1 (1969): 39–60.

Grant, Edward. *Much Ado about Nothing: Theories of Space and Vacuum from the Middle Ages to the Scientific Revolution*. Cambridge: Cambridge University Press, 1981.

Grant, Edward. *The Foundations of Modern Science in the Middle Ages: Their Religious, Institutional and Intellectual Contexts*. Cambridge: Cambridge University Press, 1996.

Hardt, Michael, and Antonio Negri. *Empire*. Cambridge: Harvard University Press, 2000.

Hardt, Michael, and Antonio Negri. *Commonwealth*. Cambridge: Harvard University Press, 2009.

Harries, Karsten. "The Infinite Sphere: Comments on the History of a Metaphor." *Journal of the History of Philosophy* 13, no. 1 (1975): 5–15.

Harriman, Benjamin. *Melissus and Eleatic Monism*. Cambridge: Cambridge University Press, 2018.

Harvey, David. *The Condition of Postmodernity: An Enquiry into the Origins of Cultural Change*. Cambridge: Blackwell, 1989.

Harvey, David. *David Harvey: A Reader*, Oxford: Blackwell Publishing Ltd, 2006.

Harvey, David. *The Limits to Capital*. New York: Verso Books, 2006.

Harvey, David. *Spaces of Global Capitalism: Towards a Theory of Uneven Geographical Development*. London: Verso Books, 2006.

Harvey, David. *A Companion to Marx's Capital*. Vol. 2. London: Verso Books, 2013.

Hegel, Georg Wilhelm Friedrich. *Elements of the Philosophy of Right*. New York: Cambridge University Press, 1991.

Heidegger, Martin. *Poetry, Language, Thought*. New York: Harper and Row, 1971.

Heidegger, Martin. *Nietzsche*. San Francisco: Harper and Row, 1979.

Heidegger, Martin. *Being and Time: A Translation of Sein Und Zeit*. Albany: State University of New York Press, 1996.

Helmig, Christoph, and Carlos Steel. "Proclus." *The Stanford Encyclopedia of Philosophy*. Metaphysics Research Lab, Stanford University, 2020.

Heraclitus. *Fragments: A Text and Translation with a Commentary*. Toronto: University of Toronto Press, 1987.

Herodotus. *Herodotus, with an English Translation by A. D. Godley*. Cambridge: Harvard University Press, 1920.

Hobbes, Thomas. *The English Works of Thomas Hobbes of Malmesbury*. London: Bohn, 1839.

Hobbes, Thomas. *Behemoth; or, The Long Parliament*. New York: Barnes and Noble, 1969.

Hobbes, Thomas. *Man and Citizen. Thomas Hobbes's De Homine*. Gloucester: P. Smith, 1978.

Hobbes, Thomas. *Leviathan: With Selected Variants from the Latin Edition of 1668*. Indianapolis: Hackett Publishing, 1994.

Hobbes, Thomas. *The English Works of Thomas Hobbes. Elements of Philosophy*. Charlottesville: InteLex Corporation, 1995.

Hobbes, Thomas. *Leviathan*. Cambridge: Cambridge University Press, 1996.

Horky, Phillip Sidney, ed. *Cosmos in the Ancient World*. Cambridge: Cambridge University Press, 2019.

Huffman, Carl. "Archytas." *The Stanford Encyclopedia of Philosophy*. Metaphysics Research Lab, Stanford University, 2018.

Huggett, Nick. *Space from Zeno to Einstein: Classic Readings with a Contemporary Commentary*. Cambridge: MIT Press, 1999.

Hume, David. *Hume: Moral Philosophy*. Indianapolis: Hackett Publishing, 2006.

Husserl, Edmund. *The Crisis of European Sciences and Transcendental Phenomenology: An Introduction to Phenomenological Philosophy*. Evanston: Northwestern University Press, 1970.

Hyman, Arthur, and James J. Walsh, eds. *Philosophy in the Middle Ages: The Christian, Islamic, and Jewish Traditions*. Indianapolis: Hackett Publishing, 1983.

James, C. L. R. *A New Notion: Two Works by C. L. R. James: Every Cook Can Govern and The Invading Socialist Society*. Oakland: PM Press, 2010.

James, William. *The Principles of Psychology*. New York: Holt, 1907.

Jameson, Fredric. *Postmodernism, or the Cultural Logic of Late Capitalism*. Durham: Duke University Press, 1991.

Jammer, Max. *Concepts of Space: The History of Theories of Space in Physics*. New York: Dover Publications, 1993.

Janiak, Andrew. "Space and Motion in Nature and Scripture: Galileo, Descartes, Newton." *Studies in History and Philosophy of Science* 51 (2015): 89–99.

Johnson, Monte Ransome. "Sources for the Philosophy of Archytas." *Ancient Philosophy* 28, no. 1 (2008): 173–99.

Kalachanis, Konstantinos, Efstratios Theodosiou, and Milan Dimitrijevic. "Aristotelian Aether and Void in the Universe." *Journal of Classical Studies of Matica Srpska* 18 (2016): 135–50.

Kant, Immanuel. *On History*. Indianapolis: Bobbs-Merril Co., 1963.

Kant, Immanuel. *Political Writings*. Cambridge: Cambridge University Press, 1991.

Kant, Immanuel. *Practical Philosophy*. Cambridge: Cambridge University Press, 1996.

Kantorowicz, Ernst. *The King's Two Bodies*. Princeton: Princeton University Press, 1957.

Keefer, Michael H. "The World Turned Inside Out: Revolutions of the Infinite Sphere from Hermes to Pascal." *Renaissance and Reformation* 12, no. 4 (1988): 303–13.

Kepler, Johannes. *Joannis Keppleri . . . De Stella Nova in Pede Serpentarii*. Prague: typis P. Sessli, impensis authoris, 1606.

Kepler, Johannes. *New Astronomy*. New York: Cambridge University Press, 1992.

Kepler, Johannes. *Epitome of Copernican Astronomy; and Harmonies of the World*. Amherst: Promethus Books, 1995.

Kern, Stephen. *The Culture of Time and Space, 1880–1918*. Cambridge: Harvard University Press, 2003.

Kleingeld, Pauline, and Eric Brown. "Cosmopolitanism." *The Stanford Encyclopedia of Philosophy*. Metaphysics Research Lab, Stanford University, 2019.

Koyré, Alexandre. *From the Closed World to the Infinite Universe*. Baltimore: Johns Hopkins University Press, 1979.

Kriegel, Blandine. *The State and the Rule of Law*. Princeton: Princeton University Press, 1995.

Kuhn, Thomas. *The Copernican Revolution, Planetary Astronomy in the Development of Western Thought*. Cambridge: Harvard University Press, 1966.

La Boétie, Étienne de. *The Politics of Obedience and Etienne de La Boétie*. Montreal: Black Rose Books, 2007.

Laclau, Ernesto. *New Reflections on the Revolution of Our Time*. New York: Verso Books, 1990.

Laclau, Ernesto. *On Populist Reason*. New York: Verso Books, 2018.

Laertius, Diogenes. *Lives of Eminent Philosophers*. Cambridge: Harvard University Press, 1958.

Landucci, Sergio. *I filosofi e i selvaggi*. Turin: Einaudi, 2014.

Lefebvre, Henri. *The Production of Space*. Cambridge: Blackwell, 1991.

Lefort, Claude. *L'Invention démocratique: les limites de la domination totalitaire*. Paris: Fayard, 1994.

Lefort, Claude. *La Complication: retour sur le communisme*. Paris: Fayard, 1999.

Leijenhorst, Cees. "Jesuit Concepts of Spatium Imaginarium and Thomas Hobbes's Doctrine of Space." *Early Science and Medicine* 1, no. 3 (1996): 355–80.

Lichtenstein, Aharon. *Henry More; the Rational Theology of a Cambridge Platonist*. Cambridge: Cambridge University Press, 1962.

Lilley, Keith D. *City and Cosmos: The Medieval World in Urban Form*. London: Reaktion Books, 2009.

Locke, John. *An Essay Concerning Human Understanding*. Oxford: Oxford University Press, 1979.

LoLordo, Antonia. *Pierre Gassendi and the Birth of Early Modern Philosophy*. New York: Cambridge University Press, 2007.

Long, A. A., and D. N. Sedley. *The Hellenistic Philosophers: Volume 1, Translations of the Principal Sources with Philosophical Commentary*. Cambridge: Cambridge University Press, 1987.

Lovejoy, A. O. *The Great Chain of Being*. Cambridge: Harvard University Press, 1964.

Lucretius. *On the Nature of Things by Lucretius*. Cambridge, MIT Classics. Accessed July 16, 2020. http://classics.mit.edu/Carus/nature_things.html.

McGuire, J. E. *Tradition and Innovation: Newton's Metaphysics of Nature*. Dordrecht: Springer Netherlands, 1995.

Machamer, Peter K. "Aristotle on Natural Place and Natural Motion." *Isis* 69, no. 3 (1978): 377–87.

Machamer, Peter K., and Robert G. Turnbull, eds. *Motion and Time, Space and Matter: Interrelations in the History of Philosophy and Science*. Columbus: Ohio State University Press, 1976.

Machiavelli, Niccolò. *The Discourses*. Harmondsworth: Penguin Books, 1970.

Machiavelli, Niccolò. *The Prince*. Chicago: University of Chicago Press, 1998.

Maistre, Joseph Marie. *Considérations sur la France*. Brussels: Editions Complexe, 1988.

Marx, Karl. *Selected Works in One Volume*. New York: International Publishers, 1968.

Marx, Karl. *Grundrisse*. New York: Penguin Books, 1973.

Marx, Karl. *Capital: A Critique of Political Economy*. New York: Vintage Books, 1977.

Marx, Karl. *Capital: A Critique of Political Economy*. Penguin Classics. New York: Penguin Books in association with New Left Review, 1990.

Marx, Karl. *Grundrisse: Foundations of the Critique of Political Economy*. New York: Penguin Books in association with New Left Review, 1993.

Marx, Karl. *Early Political Writings*. Cambridge: Cambridge University Press, 1994.

Marx, Karl, and Friedrich Engels. *The Communist Manifesto*. London: Pluto Press, 2008.

Massey, Doreen B. *For Space*. Thousand Oaks: SAGE, 2005.

Mazzeo, Joseph Anthony. "Dante's Conception of Love." *Journal of the History of Ideas* 18, no. 2 (1957): 147–60.

Meiksins Wood, Ellen. *Democracy Against Capitalism: Renewing Historical Materialism*. Cambridge: Cambridge University Press, 1995.

Meiksins Wood, Ellen. "Back to Marx." *Monthly Review* 49, no. 2 (1997): 1–9.

Meiksins Wood, Ellen. *The Ellen Meiksins Wood Reader*. Boston: Brill, 2012.

Mendelssohn, Moses. *Jerusalem or On Religious Power and Judaism*. Edited and translated by Allan Arkush. Waltham: Brandeis University Press, 2011, 13.

Michel, Paul-Henri. *The Cosmology of Giordano Bruno*. Ithaca: Cornell University Press, 1973.

Miller, Jon. "Hugo Grotius." *The Stanford Encyclopedia of Philosophy*. Metaphysics Research Lab, Stanford University, 2005.

Mirandola, Giovanni Pico Della. *Oration on the Dignity of Man*. Washington: Regnery Publishing, 1996.

More, Henry. *Philosophical Writings of Henry More*. London: Oxford University Press, 1925.

Moreira, Ivone. "Suárez in Eighteenth Century British Political Thought. Burke's Political Thought and Suárez's Inheritance." *CAURIENSIA. Revista anual de Ciencias Eclesiásticas* 13 (2018): 479–502.

Mouffe, Chantal, Ernesto Laclau, Jacques Derrida, Richard Rorty, and Simon Critchley. *Deconstruction and Pragmatism*. Abingdon: Taylor and Francis, 2003.

Newton, Isaac. *Opticks: Or, A Treatise of the Reflections, Refractions, Inflexions and Colours of Light. Second Edition, with Additions*. London: Printed for W. and J. Innys, 1718.

Newton, Isaac. "Newton's Scholium on Time, Space, Place and Motion", translated by Andrew Motte, rev. Florian Cajori. Berkeley: University of California Press, 1934.

Newton, Isaac. *Unpublished Scientific Papers of Isaac Newton: A Selection from the Portsmouth Collection in the University Library, Cambridge*. Cambridge: Cambridge University Press, 1962.

Newton, Isaac. *Philosophiae naturalis principia mathematica*. Cambridge: Harvard University Press, 1972.

Newton, Isaac. *The Principia: Mathematical Principles of Natural Philosophy*. Berkeley: University of California Press, 1999.

Newton, Isaac. *Philosophical Writings*. New York: Cambridge University Press, 2014.

Nietzsche, Friedrich Wilhelm. *The Birth of Tragedy, and The Case of Wagner*. New York: Vintage Books, 1967.

Nietzsche, Friedrich Wilhelm. *The Gay Science: With a Prelude in Rhymes and an Appendix of Songs*. New York: Vintage Books, 1974.

Nietzsche, Friedrich Wilhelm. *The Birth of Tragedy*. New York: Oxford University Press, 2000.

Nikulin, Dmitri. *Matter, Imagination, and Geometry: Ontology, Natural Philosophy, and Mathematics in Plotinus, Proclus, and Descartes*. Farnham: Ashgate, 2002.

Nikulin, Dmitri. *Neoplatonism in Late Antiquity*. New York: Oxford University Press, 2019.

Nolan, Lawrence, ed. *The Cambridge Descartes Lexicon*. Cambridge: Cambridge University Press, 2015.

O'Rourke, Fran. *Ciphers of Transcendence: Essays in Philosophy of Religion in Honour of Patrick Masterson*. Kildare: Merrion Press, 2019.

Osborne, James F. "Sovereignty and Territoriality in the City-State: A Case Study from the Amuq Valley, Turkey." *Journal of Anthropological Archaeology* 32, no. 4 (2013): 774–90.

Osta-Velez, Matias, et al. *La Filosofía y su Enseñanza*, Montevideo: ANEP, 2017.

Panofsky, Erwin. *Perspective as Symbolic Form*. New York: Zone Books, 1997.

Parmenides. *Fragments: A Text and Translation with an Introduction*. Toronto: University of Toronto Press, 1991.

Parry, Richard. "Ancient Ethical Theory." *The Stanford Encyclopedia of Philosophy*. Metaphysics Research Lab, Stanford University, 2014.

Pascal, Blaise. *Pensées. Texte établi par Louis Lafuma. Préface d'André Dodin*. Paris: Éditions du Seuil, 1962.

Pennington, Kenneth. "Lex Naturalis and Jus Naturale." *The Jurist: Studies in Church Law and Ministry* 68, no. 2 (2008): 569–91.

Philo. *On Flight and Finding. On the Change of Names. On Dreams*. Cambridge: Harvard University Press, 1934.

Philoponus, John. *Against Proclus on the Eternity of the World 1–5*. London: Duckworth, 2004.

Philoponus, John. *On Aristotle Physics 4.1–5*. London: Bristol Classical Press, 2012.

Pindar. *Pindar's Nemeans: A Selection*. Munich: K. G. Saur, 2005.

Plato. *Euthyphro. Apology. Crito. Phaedo. Phaedrus*. Cambridge: Harvard University Press, 1914.

Plato. *Plato in Twelve Volumes. With an English Translation*. Vols. 10, 11. Cambridge: Harvard University Press, 1967.

Plato. *Gorgias*. Indianapolis: Hackett, 1987.

Plato. *Plato's Timaeus: Translation, Glossary, Appendices and Introductory Essay*. Newburyport: Focus Pub, 2001.

Plato. *The Republic of Plato*. New York: Basic Books, 2016.

Plato. *Theaetetus. Sophist*. Cambridge: Harvard University Press, 1921.

Plotinus. *Ennead*, vols. 1–3. Cambridge: Harvard University Press, 1966–7.

Plotinus. "The Six Enneads." The Internet Classics Archive. Accessed January 28, 2020. http://classics.mit.edu/Plotinus/enneads.1.first.html.

Raffoul, François, and David Pettigrew. *Heidegger and Practical Philosophy*. Albany: State University of New York Press, 2002.

Rancière, Jacques. *Disagreement: Politics and Philosophy*. Minneapolis: University of Minnesota Press, 1999.

Rancière, Jacques. *Moments politiques: interventions 1977–2009*. Paris: La Fabrique, 2009.

Randles, W. G. L. *The Unmaking of the Medieval Christian Cosmos, 1500–1760: From Solid Heavens to Boundless Aether*. New York: Routledge, 2016.

Ranocchia, Graziano, Christoph Helmig, and Christoph Horn. *Space in Hellenistic Philosophy: Critical Studies in Ancient Physics*. Berlin: Walter de Gruyter, 2014.

Reale, Giovanni. *Melisso Testimonianze e Frammenti*. Florence: La Nuova Italia, 1970.

Rigby, Stephen H. "The Body Politic in the Social and Political Thought of Christine de Pizan. Reciprocity, Hierarchy and Political Authority." *Cahiers de Recherches Médiévales et Humanistes* 24 (2012): 461–83.

Ross, Jerome. "How Plagues Change the World." *The New Statesman*, May 2020.

Rousseau, Jean-Jacques. *Discourse on the Origins of Inequality (Second Discourse); Polemics; and, Political Economy*. Hanover: University Press of New England, 1992.

Ruffner, J. A. "Newton's De Gravitatione: A Review and Reassessment." *Archive for History of Exact Sciences* 66, no. 3 (2012): 241–64.

Ruggie, John Gerard. "Territoriality and Beyond: Problematizing Modernity in International Relations." *International Organization* 47, no. 1 (1993): 139–74.

Rynasiewicz, Robert. "Newton's Views on Space, Time, and Motion." *The Stanford Encyclopedia of Philosophy*. Metaphysics Research Lab, Stanford University, 2014.

Sallis, John. *Chorology: On Beginning in Plato's Timaeus*. Bloomington: Indiana University Press, 1999.

Sambursky, Samuel. *The Concept of Place in Late Neoplatonism*. Jerusalem: The Israel Academy of Sciences and Humanities, 1982.

Sambursky, Samuel. *Physics of the Stoics*. Princeton: Princeton University Press, 2014.

Sanín-Restrepo, Ricardo. *Decolonizing Democracy: Power in a Solid State*. London: Rowman and Littlefield, 2016.

Schmitt, Carl. *The Concept of the Political*. New Brunswick: Rutgers University Press, 1976.

Schmitt, Carl. *Political Theology: Four Chapters on the Concept of Sovereignty*. Cambridge: MIT Press, 1985.

Schmitt, Carl. *The Nomos of the Earth in the International Law of the Jus Publicum Europaeum*. New York: Telos Press, 2003.

Schmitt, Carl. *Tierra y Mar: Una Reflexión Sobre La Historia Universal*. Madrid: Trotta, 2007.

Schmitt, Carl. *Land and Sea: A World-Historical Meditation*. Candor: Telos Press Publishing, 2015.

Schurmann, Reiner. *Des Hegemonies Brisées*. Toulouse: T.E.R., 1996.

Sedley, David. "Two Conceptions of Vacuum." *Phronesis* 27 (1982): 175.

Sen, Jai. "On Open Space: Explorations Towards a Vocabulary of a More Open Politics." *Antipode* 42, no. 4 (2010): 994–1018.

Seneca, Lucius Annaeus. *Moral Letters to Lucilius: Epistulae Morales Ad Lucilium*. Studium Publishing, 2018.

Sextus Empiricus. *Against Physicists. Against Ethicists*. Cambridge: Harvard University Press, 1936.

Shakespeare, William. *Hamlet*. New York: Simon and Schuster, 2004.

Shapin, Steven, and Simon Schaffer. *Leviathan and the Air-Pump: Hobbes, Boyle, and the Experimental Life*. Princeton: Princeton University Press, 2011.

Shea, W. R. *Nature Mathematized: Historical and Philosophical Case Studies in Classical Modern Natural Philosophy*. Dordrecht: Springer Science and Business Media, 2012.

Shields, Rob. *Spatial Questions: Cultural Topologies and Social Spatialisations*. London: Sage, 2013.

Shields, Christopher. "Aristotle's Psychology." *The Stanford Encyclopedia of Philosophy*. Metaphysics Research Lab, Stanford University, 2016.

Simplicius, *Corollaries on Place and Time*. London: Duckworth, 1991.

Siorvanes, Lucas. *Proclus on the Elements and the Celestial Bodies. Physical Thought in Late Neoplatonism*. PhD diss., University of London, 1986.

Siorvanes, Lucas. *Proclus: Neo-Platonic Philosophy and Science*. New Haven: Yale University Press, 1997.

Sloterdijk, Peter. *Bubbles: Spheres Volume I: Microspherology*. Los Angeles: Semiotext(e), 2011.

Sloterdijk, Peter, and Hans-Jurgen Heinrichs. *Neither Sun nor Death*. London: Semiotext(e), 2011.

Smith, Adam. *The Theory of Moral Sentiments*. Indianapolis: Liberty Classics, 1976.

Smith, Adam. *Inquiry into the Nature and Causes of the Wealth of Nations*. New York: Bantam Classic, 2003.

Snobelen, Stephen David. "God and Natural Philosophy in Isaac Newton's Opticks." *Estudios De Filosofía* 35 (2007): 15–53.

Soja, Edward W. *Postmodern Geographies: The Reassertion of Space in Critical Social Theory*. London: Verso Books, 1989.

Sophocles. *Antigone*. Indianapolis: Hackett Publishing, 2001.

Sorabji, Richard. *Matter, Space and Motion: Theories in Antiquity and Their Sequel*. Ithaca: Cornell University Press, 1988.

Spade, Paul Vincent. "Medieval Political Philosophy." *The Stanford Encyclopedia of Philosophy*. Metaphysics Research Lab, Stanford University, 2016.

Steinberg, Justin. "Spinoza's Political Philosophy." *The Stanford Encyclopedia of Philosophy*. Metaphysics Research Lab, Stanford University, 2019.

Strauss, Leo. *Natural Right and History*. Chicago: University of Chicago Press, 2013.

Strauss, Leo, and Joseph Cropsey. *History of Political Philosophy*. Chicago: University of Chicago Press, 1987.

Sweeney, L. *Infinity in the Presocratics: A Bibliographical and Philosophical Study*. Dordrecht: Springer Science and Business Media, 2012.

Tamames, Jorge. *For the People: Left Populism in Spain and the US*. London: Lawrence and Wishart, 2020.

Taraborrelli, Angela. "Cosmopolitanism and Space in Kant's Political Thought." *International Journal of Philosophy* 10 (2019): 15–26.

Taylor, C. C. W. *The Atomists, Leucippus and Democritus : Fragments: A Text and Translation with a Commentary*. Toronto: University of Toronto Press, 1999.

Taylor, Charles. *A Secular Age*. Cambridge: Harvard University Press, 2007.

Thucydides. *The Peloponnesian War*. Oxford: Oxford University Press, 2009.

Urmson, J. O. *Simplicius: Corollaries on Place and Time*. London: Bloomsbury, 2014.

Vailati, Ezio. *Leibniz and Clarke: A Study of Their Correspondence*. New York: Oxford University Press, 1997.

Vatter, Miguel. "Natality and Biopolitics in Hannah Arendt." *Revista de Ciencia Política* 26, no. 2 (2006): 137–59.

Villacañas, José Luis. *La Nación y la Guerra: Confederación y Hegemonía como Formas de Concebir Europa*. Madrid: Diego Marín Librero Editor, 1999.

Virilio, Paul. *Speed and Politics: An Essay on Dromology*. New York: Columbia University, 1986.

Volpe, Enrico. "Melisso e il Problema del Vuoto: Apologia e/o Fraintendimento del Monismo Parmenideo?" *Peitho. Examina Antiqua* 1, no. 8 (2017).

Warren, James. *Presocratics*. London: Routledge, 2014.

Wear, Sarah Klitenic. *The Teachings of Syrianus on Plato's Timaeus and Parmenides*. Leiden: Brill, 2011.

Weber, Max. *The Vocation Lectures*. Indianapolis: Hackett Pub, 2004.

Weirich, Paul. "Rousseau on Equality." *History of Philosophy Quarterly* 9, no. 2 (1992): 191–8.

Westfall, Richard S. *Force in Newton's Physics: The Science of Dynamics in the Seventeenth Century*. New York: American Elsevier, 1971.

Wildberg, Christian. "John Philoponus." *The Stanford Encyclopedia of Philosophy*. Metaphysics Research Lab, Stanford University, 2018.

Williams, Thomas. "John Duns Scotus." *The Stanford Encyclopedia of Philosophy*. Metaphysics Research Lab, Stanford University, 2001.

Wolfson, Harry Austryn. *Crescas' Critique of Aristotle. Problems of Aristotle's Physics in Jewish and Arabic Philosophy*. Cambridge: Harvard University Press, 1971.

Wynter, Sylvia. "Unsettling the Coloniality of Being/Power/Truth/Freedom: Towards the Human, After Man, Its Overrepresentation – An Argument." *CR: The New Centennial Review* 3, no. 3 (2003): 257–337.

Yousef Sandoval, Laila. "Carl Schmitt y la Evolución del 'Ius publicum europaeum': interpretación y crítica desde las nuevas epistemologías de las relaciones internacionales." PhD diss., Universidad Complutense de Madrid, 2018.

Yovel, Yirmiyahu. *Kant and the Philosophy of History*. Princeton: Princeton University Press, 1980.

Zuckert, Michael P. "'Bringing Philosophy down from the Heavens': Natural Right in the Roman Law." *The Review of Politics* 51, no. 1 (1989): 70–85.

Index

EU representative:
Easy Access System Europe
Mustamäe tee 50, 10621 Tallinn, Estonia
Gpsr.requests@easproject.com

www.ingramcontent.com/pod-product-compliance
Lightning Source LLC
Chambersburg PA
CBHW070843300326
41935CB00039B/1385